COME OUT SWINGING

COME OUT SWINGING: THE CHANGING WORLD OF BOXING IN GLEASON'S GYM

Lucia Trimbur

PRINCETON UNIVERSITY PRESS
Princeton and Oxford

Published by Princeton University Press, 41 William Street, Princeton, New Jersey 08540
In the United Kingdom: Princeton University Press, 6 Oxford Street, Woodstock, Oxfordshire OX20 1TW

press.princeton.edu

Cover photo by Issei Nakaya

Library of Congress Cataloging-in-Publication Data

Trimbur, Lucia, 1975–
Come out swinging : the changing world of boxing in Gleason's gym / Lucia Trimbur.
pages cm
Includes bibliographical references and index.
ISBN 978-0-691-15029-1 (cloth : alk. paper) 1. Boxing—New York (State) —New York—History. 2. Gymnasiums—New York (State)—New York—History. 3. Athletic clubs—New York (State) —New York—History. 4. Boxers (Sports) —New York (State) —New York—History. 5. Brooklyn (New York, N.Y.) —History. 6. Brooklyn (New York, N.Y.) —Social life and customs. I. Title.
GV1125.T75 2013
796.8309747—dc23 2012049335

British Library Cataloging-in-Publication Data is available

This book has been composed in Sabon LT Std

Printed on acid-free paper. ∞

Printed in the United States of America

10 9 8 7 6 5 4 3 2 1

"Boxing is a Combat, depending more on Strength than the Sword: But Art will yet bear down the Beam against it. A less Degree of Art will tell more than a considerably greater Strength. Strength is certainly what the Boxer ought to fet [*sic*] out with, but without Art he will succeed but poorly. The Deficiency of Strength may be greatly supplied by Art; but the want of Art will have heavy and unwieldy Succour from Strength."

—CAPTAIN JOHN GODFREY, 1747

"*This* is boxing. This is the *new* boxing."

—MIKE SMITH, 2004

To

Harry and Mike, for caring when no one else does

and

Nelson, for caring unconditionally

Contents

Acknowledgments

When I wrote the acknowledgments for my dissertation, a historian friend joked that they were almost as long as a chapter. But while doing their research and writing, ethnographers rely on so many people, and incur so many personal debts along the way, that many people need to be recognized. This book is no different.

I benefited from financial support from a number of sources, which helped me conduct research and prepare this book. At Yale University, multiple Camp Research Fund fellowships and a University Dissertation Fellowship provided me with funding to perform ethnographic research. A Beinecke Rare Book and Manuscript Fellowship gave me five months of archival research on boxing training manuals from the eighteenth, nineteenth, and twentieth centuries. As an Andrew W. Mellon Postdoctoral Fellow on Race, Crime, and Justice at the Vera Institute of Justice, I enjoyed precious time to think through the manuscript and play around with different ways of organizing my thoughts. At John Jay College and the City University of New York (CUNY), several awards—a PSC-CUNY award, a Special Research Fund grant, a Research Assistance Program grant, and a Faculty Fellowship Publication Program award—provided me with course releases to research and write, forums to workshop my writing, and research assistance.

This project would have been impossible without the endless hours Harry Keitt and Mike Smith spent with me. For over a decade, Mike and Harry have given me data about boxing and, more important, about life. I cherish their friendships, and I deeply appreciate the counsel they have provided me. I am in great debt to the boxers of Gleason's Gym, whom I cannot mention by real name, but whose generosity of spirit, sense of purpose, aspirations, and daily struggles are on my mind every day. I give countless thanks to Gleason's trainers, who spent a tremendous amount of time explaining their craft to me, providing me with unguarded access to the good and bad in their lives. And I extend my warmest gratitude to Bruce Silverglade for making Gleason's Gym my second home. Bruce gave me unfettered access to the gym, and I still miss spending my days there.

Josh Gamson and his Participant Observation class at Yale University, Steven Gregory and his Epistemology and Politics of Ethnography class at Columbia University, and Mitch Duneier and his Urban Ethnography class at CUNY's Graduate Center facilitated thoughtful discussions on the practice, politics, and poetics of ethnography. Each class had a different perspective, and each helped me think about ethnography in new ways. Mitch, in particular, got me writing when I felt stuck.

My writing group—Colin Jerolmack, Jooyoung Lee, Erin O'Connor, Harel Shapira, R. Tyson Smith, and Iddo Tavory—has been invaluable in the production of this book. The group gave me beautifully detailed feedback that sometimes confronted the limits of my intellectual capabilities. I have learned so much from my ethnographic comrades and their work, and I always look forward to our meetings. Tyson and Harel, in particular, have closely watched this text come to life, and I am moved by their kindness. Participating in Columbia University/New York University's Craft of Ethnography Workshop under Sudhir Venkatesh's direction and the University of Pennsylvania's Urban Ethnography Workshop under David Grazian's leadership provided me with crucial insights. I also heartily thank Paul Willis and his Claims and Evidence class at Princeton for smart and intriguing questions and comments that helped me refine chapter 3. And immeasurable gratitude goes to Lewis Gordon and the members of the Humanities Center at Temple University, especially Heath Fogg Davis, for their engaged contributions.

Email exchanges with Loic Wacquant clarified analytical points related to boxing and boxing gyms. I value the time Loic spent reading my work, challenging my conclusions in detail, and suggesting readings. Eric Raskin, then an editor at *Ring Magazine* and a boxing expert, suggested I choose Gleason's Gym to do my research in the first place; this project literally would not have happened without Eric's recommendation. I thank Hilary Silver for being a steady and dependable source of ideas and camaraderie for the past twenty years. I also thank Gunther Kress for all that he has taught me and for his belief in me as an academic. And I appreciate the late Jeannette Hopkins for teaching me about the world of publishing.

It is hard to say enough about Paul Gilroy and Vron Ware. From the bottom of my heart, I thank them for providing me with safety under their collective wings. For more than a decade, they have gently challenged me and fiercely supported me. I have found peace inside and outside academia because of them. I have benefited immensely from the advice of Alondra Nelson and Rachel Sherman, and I treasure their friendship.

I am grateful to friends and colleagues who read parts of the book or provided other forms of input and critique. Shamus Khan and David Grazian's meticulous and astute comments helped me turn these chapters into a real book. I give them special thanks for contributing their expertise when I know they were busy. Ronald Kramer spent an incredible amount of time helping me improve this manuscript; somehow Ronald could always find a cogent idea in my muddled thoughts. Michael Driscoll read everything line by line, correcting my many mistakes and challenging me to produce a better, more accessible text. Michael Aiello, Aisha Bastiaans, Georg Bauer, Cassie Hayes, David J. Leonard, Theresa Runstedtler, and Michael Yarbrough stepped in to give me feedback and quell anxiety in the final moments of writing. My colleagues at John Jay College recommended readings, commented on my writing, and generally gave me direction when I felt lost. I thank Amy Adamczyk, Michael Blitz, Dave Brotherton, Janice Johnson Dias, Joshua Freilich, Robert Garot, Amy Green, Richard Haw, Lila Kazemian, Rich Ocejo, Susan Opotow, Jay Pastrana, Valli Rajah, Theresa Rockett, and Fritz Umbach. I am fortunate to work with brilliant and generous students, especially Michael Aiello, Alex Harocopos, Bobby Smith, Michael Sullivan, and Alex Tejada, who teach me something new each day while keeping me on my toes. My thanks also to Lynn Chancer and the members of the CUNY Faculty Fellowship Publication Program, especially Leigh Jones, as well as Tina Chiu, Zaire Dinzey-Flores, Michael Jacobson, William Kornblum, Mike Smith, Jim D. Taylor, and Jon Wool.

At Princeton University Press, a number of people worked magic to bring this book to publication. My copy editor, Molan Goldstein, transformed my manuscript into a polished text. Ellen Foos and Ryan Mulligan guided the book through the publication process, helping me with everything from permissions to indexing. David Luljak did a beautiful job with the index. Last but not least, my editor Eric Schwartz believed in this project from the get-go, and his enthusiasm not only convinced me that it was worth writing but also kept me writing when I did not. I still cannot believe I was lucky enough to capture Eric's attention and become one of his authors. I am so grateful for the time, energy, and ideas he has put into this book. No one could ask for a better editor.

Words cannot describe how much my friends and family have done for me. They kept me sane, grounded, and motivated as I wrote, often under trying circumstances. In addition to the people mentioned in the previous paragraphs, I give countless thanks to Richard Aiken, Jane Argall, Molly Braun, Peter Braun, Mal Burnstein, Roslyn Clarke, Erik Clinton, Mary Ann Deibel-Braun, Ann DeLancey, Danae DiRocco, Danielle Farrell, the late Nelson Fausto, Jason Gallina, Diana George, Craig Gilmore, Ruthie Wilson-Gilmore, Jane Gordon, Nicole Hala, Francoise Hamlin, Karen Hanna, Mark Krasovic, Leah Khaghani, Reggie and Keli LaCrete, Ben McOmber, Emily Meixner, Lauren Morris, Nima Paidipaty, Karen Press, Andres Rengifo, Besenia Rodriguez, Christine Scott-Hayward, Shawn Sebastian, Connie Sharp, Karen Tien, Catherine Ruth Trimbur, Rahul Vanjani, Cora Gilroy Ware, and Marcus Gilroy Ware, and Roxanne Willis. Tanya Jones and Beth Dever-Ryan went above and beyond what any friend should ever have to do by keeping a light burning in the darkest of hours; I owe so much to my best friends of nearly two decades. I thank my parents, Lundy Braun and John Trimbur, for their love and their politics. Their abiding insistence that society *needs to* and *can be* changed gives me inspiration and strength. My sisters, Clare and Catherine, have shown me the meaning of unconditional love. They accept me for who I am and care for me no matter what.

Prominent Participants

Female Boxers	*Gym Owners*	*Male Boxers*	*Trainers*	*White-Collar Clients*
Caitlin	Bobby Gleason	Adrian	Alejandro	Aaron
Chloe	Bruce Silverglade	Ali	Bob Jackson	Comedy Central comedian
Christine	Ira Becker	Anthony	Ed	Jack
Danielle		Cedric	George Washington	Jeff Koyen
Elizabeth		Collin	Harry	Scandinavian soccer player
Eva		Darryl	Hector	Scott Stedman
Fiona		Diego	Jeremy	Simon
Gabriela		Jeffrey	Joseph	William
Jennifer		Kenny	Karl	
Joanne		Lawrence	Mike	
Josie		Leon	Peter	
Karen		Matthew	Raphael	
Kelly		Max	Ricardo	
Layla		Michael	"Trickman" Norris	
Leah		Omar	Willie Dockery	
Lily		Paul		
Maya		Raoul		
Mila		Roberto		
Myriam		Roy		
Sunshine		Sam		
		Scott		
		Sean		
		Wells		

Preface

Four blocks off the F train at York Street, a quarter of a mile from the A/C subway at High Street, and half a mile from the Clark Street station on the 2/3 line in Brooklyn stands Gleason's Gym. The gym is housed in a renovated warehouse at 77 Front Street between Main and Washington Streets, two cobblestoned blocks east of the East River. The building is surrounded by a honeycomb of high-end clothing boutiques, chic coffee shops, specialty furniture stores, art studios, and expensive apartment buildings. Since 1996, the real estate tycoon David Walentas and his Two Trees commercial and residential development firm have turned this section of Brooklyn, now named DUMBO (Down Under the Manhattan Bridge Overpass), into a destination for the ultra rich. The former industrial area, which boasts Civil War–era storehouses that once stocked coffee beans and spices, is now one of the most desirable districts in New York City. In the late 1980s and early 1990s, when DUMBO was an unnamed district of the Brooklyn waterfront and offered cheap rents, this location was a logical choice for a gritty cantankerous boxing gym. Today, it is the last place one expects to find a serious pugilistic institution.

As I enter 77 Front Street and begin the one-flight climb to the gym, the first sounds I hear are the chirping of the timekeeping bell and the hypnotic thundering of what was once the famed boxer Jake LaMotta's 600-pound speed bag. At the second-floor landing, the voices of trainers, the laughter of fighters, and the springs of the gym's four rings become audible. The odor of sweat and toil hit me, and the air acquires an increasingly humid feel. This assault of sound and smell provokes anticipation about just what activities, happenings, and personalities lie behind the two heavy gray doors. Through these gates, the gym's owner, Bruce Silverglade, blocks admission to the gym with an old wooden desk and a smile. From this post, he greets guests and regulars alike, gently reminding tardy members of unpaid dues, and offering an opportunity for all to work out.

After passing through Silverglade's entry, I gravitate to the middle of the gym, the locus of training activity. Around this center, boxers, trainers, spectators, and other gym regulars cluster habitually in different spaces—at the domino table, beside the exercise machines, next to the treadmill, in front of a ring—socializing, coaching, working out, cooling down, reading, playing games, and dozing off. Around 11:00 a.m., when competitive fighters train, I watch Anthony practice his uppercut in front of a wall of full-length mirrors while Joanne and Maya jump rope. A spar in Ring 1 draws the encouragement, heckles, and jeers of onlookers who line up three people deep to watch Lawrence outclass an outsider. Around 2:00 p.m., when many professional and amateur pugilists have finished their work-outs, Leon studies from a textbook, Adrian flips through the pages of the *New York Daily News*, and Max shushes his toddler to sleep. Fast-forward to 5:00 p.m. and the gym is flooded with firefighters, "white-collar clients"—recreational athletes of considerable means who pay substantial amounts of money for their training—and children. Karl and Ed, two trainers, debate the weekend's championship bout with a Wall Street banker. A pair of six-year-olds mischievously avoids instruction on the heavy bag, opting instead for a game of tag; they weave in and out of the spaces between StairMasters and elliptical trainers to the dismay of their coach and the resigned disapproval of their mother.

This is Gleason's Gym.

Forty years ago, a bird's-eye view of Gleason's Gym would have produced a very different picture. At that time, the urban gym was frequented almost exclusively by competitive male boxers of color, trainers, and other men of the pugilistic industry, such as managers, promoters, matchmakers, and sportswriters.[1] Urban gyms were the domain of working-class masculinity and its historical connections to physical, powerful manhood. Boxers trained for competition; professionals worked to advance their paid careers and amateurs practiced so they could "turn pro" at some point in the foreseeable future. Trainers worked with their fighters early in the morning before work or late in evening after punching out. Unless they had retired from other jobs, trainers could not afford to forfeit employment outside the gym to spend their entire days there. Journalists and those fueling the pugilistic economy watched spars, observed fighters, struck deals, and talked amongst themselves during the gym's open hours.

Over the past four decades, Gleason's Gym has changed dramatically. In the 1980s, the gym welcomed two new groups of boxers: white-collar clients and women. As the memberships of these contingents grew, the urban gym transformed. New social practices, social relations, and relations of power emerged while novel spaces of interracial, interclass, and intergender contact and communication were created.[2] The meanings that the sport held for its practitioners diversified, and today, Gleason's Gym's 1,000-plus members—roughly 80 trainers, 450 amateur and professional fighters, 300 female pugilists, and 300 male white-collar clients—use the gym in a multiplicity of ways.[3] For some members, it is a stabilizing force; for others, it is the opportunity for intergenerational friendship. It nurtures dreams of superstardom and the need for a steady paycheck. It is a daily workout and a means to develop an identity. Gleason's is the last remaining gym from New York's golden age of boxing, and a former home to luminaries of the noble art, such as Roberto Duran and Hector Camacho. But as women and people of different class and racial backgrounds move in, the gym faces new, competing visions. It no longer functions merely as a working-class male sanctuary, though it struggles to maintain the ideals of one.

The new configuration of Gleason's Gym is the result of political, economic, and social policy changes that began in the 1960s. New market theories and practices encouraged the replacement of an economy rooted in industrial production with FIRE industries (finance, insurance, and real estate), and New York City lost a significant number of manufacturing jobs. Blue-collar workers could not find positions that paid a living wage in the "new economy," and the city experienced a rapid rise in unemployment. Black and Latino residents were disproportionately affected; poverty rates soared and produced new forms of racial inequality. Attendant policy changes included the dismantling of welfare programs, the deterioration of public education, and an unprecedented focus on law and order. The emerging crime complex mandated longer sentences than ever before, prison populations exploded, and black and Latino men with modest education were disproportionately confined. By the early 1990s, poor and working-class men of color were increasingly out of school, out of work, and in and out of prison.[4]

Longtime patrons of boxing gyms, poor and working-class men of color continued to join Gleason's Gym as amateur boxers, professional fighters, and trainers, but their participation took on a new meaning in a postindustrial era. With little access to wage labor, the gym became an important site of masculine identity formation, complete with its own set of practices and values divorced from market forces. Men used the gym not merely as athletes training in their spare time but rather as workers use their places of employment; they labored to convert joblessness into self-respect, proving to themselves and their peers that they, too, wanted to and could work. In a time of mass incarceration, the ever-present specter of imprisonment haunts the gym, and men with experiences with forced confinement joined Gleason's to reenter society and receive guidance and support from men with similar histories. With limited other opportunities, the gym remains one of the last social institutions available to them for masculine socialization and for building individual and collective forms of identity.

While poor and working-class New Yorkers experienced a decline in living standards, new subjects, objects, and spaces of commodification produced new social experiences for the upper-middle and upper classes. Wealthy men and women, primarily white, who have benefited from postindustrialism's social and economic arrangements, turned their attention to consumption and their gaze to their bodies.[5] A burgeoning fitness industry, which included health clubs and media, programs for fit lifestyles, and personal training regimes, offered products and services to an increasingly body-obsessed consumer culture. Cosmopolitanism, multiculturalism, and diversity bolstered unprecedented amounts of advertising. Black male authenticity, a new site of cultural capital, sold fitness products to men anxious about their masculinity.[6] With the enactment of Title IX of the Education Amendments of 1972, advertising firms capitalized on the increasing participation among women in competitive sporting activities. Their campaigns promoted female empowerment, bodily strength, and self-defense.[7]

Bruce Silverglade quickly recognized that to survive the pressures of gentrification and other economic restructurings, he needed new sources of revenue. He took advantage of trends in the postindustrial fitness industry by inviting doctors, lawyers, and investment bankers to Front Street to be instructed by gym trainers and fighters. Preoccupied with their masculinity and attracted to the bodily strength of black men, white-collar clients sought a powerful manhood by proximity to blackness. Women, with determination to become strong and confident in their bodies, signed up in large numbers.

And yet, if postindustrial social and economic conditions create the constellation of people at Gleason's Gym, such circumstances do not determine the gym's internal social practices, social relations, and power relations. *Come Out Swinging: The Changing World of Boxing in Gleason's Gym* analyzes how different groups of gym members use the gym in different ways. It is an ethnography of how gym enthusiasts practice boxing training, how they collectively make and mold the gym's social space, and, in doing so, how they negotiate life in postindustrial New York.[8] *Come Out Swinging* documents how Gleason's membership improvises arrangements for members' well-being and how principles such as reciprocity and redistribution are admired and flourish. It shows how value is produced in ways different from the market economy, with not all interactions motivated by the desire to make money and not all forms of value defined by the demand for profit.[9] The social practices, social relations, and relations of power in Gleason's Gym demonstrate that actions can occur both *within* and *in response to* the market and illuminate the inventive ways that some people use boxing training to answer back to forms of inequality, such as gender subordination, anti-black racism, and class stratification, as well as the ways the wealthy simultaneously use capital from new markets to forge identities and entertain themselves.

Come Out Swinging is interested in the social experience of postindustrialism as it is lived. The postindustrial is not only an economic and social restructuring but also a way of life. Accordingly, this book is concerned with how and why people construct certain identities in postindustrial circumstances. I examine one space in New York City—the urban boxing gym—where people go to create work, develop a sense of self-worth, consume, and process their social worlds. It is one site among many, but it is important in a society that is increasingly turning its attention to the body.[10] *Come Out Swinging* argues that through postindustrial changes, the ethos of the urban boxing gym has been protected, but in the process, it has been commodified. In Gleason's Gym, members relate to this boxing ethos and attendant commodification differently. Each group invests its own meanings in the gym's culture, undertakes boxing training in various ways, and produces new lived experiences. These new uses of space and reinvented ways of life illuminate how, with the right resources, postindustrial spaces can be transformed and avoid obliteration.

COME OUT SWINGING

Chapter One

SURVIVAL IN A CITY TRANSFORMED: THE URBAN BOXING GYM IN POSTINDUSTRIAL NEW YORK

OVER THE PAST FOUR DECADES, NEW YORK CITY'S SOCIAL, economic, and political structures have transformed dramatically, and the word "postindustrial" is used to describe these changes. "Postindustrial" is used in a number of contexts, and the trends that it captures are subject to myriad interpretations by scholars, policymakers, and social critics. As a result, the term is contested and not without discursive, political, and ideological problems.[1] However, "postindustrial" can be a useful way to mark the decline in manufacturing and the acceleration of the FIRE economy—finance, insurance, and real estate—in urban centers and some of the resulting social and cultural conditions and structures of feeling among city residents. This chapter, "Survival in a City Transformed," provides a sketch of the postindustrial landscape of New York City, in which Gleason's Gym and this ethnography are situated. The first part of the chapter examines postindustrial restructurings and some of the accompanying social and cultural changes, such as the elimination of welfare entitlements, the expansion of crime control, and the ascension of consumer capitalism. The second part looks at how postindustrial restructurings affected urban boxing gyms in New York City. I argue that Gleason's Gym survived the vicissitudes of the new postindustrial economy by incorporating some of its features, such as the turn to multiculturalism and diversity, the shift to cosmopolitanism and aggressive advertising, and the focus on the body and emergence of the fitness industry.

POSTINDUSTRIAL ECONOMIC AND SOCIAL RESTRUCTURINGS

New York's Labor and Housing Markets

In studies of the labor market, the postindustrial points to a specific economic restructuring that began in the late 1960s in which metropolitan centers that manufactured goods began to focus more heavily on retail, financial, and corporate services.[2] That is, the postindustrial registers a reorganization in which reliance on industrial capital was replaced by reliance on the FIRE industries. As industrial operations scattered to the global south, which offered lower taxes as well as less regulation, union organizing, and collective bargaining, cities in the Northeast and the Midwest lost a devastating number of jobs, turning them into rustbelt regions.[3] Though many urban economies suffered from this process of deindustrialization, New York City was disproportionately affected. The changes New York City endured were more exaggerated and the growth of services quicker and more extensive than in other cities.[4] Between 1965 and 1989, the number of manufacturing jobs in New York fell from 865,000 to 355,000, causing a rapid rise in unemployment.[5] Workers who lost manufacturing jobs had a difficult time finding employment of comparable remuneration in the new service economy and had few opportunities for upward mobility.[6]

While Fordist models of production were on the decline, new modes of accumulation gained ascendancy.[7] New possibilities for global trade and direct foreign investment, innovations in technology and its uses, advances in transportation, and the growing power of multinational finance and telecommunication firms shaped the postindustrial economy.[8] In her work on the globalization of economic activity, Saskia Sassen suggests that cities such as New York emerged not only as places where capital is coordinated but also as production sites. The production of financial goods and services requires what she calls "dispersal" and "concentration"; because some economic practices are decentralized, others must be more centralized.[9] For instance, as jobs moved from US metropolitan centers to peripheral low-wage areas, more coordination was necessary in central business districts. Sassen explains, "The more dispersed a firm's operations across different countries, the more complex and strategic its central functions—that is, the work of managing, coordinating, servicing, financing a firm's network of operations."[10] A new class of professionals to do this managing, coordinating, servicing and financing soon formed.

Concentration and dispersal restructured the labor market and changed the nature of work in urban areas. Workers bifurcated into "core" and "contingent" laborers. Core workers are executives, consultants, managers, and a range of specialists who manage capital. Contingent workers, or unskilled laborers in personal services, support the economic activities and personal lives of core workers.[11] The experiences of work and the financial compensation of the two groups stand in sharp contrast. Core workers enjoy higher salaries, better benefits, and more job security than contingent workers and, as a result, the former have access to more possibilities for wealth accrual, such as investment in stocks, bonds, and mutual funds.[12] Contingent workers engage in low-wage and unstable work: typically labor that has been subcontracted or that is part-time, seasonal, and temporary.[13] Though this flexibility reduces costs, it creates job insecurity and instability, benefit losses, and a reduction in investment in human capital.[14]

While the postindustrial economy promised new possibilities of profit and accumulation, wealth was unevenly distributed across society.[15] The owners and managers of capital disproportionally benefitted from the economy's splendors and a polarization of income financially distanced contingent workers from core workers.[16] An earning gap between manufacturing and nonmanufacturing, retail services and corporate services, and the outlying boroughs and Manhattan increased the gap between poor and rich.[17] Service jobs of contingent workers paid far less than did Fordist manufacturing jobs, and the remaining manufacturing jobs became low-wage and low-skill. Unionization rates plummeted and the power of remaining unions to negotiate reasonable contracts diminished.[18] Further, the new economy presented tremendous obstacles to career advancement and social mobility for contingent workers.[19] On the whole, low-income service jobs caused contingent workers to labor more and make less.[20]

New York City's economic restructuring disproportionately affected black and Latino residents and created a racialized and gendered division of labor.[21] In the postindustrial economy, black and Latino workers were excluded from the best-paid jobs. With their circumstances compounded by employers' preferences for Latino workers, women, and even white ex-prisoners over black workers without criminal records, black men faced difficulty even securing low-wage employment.[22] When they did obtain work, black men were paid below living wages. Poverty rates skyrocketed and produced new forms of racial inequality. Under- and unemployment continue to burden workers of color. In 2004, 72 percent of black men in their twenties who had not completed high school did not have work, while 50 percent of black high-school graduates could not find a job.[23] Today the division of labor in postindustrial New York is split predominantly among white men (and, to a lesser extent, white women) in professional and management positions, black women and Latino men and women working in clerical or service jobs, and Asian and Latino workers laboring in the remaining low-income manufacturing positions.[24]

The racial inequalities in the service economy reproduced themselves spatially in the form of residential segregation. The new economy required space for expanding businesses, hospitals, and universities while a growing class of core workers in postindustrial growth sectors produced new markets for luxury condominiums and Manhattan loft space.[25] Urban areas previously zoned for industry were repurposed and developed as office and residential quarters. The pace of gentrification accelerated and real estate speculation escalated. Much of the city's real estate was gobbled up by the rich, decimating the number of affordable housing units for working individuals and families. The housing market in areas of New York with large numbers of black and Latino residents—namely the Bronx, northern Manhattan, the Lower East Side of Manhattan, and central Brooklyn—collapsed.[26] Alex Vitale writes:

> Throughout the 1980s, the city's spending on homelessness-related services was directed toward providing emergency shelter and social services. Only a small amount was spent on creating new affordable housing for those on public assistance or working for low wages. At the same time, however, billions were spent on tax incentives and direct subsidies to encourage the development of high-rent commercial buildings and luxury housing, which often displaced low-income housing and low-skilled jobs. This unequal development destabilized many middle-class communities through the twin problems of rampant disorder emanating from the growing underclass and gentrification pressures coming from the new, extremely wealthy professional class.[27]

Such spending priorities precipitated a housing crisis that continues to affect families of color, who are more likely to live in overcrowded and decrepit housing than are white residents.[28]

Social Entitlements and Crime Control

Postindustrialism not only restructured the labor and housing markets but also redefined the relationships among capital, workers, and the state. The market gained enormous power in the economic and social lives of

New York City residents just as the state began shirking its responsibilities for providing social entitlements.[29] A system of governance promoting corporate deregulation, social-welfare cuts, and law and order policies supported the postindustrial economy. Contrary to the priorities of state intervention created under twentieth-century industrial capitalism, this system of governance relies on discourses of "personal responsibility," which look to the market and individual initiative rather than structural context or social conditions to solve social problems and inequalities.[30] Welfare reform, which began under President Reagan and was refined under President G.H.W. Bush, culminated in President Clinton's 1996 Personal Responsibility and Work Opportunity Reconciliation Act and obliterated three-quarters of a century of social welfare for the poor. Logistically, by annihilating Aid to Families with Dependent Children (AFDC), an outgrowth of earlier mother and widow pension programs, and creating Temporary Assistance to Needy Families (TANF), the law imposed time limits on social assistance, required clients to work in low-wage positions, and slashed compensation. Ideologically, it attacked the disenfranchised and marginalized, especially the poor of color, and blamed them for their circumstances. It also buttressed a postindustrial labor market that needed low-skill and low-wage workers to fill service positions. In doing so, it created a group of vulnerable workers who were available to capital for exploitation, a racialized process.[31]

Welfare reform was just one part of a larger conservative attack on the poor of color, especially urban youth, and dovetailed with a new focus on law and order, particularly crime control.[32] "Tough on crime" legislation and practices abolished rehabilitation, for the most part, and fixated instead on an array of new penalties, such as three-strike rules,[33] truth-in-sentencing laws,[34] victim impact statements, sentencing guidelines, and "zero tolerance." The emerging crime complex instituted longer sentences than ever before and expanded the number of nonviolent acts considered criminal, which exploded the prison population even as crime rates dropped.[35] Between 1970 and 1982, the US prison population doubled, and between 1982 and 1999, it tripled.[36] The prison industry in the United States costs roughly $35 billion and employs more than 525,000 workers, more than any Fortune 500 company other than Ford Motors.[37] It confines more than two million people and forces nearly five million additional individuals under custodial supervision, such as parole, probation, and work release.[38] Most of these men and women are low-skilled, low-income black and Latino and have been charged with low-level drug trading and consuming, even though, as Michelle Alexander documents, drugs are used and sold at comparable rates across race lines.[39]

Consumer Culture and the Rise of Urban Fitness

As the structure of the economy and governance changed, consumer culture in the US grew rapidly. Whereas many scholars focus on the FIRE industries to understand New York's transformation, others look at how postindustrial spaces and capital provided resources for new forms of cultural production. What were once wastelands and sites of decay and abandonment turned into premier locations for redevelopment and cultural attractions.[40] In an attempt to lure consumers possessing amounts of wealth unparalleled in history into spending large sums, cities promoted renewal projects and invested in upscale leisure activities, hotels, convention centers, restaurants, shopping malls, theaters, and the revitalization of downtown and waterfront areas.[41] At the same time, newly commodified cultural objects and subjects proliferated and expanded their reach in the global marketplace.[42] With more disposable income and better access to mass-produced and mass-marketed goods, individuals and families enjoyed unprecedented levels of consumption.[43] In New York, a thriving cultural economy provided billions of dollars in the forms of jobs and revenue and today employs almost as many people as finance and medicine do.[44] It is undergirded by diversity, multiculturalism, and advertising. Richard Lloyd explains:

> In contrast to theories of the city as trending toward increased homogenization and sanitation in response to the demands of new residents, diversity here is taken to be a central principle of urban authenticity, and the definition of diversity typically proffered by local artists gives value to the illicit and the bizarre. For an admittedly small but disproportionately influential class of tastemakers, elements of the urban experience that are usually considered to be an aesthetic blight become a symbol of the desire to master an environment characterized by marginality and social instability.[45]

Cultural producers sold their products and entire lifestyles by capitalizing on cultural fascinations with authenticity.[46]

An expanding urban fitness industry, of which Gleason's Gym was a part, catered to consumers eager to imagine new possibilities for their bodies. In a postindustrial social order, gender expectations became unstable and ever more fluid. As masculinity, in particular, decoupled from wage labor, generating anxiety in the process, sports and body culture provided men with a knowable and concrete means to identity formation.[47] With Title IX legislation, women had more opportunities in sport than ever before. They experimented with new ways of fashioning their bodies and looked to athletics and urban fitness as a way to try on novel gender configurations and expressions.[48] For both men and women, the body became the site of "work." It also became a profit-generating commodity that encouraged continual purchases. Programs for healthy lifestyles and products for bodily perfection promised consumers techniques to improve themselves and advertisers avenues to generous revenue streams.[49]

Over time, working on the body was infused with morality. Just as the Calvinist quest for wealth was a marker of morality in an earlier era, the postindustrial disciplined body promoted the control necessary to support the ideals of consumer capitalism.[50] While this new body culture included some New Yorkers, it excluded others, especially the poor, and reinforced an ideological divide that blamed the disadvantaged for their structural position. Shari L. Dworkin and Faye Linda Wachs suggest:

> In short, consumer culture provides continual absolution to privileged bodies through these "small successes" and the self-satisfaction of participation in a set of identity-validating middle-class and upper-middle-class lifestyles. Docile bodies fare differently. Stigmatized as immoral, lazy, and poor citizens, docile bodies are presented as failing to follow the prescriptions attended to by the readers. The structural constraints are rendered invisible as it is implying a question of "making time" or the right choices.[51]

These bodily consumptive imperatives, postindustrial governance, and discourses of personal responsibility connected. The primacy of personal-responsibility narratives in health and fitness economies perniciously supported neoliberal ideologies and practices that rendered invisible the government's contribution to structural circumstance and, more important, to serious health disparities.[52]

POSTINDUSTRIALISM AND THE NEW YORK CITY BOXING GYM

Historically, boxing gyms patronized by poor and working-class men of color have flourished in New York City. But postindustrial restructurings made it difficult for big and neighborhood gyms, for-profit and not-for-profit alike, to keep up with the pace of inflation, meet insurance premiums, accommodate rising real estate prices, and survive processes of gentrification. In January of 1996, Bill Farrell of the *New York Daily News* wrote, “It seems that just as corporations are ‘down-sizing,’ so are local gyms.”[53] Over the past twenty-five years, many boxing gyms have had to close their doors. From a high of 150 in the mid-1970s, the number of urban gyms dropped below 50 in 2000.[54] Times Square Gym, long considered one of the three most “serious” professional gyms in New York, was forced to shut its doors in 1994 by the Times Square Redevelopment Corporation in order to make room for upscale office towers, business plazas, and entertainment centers.[55] Gramercy Gym, another serious gym and Cus D’Amato’s famous institution, closed down in 1993, while trainers from the Bed-Stuy Boxing Center, the last serious gym and a legendary establishment founded by George Washington, sparring partner to Joe Louis, abandoned their gym in 1999 because of mismanagement, poor lighting, broken windows, lack of heat, and few employment opportunities. In August of 2002, Bruce Silverglade estimated that there were, at that time, ten legitimate operational gyms in New York.[56] Silverglade lamented that to stay afloat in the New York City economy, boxing gyms needed to be heavily subsidized or have a large membership to help pay overhead costs.

The number of boxing gyms in New York is difficult to assess because gyms open and close with great frequency. One way to estimate numbers is to look at the organizations registered with USA Boxing Metro, the regional sanctioning body for amateur boxing in the greater New York area.[57] In 2004 and 2005, twenty-eight boxing gyms were tallied by USA Boxing Metro.[58] However, this number does not encompass all gyms, clubs, or programs in New York City. Rather, it includes the gyms that train competitive amateurs who participate in the Golden Gloves, the country’s major amateur tournament.[59] Many boxing programs in nonprofit recreation centers such as the YMCA, or in health clubs such as Crunch Fitness, may not appear in USA Boxing Metro’s directory because they do not always send amateur fighters to the Golden Gloves. Some clubs may register with USA Boxing Metro one year and not the next; hence, the number of gyms registered is subject to change from year to year. In addition, gyms that work only with white-collar boxers will not appear on this inventory at all.

Despite difficulty in obtaining concrete numbers, boxing gyms in New York City can be divided into three categories: (1) gyms devoted to amateur and professional fighters, (2) gyms dedicated to working primarily with white-collar boxers, and (3) gyms utilized by a combination of amateur, professional, and white-collar athletes. Gyms in the first category tend to be small neighborhood-based nonprofits.[60] Because they do not enjoy revenue from white-collar clients, they usually survive, as Silverglade argues, through subsidy of some sort. Included in this category are gyms such as the New Bed-Stuy Boxing Center in Bedford-Stuyvesant, Kid Kelly Sports Boxing Gym in Williamsburg, and Morris Park Boxing Gym in the Bronx. The gyms in this category can include organizations with ties to law enforcement, such as the handful of gyms throughout the five boroughs operated by the Police Athletic League (PAL). They also include the recreational centers run by the New York City Parks and Recreation Department.

Gyms and programs populated in the second category are a more recent phenomenon and have carved out a niche based upon trends in urban fitness that have invited workout addicts to train to box but not necessarily compete. With the success of movies such as *Million Dollar Baby*, *Cinderella Man*, and *The Fighter* and TV shows such as *The Contender*, an ever-growing number of recreational athletes have expressed interest in training to box. These athletes, who are predominately white and upper-middle- and upper-class men, pay substantial amounts of money to join for-profit gyms, such as Trinity Boxing Club, established to cater to them. Or they participate in boxing programs in health clubs, such as Crunch Fitness, Equinox Fitness Club, New York Athletic Club, and Chelsea Piers. Such gyms and programs are expensive. A monthly membership at Trinity Boxing Club, for example, costs between $200 and $250, and ten private lessons cost $1,250.[61]

The gyms in the last category are also for profit but train a range of athletes—white collar, amateur, and professional. They can afford to keep their central locations (many of these gyms are located in trendy parts of Manhattan), offer better gym resources, and maintain more pristine conditions than neighborhood not-for-profit gyms because of the revenue generated by white-collar clients. Gyms such as Kingsway Boxing and Fitness, Church Street Boxing Gym, and Mendez Boxing in Manhattan train some amateurs and some professionals while being frequented by a number of white-collar clients, who sign up for either group classes or private lessons with a trainer. These gyms tend to be smaller versions of Gleason's Gym, which is also in this category. They offer similar amalgamations of amateur, professional, and recreational boxers, but their lack of space and facilities limits their ability to mobilize a sizable contingent of serious fighters.[62] Bruce Silverglade asserts, "There have been numerous pro boxing gyms throughout the city and most of them have closed down." Gleason's remains the only major boxing gym in the city that trains large numbers of amateur, professional, and white-collar boxers.

From Historic Boxing Institution to Neighborhood Fitness Center

Almost from its inception, Gleason's Gym became a mecca of serious pugilistic instruction, accommodating a legion of world champions. Prizefighters such as Jake LaMotta, Joe Frazier, and Roberto Duran regularly trained at Gleason's, while other champions and contenders exercised at the gym episodically while in New York City to fight. Muhammad Ali (then Cassius Clay) spent several weeks training at Gleason's Gym before his 1964 fight against Sonny Liston. The gym has trained more than 120 world champions and some of the country's most successful amateur athletes. Though there have been other famous and successful gyms in New York City, Gleason's Gym has surpassed its contemporaries in longevity and is currently the oldest operational boxing gym in the United States.

Gleason's Gym has lived three incarnations. In 1937, Peter Robert Gagliardi founded the gym at the intersection of 149th Street and Westchester Avenue in the South Bronx. Setting up shop in an Irish neighborhood and attempting to attract an Irish crowd to the fights, Gagliardi believed an Irish surname would help his business and changed his name to Bobby Gleason. His gym was a tiny establishment with one undersized ring and four heavy bags housed in a small loft. In 1974, a housing development chased the gym out of the Bronx and into Manhattan, and the second incarnation settled into a double storefront on 30th Street at Eighth Avenue, around the corner from Madison Square Garden. Its close proximity to the Garden positioned the gym as a highly accessible location for fighters preparing for professional bouts in the arena in the 1970s and 1980s. Bobby Gleason continued to run the gym until 1981, when Ira Becker, a New York businessman, took over. In 1983, another New York businessman with strong ties to the local amateur boxing circuit, Bruce Silverglade, became Becker's co-owner. By the early 1990s, Silverglade was sole owner.

In 1984, Gleason's Gym was once again forced out of its quarters by a volatile New York City real estate market and hopscotched across the East River to Front Street in Brooklyn, a barren area that would later be dubbed DUMBO. Though many skeptics warned that the move to a new borough and to that desolate area in particular would force the gym out of business, gym loyalists made the trip to Brooklyn, and Gleason's survived its third incarnation. In addition to being the destination for most serious amateur and professional boxers in New York, as DUMBO gentrified, Gleason's Gym became the neighborhood gym for upper-class residents. In this third incarnation boxers from sixty-seven countries sweat and exhaust themselves in the enormous 14,000-square-foot facility in four full-sized rings; on numerous heavy, speed, and double-end bags; with free weights; and on treadmills, StairMasters, and stationary bikes.[63]

POSTINDUSTRIAL CONDITIONS OF POSSIBILITY

While Gleason's Gym faced the same pressures of economic restructuring as other gyms in New York City, it was able to survive and even thrive because of the gym's reputation and the business savvy of the current owner, Bruce Silverglade, who tapped into postindustrial resources to keep the gym open. Because of its reputation, Gleason's was the first gym many fighters sought when their own gyms closed down. The fighters of Gramercy Gym took refuge in Gleason's when Gramercy was forced to shut its doors; former Gramercy owner Bob Jackson now manages his team, Empire Sports, from an office in Gleason's. When trainers from the Bed-Stuy Boxing Center looked for a new gym, they chose Gleason's, bringing their most successful and talented boxers with them. As the number of gyms dwindled, Gleason's Gym gained an increasingly captive audience among rigorous professional and amateur fighters who wanted serious sparring and an intense fighting community, as well as among trainers interested in collaborating with the most active people in the sport. As more gyms closed, Gleason's became stronger. Silverglade estimates, "I have the largest number of amateurs and pros of any gym in New York. Because of our name, reputation, and size, we attract great fighters and great trainers."

This name and reputation is not one upon which Silverglade passively relies. The gym is successful while others struggle because Silverglade spends significant time and effort thinking about how to keep the gym a major destination for amateurs, professionals, and white-collar boxers. Silverglade constantly shapes the gym's personality and institutional identity, which involves cultivating a highly profitable nostalgia in the media. Though his policy is to pay only for advertising in the yellow pages and occasionally in a local newspaper or magazine, he estimates that the gym receives $10 million to $12 million in free advertising per year through magazine and newspaper articles, TV segments, and film and music-video shoots. Some of this he attributes to the cyclical nature of and competition in the media: when one media outlet runs a story on the gym, others immediately rush to follow. He explains, "Somebody would do something about the women of Gleason's Gym and then someone else would, and it would go around and around again. And someone would do a story on a businessman and then someone else would." An abundance of successful and interesting boxers and gym programs, such as the monthly Friday night white-collar client shows, provides ample fodder for media interest.

But much of this free advertising is not simply due to the inherently interesting people who work out at the gym. Rather, it is a product of Silverglade's method of cultivating the conditions for newsworthy stories. In February 2004, for example, in order to avoid jail time, Mike Tyson pleaded guilty to a charge of disorderly conduct and promised one hundred hours of community service at Gleason's Gym teaching children to box while seeking psychiatric counseling.[64] The deal was Silverglade's idea and took over five months to negotiate with the district attorney's office. When the plea bargain was announced, it flashed around the world at lightning speed, and stories linking the former champion to Gleason's Gym appeared on televisions and radios and in magazines and newspapers domestically and abroad. The product of Silverglade's five-month toil was incalculable publicity. He says, "I didn't get any money for it, but I can't tell you, I can't even imagine how much publicity I got off that. That went around the world. Around the world. Everybody had 'Mike Tyson is working at Gleason's Gym doing community service.' And I've had call after call from media around the world." He continues, "For the past twenty-five years I've done everything I can to get the media in here."

Silverglade aims to keep as many people as possible coming through the doors of Gleason's Gym: not only the media, neighborhood residents, and athletes already invested in the pugilistic trade but also film stars, film crews, and photographers. Having this latter group gives the gym an indirect outlet for media attention. In order to prepare for her role in *Million Dollar Baby*, Hilary Swank trained at Gleason's Gym. In January 2005, when Swank won a Golden Globe, and in February 2005, when she won an Oscar for her performance, she thanked her Gleason's trainer, her sparring partners, and "the boxers of Gleason's Gym," bestowing more high-profile attention to the gym.[65] Photographers working for companies such as Ralph Lauren and Calvin Klein use the gym as the background for photo shoots. And the gym has been the site for numerous films—among them *Raging Bull* and several Woody Allen movies—and TV shows, such as *NYPD Blue*. Silverglade offered Gleason's for the book launch of a writer for the *Irish Echo*, who had penned several stories about the gym. He scheduled the launch to coincide with the monthly white-collar show, and the author immediately sold all the copies of his book that he had brought with him. When the publisher realized how successful the launch was, he asked if they could do another. Silverglade agreed but charged a fee for using the gym the second time.

Having film crews and photographers shooting in the gym provides the added advantage of supplementing the gym's income with location fees. Silverglade does not regularly depend on this income—he calls it "plus money"—but it does help dull the sharp pain of an ever-increasing rent. Silverglade is careful to make sure that such filming and celebrity visits do not adversely affect the everyday functioning of the gym. He ultimately envisions Gleason's as a community center and tries not to close his doors during filming, shoots, and celebrity cameos. During *Vanity Fair*'s visit to Gleason's Gym to do a photo shoot with Muhammad Ali, Silverglade kept the gym open in order to perpetuate its image as a place where the average person can train alongside famous ex-champions and movie stars. Silverglade says, "I wanted the neighbors to say, 'Hey, you can walk into that gym and Ali will be there! And I went in and had my picture taken.' " Similarly when Hilary Swank and Craig Bierko, who prepared at Gleason's for his role as Max Baer in *Cinderella Man*, frequented the gym, they trained on the same heavy bags and in the same rings as other gym regulars and did not receive special treatment from the gym's management.

Silverglade also refuses to close the gym for reigning prizefighters, many of whom request total privacy while training for big bouts and expect solitary training sessions. Silverglade likes the fact that no one gets preferential treatment and he works very hard to develop and control this personality of the gym. He reflects,

> It's a community center, and that's what I like. I like the kids who come up here. I like the fact that the parents will bring their kids up here. They like this place. They trust this place enough to bring their children up here. Many gyms are stricter and not as loose as it is up here. But I think that my attitude and the way I run this is what makes it a success. People want to come over here.

Possibly more important, taking cues from the emerging urban fitness economy, Silverglade makes the gym accessible to people who, historically, are unusual for a boxing gym: white-collar clients and women. Over the past thirty years, he has cultivated a new type of gym enthusiast—whom he calls the "nouveau clientele" and whom trainers call "clients." Clients often have little to no interest in competitive boxing but nonetheless seek a rigorous workout under the watchful eye of an "authentic" trainer. Recreational athletes have always frequented boxing gyms in small numbers, not only to observe but also to work out. Ernest Hemingway boxed, and Miles Davis worked with a professional trainer at Gleason's Gym in the mid-1950s.[66] But Silverglade was the first gym owner to market directly to these upper-middle- and upper-class men and to create special training programs for them. As the numbers of these boxers increased, he realized that they had few opportunities to showcase their skills. He remembers, "I had all these people training here and, as you know, it's an addictive sport, so they say, 'What am I doing this for? What's next?' So I had to have a reason for people to stay here and train." The result was a white-collar boxing league, in which participants fight in three two-minute rounds. No winners and losers are declared. Rather, both participants' hands are raised at the end of the bout, and both boxers receive trophies. Silverglade's appeal to this nouveau clientele has been extremely successful, and the shows continue to run. White-collar cards draw crowds of between 100 and 200 people monthly, and sister leagues run in cities such as London, Tokyo, and Dubai.

Finally, much of Gleason's survival of postindustrial restructuring is due to Ira Becker and Bruce Silverglade's decision in the mid-1980s to allow women to train at the gym. For years, women who had visited the gym in Manhattan as part of video and still-picture shoots had inquired about training possibilities for female athletes. At that time Becker was adamantly opposed to a female membership. Silverglade recalls, "There were always women who said, 'Jeez, we want to do this.' And we kept saying, 'No. You can't come into our place.'" Though Silverglade wanted women to participate in the sport—and more specifically to pay membership fees—he deferred to his older partner, who preferred to keep the gym's identity as an old-time professional boxing gym, reserved for working-class masculinity and the gruffly male sensibility of smoking sportswriters. But over time Silverglade recognized that women's memberships were a financial opportunity that the gym could not afford to forfeit, and he eventually persuaded his partner of its economic necessity. The gym opened its doors to women in 1983. Because Gleason's Gym in Manhattan had only one shower room, two shower stalls, and a very small dressing room, Silverglade and Becker closed the gym early three nights a week to allow women to use the facility. The arrangement was an instant success, and women became a permanent fixture of this urban community's landscape. When the gym moved to Brooklyn, a separate locker room was constructed for female members so that they could have access to the gym at the same time as male members.

Financially, white-collar clients and women are invaluable to the gym. They tend to be steady and consistent patrons, and their memberships are responsible for keeping the gym afloat in turbulent economic times. Silverglade calculated, "If it weren't for the white-collar men and women, Gleason's would be a much smaller gym or . . . nonexistent."[67] The number of women and clients not only helps the gym function smoothly but also employs gym trainers, which helps boxing coaches generate an income. Whereas boxing trainers historically coached in the evening hours and worked day shifts elsewhere to make ends meet, many trainers at the gym now don't have to work outside the gym and can devote all of their time and energy to training. The new clientele has made this decision financially feasible as they pay between $20 and $75 per hour for boxing instruction.

Gleason's celebrity in pugilistic circles and its popularity with male and female residents of DUMBO helped it survive the economic restructurings of postindustrialism. This survival, in turn, has made possible new sets of social relations and practices of the gym. In the chapters that follow, I consider some of these uses of the gym.

Chapter Two

WORK WITHOUT WAGES

"The first thing to be learnt in Boxing is the Attitude or Guard."

—A PUPIL BOTH OF HUMPHREYS AND MENDOZA, 1784

ON AN AFTERNOON IN LATE AUGUST, ADRIAN AND I STROLL leisurely along Court Street in Brooklyn from the public library, where we have checked our email. Adrian, a twenty-two-year-old amateur boxer, is fresh from a humiliating loss in a fight that everyone in Gleason's Gym agrees he was physically prepared to win. His training has been rigorous and focused for the past several months, but he has suffered defeat after defeat to athletes he is talented enough to dominate in the ring. In a somber tone, he tells me that he has given up too much not to see any results and that the costs that boxing demands now outweigh the benefits. The series of failures threatens his reputation as a man and his status in the gym, while the burden of meeting the monthly membership dues has become exhausting.[1] To preserve his dignity and cope with limited funds, Adrian has decided to quit the sport.

Up until now, Adrian has found success in the gym. He is known as one of the hardest working fighters and is reputed for his discipline, regimentation, and asceticism. He is not the most physically gifted athlete, but his quick thinking in the ring and his ability to thrive during grueling training sessions have earned him respect as a pugilist. Socially, he is a fixture of gym life. Years earlier when he arrived, he could not so much as make eye contact with anyone. Physically abused by a parent, emotionally neglected by teachers, and teased by students, Adrian preferred his own company, had few friends, and trained by himself rather than with a coach. Yet slowly he inched his way into the community and over time bonded with trainers and other boxers. He found he could hold conversations, ask for and offer advice, and participate in the gym's vibrant culture.

With few social and economic opportunities outside the gym, Adrian threw himself into the gym, spending long days there. Though he tried to find work, he had difficulty locating anything stable or financially adequate. If contacted by a department store that episodically asks him to unload merchandise, he will put in several hours at minimum wage. But these earnings leave him unable to afford housing and often food and transportation fees. Adrian reconciled himself to living in a cramped, rundown one-bedroom apartment in a remote section of the Bronx with his mother and sister. He resigned himself to eating rice and beans, drinking coffee to suppress his appetite, and skipping meals when necessary. And he has resolved to walk to Gleason's from the Bronx and back, a roughly fifteen-mile journey each way, when there is not money for a metro card. For these sacrifices, he invests his time at the gym, developing a sense of self and socializing with other men in similar social predicaments in order to be part of a community. But these identities and standing, which he has worked fiercely to construct, currently are jeopardized by his athletic disappointments.

Our conversation drifts from Adrian's athletic, psychological, and financial frustrations to the hardships of his teammates. The discussion is glum. One fighter has lost an important bout, another his job, and still another has been remanded to jail. Adrian remarks that our conversation is precisely why he does not want to read my book about gym life: it will expose too many disappointments and be too depressing.

Though bleak, my talk with Adrian is an apt frame through which to begin to analyze how amateur boxers use Gleason's Gym, because it touches on some of the social circumstances that shape the lived experiences of young men of color in New York City: the lack of formal work, the burden of economic struggle, and the constant threat of imprisonment.[2] Our conversation also demonstrates some of the ways in which amateur boxers utilize the urban gym to respond to their social-structural position: the meanings they derive from their punishing workouts, the hopes they have for achieving victory in the ring, and the admired forms of masculinity they long to possess. This chapter looks at the work that male amateur fighters undertake in Gleason's Gym. It examines the physical practices amateur boxers improvise, the meanings of those practices, and their connections to the transformation of social space in postindustrial New York. I argue that although amateur fighters are unpaid, they consider boxing to be their job. They approach training with the insistence and purpose of an occupation rather than as a pastime or hobby, and they use pugilism to implement discipline, create identities, and earn respect from others. By engaging in amateur athletics, young men are able to see themselves as a different type of laborer and produce a new kind of work—bodywork—and attendant forms of value.[3]

Amateur boxers disentangle traditional moral and emotional features of work from economic compensation. In the case of the amateur, the social status and cultural recognition achieved from training one's own body is neither the product nor the source of financial gain. Yet value *is* engendered through gym practices when amateur pugilists invest in the sharp, intellectual training of their minds and the strength, skill, and agility of their bodies. Whereas social scientists understand value primarily as the by-product of formalized work, amateur fighters illuminate that status and recognition can be generated in alternative institutions in a postindustrial landscape—but without wages.[4]

THE AMATEUR BOXERS OF GLEASON'S GYM

The amateur male fighters of Gleason's Gym are primarily men of color between seventeen and twenty-seven years old, with the majority clustered between nineteen and twenty-four. They travel to the gym from similar neighborhoods—Bedford-Stuyvesant, Brownsville, Bushwick, Canarsie, Crown Heights, East New York, and Flatbush in Brooklyn; the South Bronx; Far Rockaway in Queens; and Harlem and the Lower East Side in Manhattan—and grew up in families that used social-welfare programs. Most live in social housing, and if they can, many continue to cohabit with family, as they cannot afford their own apartments.

The most notable commonality of this group is the shared experience of imprisonment or of having spent time in the custody of the state, such as in juvenile detention centers, prison schools, and boot camps. Mike, one of Gleason's most expert trainers, says, "Most of the guys I work with have been locked up at one time or another." Many amateur boxers have engaged or do engage in criminal labor—most frequently the drug trade—and have been sentenced to time in jail and prison for drug, drug-related, parole, or probation-related offenses. Because they came into contact with the criminal justice system when New York City and the rest of the country were getting "tough on crime" and implementing "zero-tolerance" policies, teenagers were tried not as juveniles but rather as adults.[5] Anthony served a five-year stint in a number of maximum-security state prisons as a sixteen-year-old, and Kenny entered prison at the same age.

As a result, Gleason's amateur boxers pass much of their adolescence in prison cells. While their nonincarcerated peers are learning "how to be men," as they say in the gym, by figuring out how to relate to romantic interests, differentiating from peers, and separating from parental households, many of Gleason's amateurs wither away in solitary conditions or in recreation rooms with men much older than them and with little to no contact with others their age. Other men bounce in and out of prison throughout their teenage years. Even those who reject participation in criminal economies and make a concerted effort to avoid breaking the law have a difficult time avoiding incarceration. They are arrested for what ethnographer John Horton's participants call "suspicion of suspicion": being in the wrong place at the wrong time without identification, such as during New York Police Department (NYPD) Technical Narcotics Team (TNT) raids in their buildings, or lacking proper documentation while driving.[6] When they cannot afford bail, they are held in jail—usually on Rikers Island, one of the world's largest penal colonies—until the charges are dropped.[7]

Because amateur fighters are incarcerated as teenagers, most young men who have been imprisoned earn their highest educational degree—the general equivalency diploma (GED)—behind bars. As the majority of amateur boxers who had not been forcibly confined terminated their education at some point in high school, New York State prisons are among the largest educators of amateur athletes in Gleason's Gym. In 1994, the crime bill, or Public Law No. 103-322, cut the eligibility of prisoners for Pell Grants, forcing most degree-granting college programs located in prisons to shut down.[8] As a result, very few men have experience with higher education programs. Roy completed college, while Paul, Leon, Collin, and Anthony worked full-time, trying to balance boxing and completing their degrees. These five boxers either received assistance from their colleges or had strong support networks. Roy, the one college graduate, had earned a basketball scholarship from a small school in New Jersey, whereas Paul, Leon, and Anthony received emotional or financial help or both from families or trainers. Even with such support, the demanding schedule burned out aspiring students. Anthony left school; and Paul and Leon spent years trying to complete their degrees. Those without support had an even more difficult time. Collin left school after he suffered exhaustion from working full time and going to college full time. Max dropped out due to cost; he found paying for community college feasible while selling heroin but could not meet his tuition and living costs after he stopped working as a drug salesman.

Related to time in prison and modest educational backgrounds is the difficulty that amateur boxers have finding employment. Mike, the trainer, reflects, "The majority of these guys are at minimum wage. But most don't work." Anti-black racism in employment procedures and the lack of existing wage labor combine to limit the availability of adequate work for young men of color. Christian Parenti argues that racial discrimination has intensified in the postindustrial era, observing that "[h]iring and firing practices in the service sector are more racist than in industrial employment."[9] Devah Pager finds that white men with criminal records are more likely to get hired than black men *without* criminal records.[10] During my fieldwork, roughly half of the amateur boxers were unemployed, despite actively seeking jobs. Those who could secure work had to settle for jobs that paid below living, minimum, or subminimum wage, laboring as janitors, security guards, mechanics, restaurant workers, delivery drivers, and stockroom clerks, which paid between $3 and $12 per hour. As mentioned earlier, Adrian could obtain five to eight hours per week unloading merchandise for a department store at minimum wage. At $5.15 per hour this left him with, at best, $165 per month. After getting kicked out of his mother's apartment, he became homeless, spending five years unhoused. Hungry, he attempted to steal food from a restaurant but was caught and incarcerated on Rikers Island. It was only after he was diagnosed with a psychological disorder that made him eligible for accommodation through a nonprofit organization that he found stable lodging. Diego was offered a dishwashing position in a neighborhood restaurant for three dollars per hour, a position he felt he had to take to satisfy the conditions of his parole, which required that he held a job.[11] He realized very quickly that it was impossible to support his girlfriend and daughter on this salary on the Lower East Side of Manhattan, even though his family lived with relatives to defray housing expenses. He soon looked to extra-legal economies to supplement his income.

Those who can locate adequate lawful labor find it challenging to keep, and their positions are the first to be cut when their companies downsize.[12] Max found work at a home furnishings retailer through a white-collar client at Gleason's Gym and held the job for over a year. When the US economy slowed, he was laid off and, despite aggressively searching for employment, could not find a way to support his girlfriend and child. Kenny experienced similar difficulties; he worked as a security guard in a women's shelter in the Bronx for years, but after being let go, he could not secure comparable employment. Much of the persistent trouble maintaining adequate work could be attributed to criminal records, but even those who had not been convicted of a misdemeanor or felony found it very challenging if not altogether impossible to capture a stable job.

The combination of histories of incarceration, short educational backgrounds, and difficulty finding employment means that young men of color—both with and without criminal records—lose access to work and the educational capital required to secure it.[13] Without jobs, they cannot acquire the material resources necessary to build and support households, which Paul Willis argues is "the main living embodiment of the labourer's 'freedom and independence' from capital."[14] The absence of wage work and educational opportunity then shapes possibilities for building forms of identity. Willis asserts that labor "brings a sense of self and maturity which is achieved through insight and experience rather than through the mere acquisition of years, or through someone else's say so."[15] In other words, without jobs, men cannot create the individual identities traditionally associated with wage labor, as well as the benefits of those identities, such as social knowledge, recognition, and status. Without a work site, they also cannot build collective forms of identity.[16]

Because amateur boxers are not in school or at work, they have a significant amount of time on their hands. There are also a limited number of places they can go. Men who have participated in criminal economies but want to avoid returning to them after prison face a challenge passing their days; they cannot return to their neighborhoods and former "places of work" because of the financial and social pressure to reengage in crime, as well as the risks of associating with "known criminals" and being suspected of criminal behavior, both of which are technical parole violations. Men who want to avoid re-incarceration say that before joining the gym, their only option was to "sit up in the house." But the sustainability of staying in one's apartment is tenuous. Shari Dworkin and Faye Linda Wachs suggest that the collapse of work in postindustrial spaces is marked by a renewed interest in bodywork, while Paul Willis wonders if men will "convert male working-class culture to individual body culture."[17] At Gleason's Gym, amateur boxers do just that. Amateur fighters recast traditional features of the wage to create a new kind of physical work in the gym—bodywork—which allows them to develop the identities traditionally associated with formal work, but in a postindustrial landscape.

"FOR THE SHEER LOVE OF IT": THE ART OF THE AMATEUR

Gleason's Gym is open Monday through Friday from 6:00 a.m. to 10:00 p.m. and on Saturday and Sunday from 8:30 a.m to 5:30 p.m. Members can train at the gym when they like, but because of employment and school schedules, various groups congregate at particular times. Gym enthusiasts who have traditional 9:00 a.m. to 5:00 p.m. workdays, such as white-collar clients, firefighters, and police officers, frequent the gym between 6:00 p.m. and 10:00 p.m. Children visit the gym after school, arriving between 3:00 p.m. and 4:00 p.m. Gym regulars commonly refer to the period of time between 10:00 a.m. and 2:00 p.m. as "pro time" because it is when professional fighters come to receive the quiet, undivided attention of their trainers, to spar with others of similar ability, and avoid the chaos that the previously-mentioned groups can generate. Because amateurs are not at work or in school, they, too, can train between 10:00 a.m. and 2:00 p.m. Even amateur boxers who are employed frequently take night shifts to make pro time. Jeffrey, for example, worked for the sanitation department at night in order to train during pro time. Many determined amateur fighters go to the gym during pro time in order to train alongside the sport's most successful professionals, to learn from them, and even to outclass them. "Pro time," then, could just as easily be considered "amateur time."

Amateur fighting differs from professional boxing in that amateurs are not allowed to fight for money and cannot accept financial compensation for any of their athletic activities. Amateur boxers are regulated by USA Boxing, while professional fighters are sanctioned by the various state athletic commissions, and the rules of the amateurs differ from the pros. Amateurs box three or four rounds of two or three minutes, depending on whether they are considered "novice," which is defined as a fighter who has fewer than ten fights, or "open," an athlete with more than ten fights. The amateur boxing scoring system is more formal and rigid, as it is computerized and registers a point for each punch landed cleanly, regardless of degree of difficulty or force, leaving little room for leading off, which means making the first move, or style.

The physical components of amateur and professional training sessions are, for the most part, the same, but because the scoring system and rules of amateur boxing—and, consequently, ring strategies and styles—differ from those of professional fighting, each group may emphasize different components in their training.[18] For example, amateurs can be penalized for fighting on the ropes, where they can throw fewer punches (such as Muhammad Ali's famous "rope-a-dope" strategy), so they may devote more time on footwork drills to enhance their ability to move forward and cut off their opponent in the ring. Or they may practice jabs to their opponents' heads rather than to their bodies since the latter punches are more challenging to land but earn the same amount of points as any other type of punch. Professionals box more rounds than amateurs and need more aerobic stamina, so they might run more miles—known as "roadwork"—and more frequently. The roles of trainers are also more circumscribed in amateur boxing, as trainers are not allowed to yell or advise from the corner during a round, a restriction that usually does not appear in professional rules. And finally, amateur athletes are required to wear protective equipment during spars and fights, such as headgears, and their gloves are heavier than those of their professional counterparts.

But a deeper divide than how the two groups are compensated, sanctioned, judged, trained, and instructed from the corner separates amateurs from professionals. Amateur fighters have a different set of orientations to and investments in the sport, largely because their primary motivation for fighting is not money. This is not to suggest that every professional fights only for the money or that amateurs do not have professional ambitions or hope to draw a salary from the sport at some point in the future. But because amateur boxers are unpaid, their immediate goals are not economic. When I first started visiting the gym, I was surprised that many amateurs do *not* intend to become professionals and do not see themselves as "in training" for professional careers. Amateurs box for reasons unrelated to monetary compensation and, through their devotion to pugilism, express desires, commitments, and solidarities removed from the world of making money and becoming famous but still related to the world of work, capital, and value.

In his treatise on "amateuring," literary scholar Wayne Booth argues that the overarching reason amateurs practice their craft is love. Booth laments that discussions of amateurs of any type—athletic, musical, artistic—are laced with dismissive subtexts and devalued when implicitly compared with the professional who is expert and skilled.[19] By contrast, Booth suggests that amateuring can be rigorous and reveal intense investment. He writes that, "although most true amateurs will never entirely escape being amateurish, they don't just dabble at something that they sort of enjoy doing occasionally. Instead, like any serious professional, they work at learning to do it better."[20] Amateuring demands time, labor, and aspiration, and inherent to this process is love. To Booth, amateuring is "a celebration of what it means to do something worth doing for the sheer love of it, with no thought of future payoff—in a world where you can't even survive unless you do some thinking about payoff."[21] For the amateur boxers of Gleason's Gym, money is not the end. It is the love of the practice itself and the social possibilities that the practice offers that drives their amateuring. Love in this context is about improvising a kind of work and producing a form of value that I spend the rest of the chapter describing.

THE WORK OF TRAINING

Amateur boxers travel long distances to Gleason's Gym instead of training in their neighborhood gyms. As discussed in chapter 1, the number of gyms in New York City has declined, but urban gyms do still exist. It is not an accident that amateur pugilists seek out one of the most famous boxing institutions in the country and not their sleepy local establishments. Gleason's Gym gives amateur boxers important access to a work site; it is open for sixteen hours a day, which is important to men who want to train with their coaches without interruption from other gym goers. While the New Bed-Stuy Boxing Center is open from 10:00 a.m. "until the last fighter goes home," trainers there say that they will not let anyone under the age of eighteen into the gym until 3:00 p.m., when school lets out, in order to discourage kids from terminating their education.[22] Other gyms, such as those operated by the Police Athletic League (PAL) and the clubs of the New York City Parks and Recreation Department, are often only open in the evenings and are perceived as overcrowded, underresourced, and inconvenient. These gyms also are associated with law enforcement (PAL) and the city (the Parks and Recreations Department). For men who have histories with the criminal justice system or who are unimpressed by the limited allocations to New York City athletic programs, these gyms can be unappealing options.

More than hours of operation and social and economic associations, amateur boxers say they join the most well known gym in New York City because of the professionalism associated with it. Nostalgia and pride are invested in working out at and being a boxer of Gleason's Gym. Boxers build individual and collective forms of identity at Gleason's because of its historic connection with labor and manhood. For amateur boxers who have trained in neighborhood gyms such as the Bed-Stuy Boxing Center, which funneled a large number of fighters to Gleason's in the late 1990s, the latter gym has a different feel. Omar feels that "Gleason's is more of a professional atmosphere." When I ask if he misses the Bed-Stuy Boxing Center, where he spent a large portion of his amateur career, he replies, "No. Not at all because my era is over. There isn't nothin' for me there no more. They can't do nothin' for me no more." Gleason's is described as less communal and social than the Bed-Stuy gym. It is called "more corporate" and "more commercial" with its abundance of white-collar clients and its many professional fighters, complete with financial managers, matchmakers, and promoters. The gym also accepts women, whom many male boxers consider an inappropriate distraction for a boxing establishment, but this has the curious effect of lending a sense of legitimacy through a more restrictive interactive structure. Every male boxer must sign a sexual harassment waiver, so, at the very least, the presence of women has introduced some manner of formality and bureaucracy into the gym's culture.

Gleason's enjoys far more resources than other gyms and is able to offer amateurs more amenities. It boasts four rings, while the New Bed-Stuy Boxing Center, Kingsway, and Kid Kelly each has one. It is also much larger in square footage. To amateur boxers, having access to these resources means that, by definition, one is a serious fighter, even if turning pro is not desired or an option. Lawrence, who also trained at the Bed-Stuy gym, sees those who train at Gleason's as "hand-picked." Whether amateur or professional, the boxers of Gleason's have been carefully selected because they are more determined and rigorous than the fighters who work out in neighborhood gyms. This is a point of considerable pride: Not only do Gleason's boxers get better sparring and rise to the level of the athletes around them but also they are associated with the legacy of Gleason's as an institution. Participating in this legacy is an accomplishment unto itself and brings status and prestige to amateur fighters.

The amateur boxers I worked with enter the gym sometime in the late morning and make their way to trainers Mike and Harry's corner. Once there, and depending on how sociable the fighters are or how impatient the trainer is, they sit around and chat as they apply Albolene, a makeup remover that boxers coat their arms, chests, backs, and legs with in order to open their pores and help them sweat, and wrap their hands, discussing their problems, expressing disbelief at interesting current events, or recapping fights.

The first part of an amateur's work is either jumping rope or shadowboxing. On Tuesdays, Thursdays, and Saturdays, popular days for sparring, an amateur will spar for six to ten rounds, depending on the trainer's philosophy and assessment of need. The form of sparring varies according to the fighter's weaknesses and the trainer's judgment, but staggering the fighters—bringing them in and out of the ring at intervals (i.e., Max spars Adrian, Adrian spars Michael, Michael spars Diego, Diego spars Max, Max spars Michael, etc.)—is a popular way to give all fighters different kinds of work. If a boxer has an upcoming fight, his trainer might keep him in the ring for the duration of the ten rounds and alternate his sparring partners, a technique that trainer Joseph uses. After sparring, the athlete does padwork (hitting padded mitts that the trainer wears as gloves) either in the ring or on the floor. Following this, although he is still supervised by his trainer, the athlete is released to work on his own. He moves to the heavy bag for six to eight rounds and then to the speed or double-end bag for another six to eight rounds. Later, he will do hundreds of stomach exercises and weight training, and at some point—either in the morning or in the evening—he is expected to run three to eight miles.

The gaze of the trainer follows the boxer as he labors. As will be discussed in chapter 3, the ideology of training demands that the flow of knowledge is unidirectional from coach to athlete. There is no negotiation. A boxer must comply with his trainer's orders, and there is very little he can say or do to alter his work practices. If he is tired or has come into the ring without warming up, his trainer will ask him why he did not stay home. Or his trainer may ask him to clean out his locker, threatening to drop the fighter from his team altogether if he does not perk up, which is one of Mike's favorite coaching strategies. Once under the rule of the trainer, fighters must leave their own perceptions of and perspectives on their training behind.

The fastest period in which a workout can be accomplished is two hours, though it is far more common for it to take between three and five hours. Fighters are working for the majority of this time. Given that each round is three minutes and that there is only a one-minute rest between rounds, this is arduous work. Why might boxers undertake such demanding training? Despite not being compensated for their time, amateur boxers consider this pugilistic work to be their job. This is true for fighters who have professional aspirations—those who will be permitted to make money in the future—and for those who do not have any plans to go pro. It is is true for amateurs who can secure jobs; despite holding part-time and full-time positions, they consider themselves, by vocation, to be boxers. And it is true for men who participate in extralegal and illegal economies outside the gym. Kenny is categorized as an amateur, and when I first interviewed him, he was employed full-time as a security guard. He worked nights at a shelter for survivors of domestic violence in the Bronx and trained at Gleason's Gym during the day. He told me, "I box for a living. It feel good when a lot of people recognize you for what you do." His self-description is telling because he is not paid for his boxing, so the "living" he refers to is not about financial reward. And when talking about "what you do," he is referring to his time in the gym and not his full-time security position.[23]

WORK WITHOUT WAGES

Amateur athletes want to be known as "boxers," which allows them to receive recognition for their labor, and, in doing so, they express a desire to be defined by their "job." This is evident when Kenny remarks that he likes the identity-defining acknowledgment from others that he *is* a boxer. When talking about his labor, Adrian explains that there are different types of intelligences. Some people "have brains" and are good in school. Other people are "intelligent" when working with their bodies. Boxing allows the latter to demonstrate their bodily acumen or aptitude. Adrian trains and fights to demonstrate his mental and physical intellect, and he earns respect on the basis of this type of bodywork.

Others box to identify and showcase their own admirable qualities; just stepping into the ring reveals something to boxers about themselves. "Having heart" is considered one of the fundamentals of being a true fighter and is understood as necessary for success. Pete Hamill suggests:

> By "heart," they don't mean simple courage. They know that it requires a certain amount of courage simply to climb into a ring in front of strangers. The mysterious quality called "heart" is about the willingness to endure punishment in order to inflict it. . . . And so "heart" is about getting up. It's about seeing the cut above your brow . . . and calling on some secret reservoir of the self to dominate and win.[24]

Echoing Hamill, Max reflects: "When I step in the ring I feel relaxed, but I feel proud because not everyone can do it. Some people have heart problems. And that's one thing—I don't have a heart problem." By participating in competition—and especially continuing when the fight is difficult—he simultaneously learns about and professionalizes himself.

Being defined by their work facilitates boxers' attempts to establish some sort of a legacy, which is important to fighters with children. Max, the father of a one-year-old baby boy, philosophizes:

> I want my son to see—I want him to be proud. "Look at my father. He's a boxer. Look at him." That will *excite* me. I want him to go to his friends and say, "Yeah, well, your father can't beat my father." That's what little kids do, and I want to provide for my son.

Desiring to make their children proud is discussed by amateur boxers in the context of not having known their own fathers and trying to interrupt a pattern of fatherlessness among black men. Max continues, "I really didn't have a father there for me. So I'm trying to show that for my son: that there are fathers out there that is trying. And I may not see you that much, but I love you and I'm trying. I am always gonna be there for you." With boxing as a purpose, Max feels he is a better parent because he can demonstrate goal setting and ambition to his child. Max's discussion of his boxing also reinforces a kind of superiority comparison between him and other boxers and fathers. As Rachel Sherman points out in her work on luxury-hotel employees, such comparisons help workers construct themselves as skilled.[25]

Omar fights "to build a legacy. I always wanted to be like my father. Every kid, they always are gonna talk about they parents. And all my life I been messing up. And I got a son now, and I got two girls that I look after, my two stepgirls. You know what I'm saying?" Omar remembers that one of his losses was even more devastating than usual because his wife and children were watching. Losing a fight in front of his family made him feel undignified because it publicly illustrated a setback to his goals of establishing a legacy and taking care of his family.

For amateur boxers who have spent time in prison, there is a sense of urgency with which they discuss their training in the gym. Many feel behind in life and are in a hurry to establish themselves. Boxing is an alternative identity to both "criminal" and "ex-con," two identities the men in the gym feel are projected onto them. Being recognized as boxers allows fighters to prove to themselves and to suggest to others that they have taken up a highly disciplined occupational alternative to crime, which, again, is especially appreciated by fighters with kids. When thinking about boxing, his son, and crime, Max says, "That's what I want him to see—that just 'cause you live in New York don't mean that you have to do crime. There's other things out there, and I want him to see the bigger picture."

Amateur boxers want to leave social status and cultural recognition behind for their children. In lieu of economic capital, they want to pass on their knowledge, accomplishments, and prestige in the ring to their children. While sociologists understand accumulation as traditionally financial in nature, in this case, amateur fighters want to accumulate *reputations* for which their children can respect them and by which they can be remembered. Omar and Max see possibilities for taking care of or providing for their families without material resources. This is not to suggest that they would not provide economic capital if they could, but rather that Omar and Max belong to a group of men for whom those possibilities of lawful paid work are almost occluded in the racialized postindustrial landscape of New York City. In the absence of such work, they find alternative ways to generate value.

To do their work and produce such value, amateur boxers develop a rigorous work ethic. This ethic involves the rigid application of rules, restrictions, and disciplinary practices. Self-regulation is the norm, and the boxers do not drink alcohol, do drugs, smoke cigarettes, or socialize outside the gym. They wake up early, limit their television viewing, and are avid readers in their search for self-improvement. They impose dietary restrictions, such as eating vegetarian or even vegan, and will not consume over-the-counter or prescription medication. It is the nature of discipline in boxing, in particular, that attracts many fighters. They build and rebuild their lives through and around strict regimentation. Anthony, an ardent proponent of discipline, regimentation, and other forms of self-control, defines discipline and explicates its importance:

> Discipline is simply, in general, instilling or imposing your rules and regulations on people so people understand your rules and regulations. . . . I think a disciplined person has something to live for. When you are disciplined, you stand for something. . . . Right or wrong, you stand for something. . . . Without discipline, you are a leaf in the wind.

Anthony believes that for the first several years of his prison sentence, he resisted the discipline of forced confinement. He socialized with former colleagues and got caught up in the "culture" of the prison. But after being sentenced to additional years for institutional misconduct, he decided to make a radical transformation and refrain from engaging in any form of criminal activity. His method was to exceed the disciplinary requirements of prison life and to self-impose additional dietary, social, and physical restrictions. Anthony out-confined his confinement: He stopped hanging out with friends, started reading, worked out as much as he could, and avoided certain foods. When he implemented these disciplinary practices, it gave him a sense of power and of control:

> It felt so good because it felt like I could overcome these things, right? It's like when you have a bad habit or anything, and you tell yourself, "I'm not gonna do that anymore," and you just make up your mind, and it feels good when you tell yourself, "You win." You won over whatever it was. Even if you get a feeling that you want to do that, and you tell yourself, "For what?"

The sense of routine derived from the discipline of boxing training is highly valued among men who have spent time in prison. Anthony argues that boxing gave him structure after his release. He says, "I fell in love with it. So it was like part of a regular routine for me. I already loved working out. I worked out endlessly, like a madman everyday. So it was just a different kind of workout." Kenny implemented similar practices when he came home from boot camp, reproducing, in effect, the schedule of forced confinement outside the prison's walls:

> I set my curfew. On weekends, nine o'clock 'cause I work on weekends, and I gotta get up at like five o'clock. And then after I go to work, I go straight to the gym. I don't have time for nobody. And I go runnin' and come home from runnin', and I gotta take a shower and eat. I watch the news for ten minutes, and I be sleepin'.

This regimentation is empowering for Kenny because it orders his life and, as it does for Anthony, provides him with structure. He believes that boxing helps him "follow a plan. I know I gotta go to work, go to the gym, and go home and go running. It allows me to follow everything step by step." Max, Omar, Diego, and Harry describe similar impulses toward schedules and discipline after incarceration. Max says the structure helped him mature; after being released from prison, boxing's routine "made me think about life and growing up to be a man and to handle my responsibilities as a man." As Max's reference to the requirements of manhood suggests, this regimentation process is seen as gendered.

Being a boxer allows young men to continue to learn and self-improve, another feature of the work ethic. When I ask Anthony what drew him to boxing, he explains:

> It was an educational process. I enjoyed that: learning new things and applying them. Whenever I apply them, I feel like I'm getting better. I feel like I'm

> learning something new, and I just love utilizing it and using it. I'm not afraid to hit, and I hit pretty hard. I learn anything easy, and I love to learn. Anything, I'm willing to learn if someone's willing to teach me.

How boxers understand victory and defeat highlights the importance of learning and professional development. Perceptions of the outcome of a fight are not always as simple as feeling happy when one wins and feeling bad when one loses. The interpretation of a bout is shaped by how well a fighter thinks he has performed: that is, whether or not he has used the knowledge his trainer has given him and whether or not he can find room for improvement. A win, for example, can be both a chance to experience accomplishment and a chance to discover more about one's self and the sport. Max explains, "A win feels like—oh man! A win feels like when you first have sex. 'Cause you're like 'Oh! I did it! I accomplished it!' You can't explain it." He continues:

> A win also helps you get into what you gotta work on. What's the things that you didn't do? What did you do that was wrong? So you can't take the win like "Yeah, I did this." You gotta know why you won and why you could have lost. 'Cause you did this and could have lost.

Similarly, there is no dignity in dodging a difficult opponent or in gloating about an easy win. After knocking out a competitor early in the first round, which is rare in the amateurs because of the weight of the gloves and the requirement of headgears, Anthony is disappointed. He tells me, "When I knocked that guy out in thirty seconds, I was hoping he was getting back up. I would hope that he would get back up, so I could try other things that I've learned."

If a fighter loses but worked hard, executed what he knew, learned something, and found new things to improve upon, the fight is generally considered a success. This is even more accurate if an opponent's trainer and teammates acknowledge the effort. Diego remembers:

> I fought this kid, and I did really good. Everybody said I did really good. Even his teammates was like, "Yo, you did really good." And they was like, "You only have one [previous] fight?" and I said, "Yeah," and they said, "You did *real* good." So I felt that I did good in the fight even though I lost. I felt good about it. I fought somebody who was already experienced.

When I ask if his optimism comes from the process of learning, he responds, "That's what counts. That's what counts for me because it's a learning experience. You learn from everything, and that learning experience made me feel real good."

In the constant quest to self-improve, some boxers like the opportunity to *find out* how they can improve. After a devastating loss, Anthony begins to appreciate the defeat for demonstrating what he needs to work on:

> I felt like since I lost that fight, I've become a much better puncher. I feel like everything has actually taken a step up because everything I learned from that loss was valuable. I think there was a reason for me to lose. . . . Confucius said, "When you make a mistake, if you don't learn from that mistake, you're making a mistake." So it was like, from that loss, I felt like that's what I needed to focus on: learn and correct it.

Kenny echoes these sentiments, "I learned to appreciate a loss more than I do a win because when I win, I feel, 'Okay, I won, I'm on top of my game,' and when I lose, it's like 'Wow. I need to dig deep in myself.' And I question myself: 'If I'm gonna do this, I gotta do it right.' " A loss to someone considered better is a chance to test oneself and to learn more. It is also an opportunity to earn respect from spectators. Kenny thinks,

> It feels good when I'm doing my best and the guy is just better than me. You know? It feels good . . . when somebody is better than me and only thing I could do is my best. I'm human, and I'm not tired, and I'm in shape, and he still wins—that's pushin' me more.

A loss that is "given away," however, is humiliating. Kenny explains: "It's harder when I beat myself. When I lose 'cause of somethin' I didn't do. That's the worst feeling 'cause I can't take it back. We can't start over and we can't box again. I have the L [loss] so that hurts." Kenny's comments also reveal a commitment to a natural, essential identity of bootstrap individualism and personal responsibility, which he seeks from his boxing practices. "Getting robbed"—unofficially winning the fight but officially losing it—is usually attributed to anti-black racism in judging but is still considered the fault of the boxer who has lost the bout. The perception is that the lighter the skin of the fighter, the greater the likelihood he will win if his opponent does not shut down the fight by knocking him out. In response, Mike and Harry instruct their fighters not to leave any room for racist officials to discriminate by dramatically outperforming their opponent and thereby asserting their individual agency. During the Golden Gloves, Max loses in the semifinals to a white firefighter and is blamed by his trainer and peers for being "robbed." While everyone acknowledges that he should have won, based on how well he fought, it is considered Max's responsibility to foreclose any opportunity for anti-black racism, which is naturalized by those in the sport as an ordinary feature of amateur judging. After the fight, Lawrence gives his perspective on Max's fight and shifts the responsibility of the verdict from the judges to Max, declaring, "He really should have knocked that kid out."

What is particularly significant about the identities boxers derive from their work is that they are not the opposite of other identities that amateur fighters may form or possess at different moments in their lives—hustler, dealer, prisoner. Rather, the identity of the boxer can coexist in a fluid way with other identities and adapt to social circumstance. Though many amateurs seek out the gym in order to leave behind lives of crime, the movement from crime to legality is not always unidirectional, and not all boxers can avoid criminal reengagement. Though the boxers of Chicago's Woodlawn Boys Club, chronicled in Loic Wacquant's *Body and Soul*, were fortunate enough to actualize crime cessation, in New York City generally and Gleason's Gym in particular, the lines between legality and illegality are always shifting, and sometimes the two are indistinguishable.[26] Many amateur boxers find it impossible to support their families with the jobs available to them or by means of the city's rapidly diminishing safety net. They may deal drugs episodically or chronically while employed, underemployed, or unemployed or may participate in other aspects of informal economies in order to make ends meet.[27] When I ask about the financial circumstances of his amateur athletes, Mike wearily shakes his head and mutters, "People don't understand that these guys don't go out to be a drug dealer. It's *financial necessity*." Even those who do not participate in illegal or informal economies find it difficult to meet the stringent conditions of parole and are sent back to jail for minor infractions, such as being arrested even if not charged.[28]

In the case of incarceration, boxers find that their work can be maintained behind bars and that, once established, boxing identities can travel in and out of prison, which, in turn, helps some men survive the injuries of confinement. Fighters can undertake rigorous training regimens while in prison and attempt to reproduce their athletic image in the eyes of other prisoners. During one of his early jail sentences, Diego remembers:

> When I was inside everybody called me "the boxer" 'cause they seen me spar. I did my own training. I shadowboxed in the bathroom for ten rounds. . . .

> When I was in the yard, I lifted a bit of weights. I ran about three or four miles. I was doing that Monday through Friday. Saturday and Sundays were my days off. In the winter I was shadowboxing in the yard, but once it got to be summer, and there was a lot of people there, I didn't feel comfortable 'cause people will be like, "Oh, he's a show-off," and I didn't want that. . . . In the fall, I was playing a lot of handball to keep my hand-eye coordination. I was practicing my left a lot because I'm a right-handed boxer.

Being considered a boxer in prison also protected Diego from the harassment and violence of other prisoners. He says, "I think that people felt intimidated because of that [being a fighter]. They felt that I was gonna fight back, 'cause in jail, a lot of people take advantage of you." This is especially important for Diego, as he has a slight build and smaller men are preyed upon in spaces of forced confinement.[29]

Omar was considered the "Iron Man" while in prison. He continued to train and recounts:

> I was training everyday. *Every day*. First rec in the morning because I had a night program. . . . In morning rec, I would go out there and run five miles. After the five miles I would do my calisthenics. I would go two sets "around the world." Around the world is what they call it when you do everything—ten sets of everything, push-ups, dips, and pull-ups. I was kind of ripped up. . . . When that was over, I would come back for the afternoon rec period, and I would hit the bag and do my stomach and stuff like that.

Fighters can actively maintain their ties to the gym while incarcerated. While Diego was in jail, he called his trainer in the gym—pay phone to pay phone—to provide progress reports on his GED studies and his training regimen. The gym was the first place Diego visited immediately after his release from Rikers Island after nine months. One hour after coming home—before seeing his girlfriend and his daughter—he relaxed in Mike and Harry's corner of Gleason's Gym talking, joking, and celebrating his homecoming with his coach and teammates. He was greeted with warm enthusiasm and peppered with questions about his health, especially his weight and diet, while incarcerated (he looks skinny—did they only feed him tuna?). He began to train that same day. When I ask him why he came to the gym before seeing his family, he construes "family" as referring to his teammates and trainer. He smiles and answers, "Yeah, I love the gym. It's all I thought about. My girlfriend, she bought me a history of boxing, and I used to read about the first boxers and all these heavyweight boxers. And my girlfriend bought me magazines so I stayed up with all the fighters."

Diego intended to fight immediately upon his release. Before he went to Rikers Island, Mike and he developed a plan and set goals, a reentry plan of sorts, which helped Diego not only to stay in shape but also to envision life after jail. He tells me, "I'm never going back over there, but I knew when I was there that I was going to fight when I came out. I knew I was going to fight in the first month. Mike told me that I was going to fight in the first two months." Omar also kept up his ties to the gym community while imprisoned. His trainers met him when he was released from a correctional facility in Connecticut and drove him back to New York City.

RETHINKING LABOR AND VALUE: THE POSSIBILITIES AND LIMITATIONS OF BODYWORK

The work that amateur boxers do in Gleason's Gym does not fit a standard notion of work. Amateurs are not employed in the formal sense, their labor is not paid, and their toil is not recognized by most sectors of society. Rather than making a product or a good, as in a manufacturing economy, or delivering a service, as in the new economy, the amateur works on his own body—training, challenging, and improving it in a quest for skill and conditioning perfection. This is work of a very different kind, quite different from the work of paid wage labor. It is not fictional work nor is it simply the passing of leisure time. Amateurs approach their boxing activities with the insistence and purpose of a job rather than as a pastime or hobby.

Amateur boxers borrow some of the features of traditional wage work—such as regimentation and disciplining—and recast these features to create a new kind of labor, which allows young men who cannot participate in lawful work or have spent time in prison to forge new identities. Amateur pugilists are able to find meaning in their daily routines and to fashion the conditions by which they can learn, be challenged, and succeed. They create the rules and systems of meaning in the gym, such as prizing determination and "heart" and investing worth in the practices and social relations of pugilistic training. Fighters who work hard are rewarded with admiration and status whether they win or lose. Their work is done with the supportive help of the trainer, an educator who prepares, encourages, and disciplines. These activities and conditions allow men who have been left out of the socializations of traditional institutions to enjoy some of the benefits that might otherwise be formed through paid labor.

Through their work, amateurs conceptualize their time, their bodies, their labor, and their lives in novel ways and reclaim their bodies from the lack of a wage, from prisons, and from "failure." Amateur boxers engender their bodies with value and recognize that value after enduring postindustrial social and economic injury—unemployment, underemployment, imprisonment, and racial exclusion. The bodywork they style demonstrates how young men develop dignity and earn respect in a postindustrial landscape, as well as how they intervene in their own lives and attempt to control the conditions of their experiences when maneuvering room is severely constrained.

Amateur boxers re-create within the gym opportunities for work, which they have been denied outside the gym, and find ways to engage those opportunities. In other words, when there is no lawful or paid work, these men improvise work. Their improvisations reveal that they recognize the ability to work as fundamental. The kind of labor they create and embody offers them opportunities to learn, to be challenged, and to succeed. It is about the process of doing and of making the self rather than about achieving any particular outcome. As will be seen in chapters 3 and 4, the types of social relations they develop while undertaking this work actualize other benefits of bodywork in the form of homosocial bonding, collective identity, and intimacy with other men. Amateur boxers have found a way to meet their own unspoken demands for work, and in a worksite that is fair and instructive and that supports them.

Since amateurs' lives do not fit into a wage-labor time structure, amateur fighters carve out time for both work and play. This is not to suggest that the sufferings of postindustrial racial, gender, and class hierarchies do not penetrate the walls of Gleason's Gym. As chronicled in chapter 1, such forces are largely responsible for the social circumstances that motivate young men's decision to join the gym and, as will be examined in chapter 3, these forces shape the neoliberal discourses of personal responsibility that are used in training. But it is to suggest that amateur boxers find ways to buffer the damage of certain features of late capitalism by creating new spaces where *they* define the rules of engagement. The effects of unemployment and imprisonment are quite real and deeply affect how these men think and feel about themselves, but they also find meaning and create identities in ways that are not overly determined by social structure. The work they do is an answer to capitalism and to a hyper-penal society and is unique in its own right. It is not just a stopgap measure, and in that way, it forces a reconsideration of the idea of work itself.

For example, winning at any cost is not admired. Amateur boxers see Gleason's Gym as a meritocracy. The rules of the gym are legible and reasonable to follow. The work undertaken there is educational and supported by the community, and the benefits are considered important. The ring is a place where men can fight—literally and metaphorically—for a different life experience. It is perceived as a level playing field: in it, the fighter who works the hardest usually wins. Fighters re-create the discourse of meritocracy, in which they are guided, and can succeed on the basis of their own level of determination, rather than the social or economic capital they possess prior to entering the ring.

Since collective intervention into the world of paid work is considered impossible, amateur boxers intervene at the individual level.[30] The object of their focus becomes their own minds and bodies, and their goal becomes to work hard and succeed despite the acknowledged structural odds. The work they employ to do this uses the body in a way that preempts any critique of institutional anti-black racism or the social limitations to their freedom, because the body can always be worked on more and improved upon endlessly. This form of bodywork is predicated on noncomplaining and acquiescence to the expertise of the trainer, and training is transmitted in a way that forecloses negotiation. The work amateur boxers undertake, then, acknowledges the importance of work, but because that need is met by the body culture of the gym, there is no formal indictment of society or demand of the larger society to guarantee possibilities for lawful labor.

In the context of the individual types of injury amateur men have endured, the primacy of individual experience and bodily control suggests that experiences of suffering—such as the humiliations of forced confinement and unemployment—are profoundly personal. Though racial and class exclusion are systematic and structural, they are borne on an individual level. The way to negotiate and respond to these experiences is to return to the body. Bodywork is a way to reconcile the burdens of structural inequality with goals of individual forms of power.

But what about that economic capital amateur fighters have been denied outside the gym? As Adrian, who was unable to actualize the benefits that Gleason's can offer, shows, the gym cannot hold all the amateurs who seek it out. Bodywork is not available to all who might want to engage in it. Differing levels of talent, emotional wellness, and financial stability affect individuals' abilities to take advantage of the gym's social possibilities. More important, though the gym can fulfill the social role of work through identity, self-worth, and individual discipline, it does not fulfill the economic role of work. That is, bodywork does not pay and leaves amateurs vulnerable to failing to reproduce the material conditions of their existence. In postindustrial New York, work can be improvised and fashioned in inventive ways, but only in the narrow confines of the urban gym and without wages.

Chapter Three

TOUGH LOVE AND INTIMACY IN A COMMUNITY OF MEN

> If your friend is ignorant of the science of manual defence, which I have taken for granted, you ought both alternatively to officiate, the one as a teacher, and the other as the pupil, and thus prove the means of mutual assistance.
>
> —A PUPIL BOTH OF HUMPHREYS AND MENDOZA, 1784

"THE ONLY PEOPLE OUT AT THAT TIME OF NIGHT ARE COPS and robbers."

Harry is at it again.

Reclining in a plastic chair with his arms folded behind his head, ankles crossed, and heels propped up on a table, Harry, a gym trainer, is beginning to lecture Cedric, a tall and quiet fourteen-year-old. Cedric has no idea that he is perched on the precipice of a sermon, but others do. Sensing Harry's fervor, several gym regulars exchange warning glances and slink away. Cedric also has no idea that after just months of working with Harry, he is already one of his coach's favorite boxers. This status will position him as the charmed beneficiary of a number of lectures in the time to come.

Several months before, Cedric was brought to Gleason's Gym by one of his middle- school teachers, who saw in him great promise but little guidance. Cedric's mother has abandoned her formal parental responsibilities while his father, who is incarcerated, is unable to intervene in his son's day-to-day activities from behind bars. Harry has taken Cedric under his wing and assumed the role of mentor. It is a job that Harry takes seriously, and to fulfill it, he will rely heavily on lectures. Today's starts when Cedric innocently mentions that he hurt his hand playing basketball until 1:30 a.m. the night before. With an injured wrist, he cannot hit the heavy bag. But it is not the injury that concerns Harry: it is Cedric's lack of a curfew.

Harry's first move is fact-finding, so he grills Cedric: Why was he out so *late*? Who was he out *with*? And what time did his *mother* want him home? Harry responds with a dramatic sigh and eye roll at each of Cedric's answers until he has heard enough and begins his speech. Life in the projects is very dangerous, Harry argues, far more than Cedric probably realizes. The only people out at 1:00 a.m. are cops and robbers, and as a black youth in Brooklyn, Cedric is likely to get shot—as much by the cops as by the robbers. Hanging out late will get Cedric into serious trouble, and Harry predicts that if Cedric continues such dubious escapades this summer, he will land in jail before it is over. If Cedric doesn't believe Harry, he should talk with Kenny, another of Harry's amateur boxers, who recently has endured this very trauma.

Harry then prescribes a remedy: Cedric needs a summer activity. Harry has been trying to find Cedric employment but has been unable to find anything yet. As a substitute, Harry promises to show Cedric the world, and so the ultimate consequence of the curfew infraction is that if Harry can pull together some money, he will take Cedric with him on his next boxing trip.

The lecture's conclusion is Harry's specialty, and even he acknowledges that he saves the best for last. Does Cedric know why Harry is so intimately acquainted with the dangers of social housing life? It is because Harry *was* one of those late-lurking robbers. Harry rehearses a history of wine drinking and pot use and cocaine and crack addiction. A parallel history of crime is detailed: pickpocketing, mugging, robbery, and attempted murder in Marcy, Tompkins, Sumner, and Gowanus Housing Projects. Crime led to prison, prison to homelessness, and social exclusion to racial exclusion. Harry ends with a pronouncement: Cedric does not know the dangers of project life because he cannot see beyond it. Harry implores him to try.

Oration, like the discourse bestowed on Cedric, is a rhetorical technique that gym trainers use when they work with amateur fighters. This particular lecture illuminates the kinds of problems—not directly related to the sport of boxing—that trainers mediate. And it illustrates some of the difficulties trainers have addressing these problems. Harry's vacillations, for example, between social-structural arguments that hold racial segregation and urban marginality responsible for Cedric's lack of opportunities and arguments that prize personal responsibility to overcome disadvantage reflect the tensions trainers manage when they mentor young men. Harry's hopes for Cedric show the worth that trainers see in the amateur boxers they train.

At Gleason's Gym, trainers coach amateur fighters both inside and outside the ring.[1] In the ring, trainers prepare amateurs for competition and help their boxers develop masculine identities. Outside the ring, they provide desperately needed forms of social, psychological, and material support. This chapter analyzes the social practices trainers undertake when they work with amateur boxers and the social relations generated from them.[2] It examines how trainers collaborate with fighters and how trainers' life histories shape the intellectual and physical rigor they demand, the forms of knowledge they impart, and their philosophies about racism, late capitalism, and patriarchy. I argue that trainers perform a unique type of mentoring in which the relationship between mentor and mentored is predicated upon and successful because of shared experiences. This mentoring is an expression of trainers' political consciousness about society's failure to provide young men of color with resources and guidance in a postindustrial landscape and frequently becomes an expression of kinship.[3] Through kin relations, trainers encourage young men of color to view their worth in different ways, to create and measure the meaning of their lives in different spaces, and to see that no identity is final.[4]

IN THE RING: TRAINING AND THE TROPE OF "TOUGH LOVE"

In the ring, a trainer's athletic goals are to teach boxers the sport's techniques, develop their skills, and prepare them for competition. Though most coaches agree on the basics of boxing, it is up to an individual trainer to ascertain how to accomplish these goals with particular fighters. Trainers take an enormous amount of time learning about their amateur pugilists—what works for one will not always work for another—which requires determining when and how far a fighter can be pushed. Not pushing a fighter may make for a comfortable training experience but inevitably produces a brutal wake-up call in a bout. Pushing an athlete too far will, at best, demoralize him; at worst, it will place him in a life-threatening situation. But pushing a fighter just the right amount can precipitate a breakthrough in confidence, paving the way to success.

One of the most important practices used to teach boxers is the spar. Sparring is typically done on Tuesdays, Thursdays, and Saturdays, when fighters are considered the most focused and rested.[5] The coaching that Harry, one of Gleason's most prominent trainers, imparts in spars follows a formula. In the early rounds, Harry gives very little praise and an almost overwhelming amount of criticism. When they err, the sparring partners' masculinities are challenged and they are taunted for their lack of effort in the ring. They are feminized and degraded as "women" or "little girls" and mocked as "sleeping together" when they clinch one another in exhaustion. If the boxers protest or offer excuses, including serious injury, they are chastised until silenced. In the middle of the spar when visible signs of exasperation and dejection present themselves—heads, shoulders, and hands sag while footwork slows—Harry might threaten to drop them from his team if they do not comply with his instruction. With little choice, they rally, and more times than not succeed in throwing the number and quality of punches demanded. In the last rounds of the spar, as they push through fatigue and pain, their determination wins Harry's approval. He compliments and encourages them, and when the spar is finished, they climb out of the ring drenched in sweat, bodies slumped in exhaustion, and faces beaming.

A spar between Wells and Ali illustrates this pattern:

> HARRY: Come on, let your hands go! Let your hands go! Come on. Bend. Double your punches and work. Work! You waiting too long, you ain't fightin'. You aren't fightin' amateur [meaning that Wells is not executing the techniques necessary for competing in the amateurs]. Move your head. Stop reaching! Bend your legs, jab. Come on, work, work, work! Both hands. Bend your legs and work. Work. Stop swinging wild and back him up. *Work*. Back up his punch. Come on! You'd better not drop the right hand to the body. You wait too much, man. Why you wait?

This, like most of Harry's questions, is intended to be rhetorical, but Wells cannot resist the urge to explain himself.

> WELLS: My hand hurts.
> HARRY: What?
> WELLS: My *hand* hurts.
> HARRY: Then why are you boxing, Wells, if you hand hurts? Look at me. Come here. Let me put some grease on your face, man. What are you going to tell the guy next week? That your hand hurts?

A trainer gives athletic instruction to a male fighter during a break in sparring. Photograph by Issei Nakaya.

WELLS: [*sulking*] No.

HARRY: Right now, forget about your hand. You ain't got one.

Wells complies and boxes as if he has, quite literally, forgotten that he has a hand, lowering his right glove and using only his left jab. He executes Harry's instruction virtually word for word, which earns him praise. When the spar is over, Wells descends from the ring with a big smile, and he and Harry begin joking. Sitting on the ring's edge, they discuss how Wells's accomplishment, produced through bodily trauma, will benefit him in his next fight.

In boxing training, trainers ask their athletes to disregard their assessments of the situation and context—that they are in pain because they have been hurt—and instead take up their trainers' understandings—that boxers can fight through the pain. That is, rather than focusing on the fact of physical suffering, fighters are asked to respond to that suffering by summoning will and determination. Joyce Carol Oates observes that "[t]he boxer must somehow learn, by what effort of will non-boxers surely cannot guess, to inhibit his own instinct for survival; he must learn to exert his 'will' over his merely human and animal impulses, not only to flee pain but to flee the unknown."[6] Trainers must teach their fighters to endure when in pain. And as seen in the case of Wells, this process is not seamless. Wells does not believe that he can execute Harry's instruction.

He gets angry and even challenges the soundness of Harry's reason. But he eventually capitulates, adopting Harry's interpretation of the spar. He ignores his own reading (i.e., that he cannot fight because of a severely injured hand) and trusts Harry. When Wells prevails in the final rounds of the exercise, both trainer and boxer are delighted.

This process can be troubling to watch. The amount of criticism a fighter sustains during a spar is crushing for any sporting activity but especially for one in which athletes endure considerable bodily harm. I watched with incredulity as fighters had their noses, fingers, and hands broken, their shoulders dislocated, and their ankles twisted, only to be blamed for their injuries and told to continue. Following Wells's spar, I ask Harry why he would demand that Wells persist when he is clearly suffering. Couldn't that ultimately be detrimental by causing long-term injury? Harry explains, "I want to put them in the frame of mind that if you hurt your hand in a fight, what are you going to do? You gonna quit? Or you gonna continue? Life is only over unless you give up and give into it. There's a thing called 'tough love.'"[7]

Tough love is the most commonly articulated trope of training practices. The trope bespeaks the care, devotion, and responsibility that trainers have for their amateurs while acknowledging the particular demands and realities of the sport. The "love" in tough love derives from trainers' responsibility for their fighters' well-being in the ring. A boxer, especially an anxious or young athlete, cannot always judge a fight—how much injury he is sustaining, what punches are working, which combinations are not, where defenses are failing. Trainers say "the corner wins the fight for you" meaning that a trainer can better assess the bout than the competitor: the strategy, skill, and danger. Trainers take this evaluation seriously, and in order to keep their athletes safe, trainers assume control, dictating fighters' actions as well as their understandings of those actions.

An exchange between Harry and Kenny, an extremely talented amateur boxer, demonstrates the gravity of trainer responsibility. After Kenny is hit too much for Harry's liking, Harry pulls him from the ring. Stopping a spar abruptly is unusual, and in this case, signifies that something is very wrong with Kenny's performance.

HARRY: Listen to me, come down. Come down for a minute. The reason why you're getting hit is that you're too tight. Relax. When you throw a jab, you're dropping your jab. Pop *pop*. *Pop pop*. You know what I'm saying? Don't jab and do this [*drops his hand to demonstrate*]. The man going to hit you with a right hand. Jab, jab, and move your head from side to side. That's all you gotta do.

KENNY: But the first round, I always be cold, Harry.

HARRY: I understand that, but you can't come out cold in boxing. People get knocked out in the first round. That's the most dangerous round of the fight—the first round. You gotta come out hot and smoking in the first round because that's how people get knocked out in the first round. You see first-round knockouts? It's because people come out cold. You can't come out cold. This is not a sport when you can afford to come out cold. Because if you're a slow starter, they ain't gonna wait for you to start. They gonna get off [on] you.

Harry removes Kenny from the ring because Kenny's physical safety is at risk. Harry worries that Kenny is accustomed to warming up in the first round, and if not broken, this habit will become a liability in competition. But Harry's quote indexes another investment in tough love. Harry fears that opponents will "get off" on Kenny if Harry does not get him into the best possible mental and physical shape. Hence, trainers also see themselves as responsible for protecting their fighters from failure. The "love" in tough love tries to shield amateurs from disappointment as much as from injury.

The "tough" in tough love emerges from trainers' belief that their amateur boxers' general inclination is to back away from difficult situations. Their job is to teach fighters how to call up the will Joyce Carol Oates describes while in physical agony.[8] This is a gendered, heteronormative process. Harry frets that if he entertains his fighters' excuses, they will become weak and emasculated, losing some of the inherent masculinity deemed necessary for success in the gym. He tells me,

> If I make a way out for you, you gonna take an easy road. You don't pet grown men. I'm not saying men don't deserve hugs and stuff like that. But you can't treat a man like he a woman. You gonna ruin him. You gonna take what's naturally in him and turn it into something else.

Entertaining fighters' complaints of painful experiences—"petting" them—is demeaned and dismissed as feminine. Harry's reference to "hugs" suggests that a particular type of physical intimacy threatens masculine toughness, and so the task of the trainer is to ensure that the masculinity "naturally" constitutive of men is not lost through feminine coddling.[9]

Racial, gender, and sexual aspects of subject formation are used as a way to develop and maintain physical power.

On the "hard road" that Harry mentions, fighters are held responsible for the injuries they sustain. When Cedric is hurt in a spar, Harry casts the injury as Cedric's failure:

> I got this kid Cedric . . . and he got hit in the throat and the stomach. He fell down. "I'm getting [out of the ring]—." "No you're not. Finish. Finish the round." "But my throat!" I say, "Your throat is hurting because I always told you, 'stop picking your head up.' And you won't. And your stomach hurt because you won't do no road work.' "

Cedric was harmed not because another fighter punched him in the throat and stomach. He was hurt because he failed to protect himself through rigorous aerobic training and defensive skill. He had a choice, exercised the wrong option, and was at fault. Through tough love, the context of injury is naturalized and the individual response to injury prioritized. The fact of physical suffering is accepted as is, as an inevitable feature of gym life, and fighters are constituted as having a choice in the midst of bodily trauma: they can either quit or continue. Possibilities for expressing agony or even critiquing the exercise at hand are structured out, and instead the fighter's actions are scrutinized.

Tough love allows trainers to instill confidence in their fighters by pushing their bodies far beyond where fighters (and even the audience of a spar) think they can go. There is immense care, thought, and attention in the assessment of boxers' abilities: what fighters will react to, how they will execute the task, when they will need to be encouraged. Implicit in tough love is an underlying confidence that fighters can and will accomplish the task they are asked to undertake. Wells, for example, does not have a hand, but he can still fight on. Trainers demonstrate their belief in their boxers and that the expectations they have of their athletes will surpass even fighters' own expectations. When pugilists complete difficult spars, or even when they do not perform as well as they could have but are criticized in a way that assumes they will next time, self-worth is generated. Athletes develop a new level of confidence in their abilities. Fighters also demonstrate a corresponding trust in their trainers when they lift their slumped heads and shoulders, straighten their disheveled headgears, and start bouncing on their toes again.

One could argue that the commitment to individualism and individual will are necessary in a sport as highly individuated as boxing. A corner may coach, advise, and encourage, but it is up to a boxer to battle through the difficulties of the bout on his own. However, this same commitment to the response to suffering rather than the fact of injury presents itself outside the ring. As trainers mentor boxers, they take seriously the idea of personal responsibility and hold close the notion that "anyone can do it."

IN THEIR CORNER: THE SOCIAL PRACTICES AND RELATIONS OF MENTORING

The boxing experience is used as a theoretical template when trainers intervene in the social lives of their fighters. Trainers often connect experiences in the ring with life outside it. Harry, for example, likes to give boxing-related object lessons by linking performance in the ring with other aspects of a boxer's life in order to prove personal failings. He chides Cedric:

> What I'm telling you now, didn't I tell you both [his predictions about boxing and school]? It's the same situation you got in school. Your teachers tell you, "If you don't do you work, you gonna fail." I tell you, "If you don't do this, this will happen." But I forewarned you.

But trainers go beyond merely drawing parallels to undertaking social practices outside boxing: from providing material resources to acting as educators to imparting romantic advice to serving as father figures. When engaging in these practices, trainers become the structure in their fighters' lives, and trainers and fighters develop relationships centered not on pugilism but on intimacy.

Trainers develop for their boxers a social network, which involves the important practice of finding their athletes work. Because amateurs are usually unemployed or are in insecure positions, and because trainers know it is unlikely that their fighters will ever make substantial money from the sport, trainers are constantly on the lookout for suitable employment.[10] They discuss with other gym goers job vacancies and consult with their white-collar clients about potential openings. When a popular home-furnishings retailer moves into the area, Harry urges Max, one of Mike's amateur boxers, to put in an application. Mike realizes that the manager of the store is a white-collar client of his fellow trainer Ricardo and lobbies for Max, ultimately securing him the position. When Harry learns that Scott is unemployed, he uses his connections in the neighborhood to locate a job for him, which is particularly difficult as Scott does not have work papers. Peter, one of the gym's most established trainers, routinely passes along episodic security and construction work to amateur fighters. And Ricardo, who also works as a stunt double, frequently recruits amateurs as extras in film and television.

Locating employment for fighters may require that trainers forgo the jobs themselves. When a Manhattan boxing gym offers Mike a position that pays $10 per hour and guarantees twenty hours per week, Mike is tempted to accept, as he is homeless at the time and trying to save money for an apartment. However, knowing that Anthony has been searching for work for more than six months and concerned that the difficulty may be due to his criminal record, Mike gives him the job. After working with a *Comedy Central* comedian for almost a year and making a dependable salary, Harry gives up the position to Leon, an amateur he has trained for more than thirteen years. When I ask Harry if he can afford to relinquish a job that adds over $10,000 to his income per year, he shifts the focus of the discussion to Leon and tells me, "It's a good job for him."

In addition to giving job referrals, trainers frequently oversee their boxers' careers, weighing their options and establishing long-term goals. Mike always has employment plans for the members of his team. When Ricardo refers Anthony to a casting agent who needs a heavyweight boxer for a commercial with Mike Tyson, Mike sees an opportunity. He encourages Anthony to pursue acting or modeling and even sets him up with two of his white-collar clients to jumpstart the process. Mike thinks,

> He should get headshots because if you look in the magazines, it's the same profile. It's him . . . so he should get some headshots together. You know, if you know how to read a part, he'll get into movies. He could do runway, but he'd have to trim down a little bit. He'd have to be, like, 160. He's too big. But like Tyson Beckford? That's the *same* look. He could do that. Then he boxes for real and that's even better! He should talk to Simon [one of Mike's white-collar clients]. He know a lot of agencies. Simon know a lot of models 'cause he in advertising. It's all set up for you. Mila [a female boxer] husband do model pictures. The whole thing is set up for you. It's not like, "Oh I don't know who to go to." It's set up for him. I'm like, "Do it!"

When Max is working in a stockroom, Mike urges him to press the management for a store clerk position, which Mike considers a better career opportunity. And Mike routinely harasses Adrian to get his GED so that he can go into the military. Though Mike, a veteran himself, has serious reservations about the armed forces, he believes Adrian's love for discipline, regimen, and hard work would be rewarded in the military. Mike even contacts the head of the army's boxing program about opportunities. Mike does not try to fit all of his boxers into one employment trajectory but rather develops individual plans for his boxers, contingent on their histories, needs, strengths, and interests.

Much as they work as advocates from the ring's corner, so too do trainers work as advocates in the lives of their fighters. This involves supporting amateur boxers in manifold ways as they engage a number of institutions, among them family, work, and especially the criminal justice system, in which amateur athletes feel particularly disempowered. In doing so, trainers teach their fighters how to navigate and negotiate the tricky procedures of these social and economic spheres. Max and his partner have problems adjusting to their new baby and familial arrangement, so Mike speaks to each of them about the stresses of childrearing, urging each to consider the other partner's burdens. When Kenny is fired from his job without being given a reason, Harry calls his employer to ask about his severance and his final check. Peter advocates for a lesser sentence for Darryl, who has changed his life by dedicating himself to boxing, years after being charged with a felony. When this does not work, Peter uses his years of experience as a corrections officer to try to protect his boxer when he is in prison:

> Those troubles were way before he ever came here. He came into boxing to change his life and did. But the judge said—we wrote letters, me, Bruce, everybody—and the judge said, "Look, these are letters from very reputable people, and here's a guy with thirty-five years in the correctional department. You're a good risk, but I just can't ignore what went down." It was a woman. There were two charges. One was a gun charge—very serious. She gave him the minimum on both charges to run together. So it was three years for one, five for the other, which means he's got to do three years.
>
> So I tell him, "OK, this is a bump in the road that you gotta get out of the way." "Oh I wasted—" "You didn't waste anything. You changed your life. You got a different view. We saved you from the streets. That's our job here." . . . Well, I'm prepared to deal with anything in life. Life—there's no shocks or surprises for me. I knew this was coming. And I was really trying to prepare him for it along the way. "Maybe this could happen, maybe that could happen." He'd come up with ideas along the way. "Maybe the judge will. . . ." I wouldn't say, "Never." I'd say, "Well, Darryl, the bottom line is: be prepared for the worst. And then you can accept whatever comes down. But if

you prepare for the worst, it won't crush you." Now when I talk to him, he's not crushed.

I called—nothing dishonest, I still know people—a very, very dear friend of mine who worked under me and is now a big guy in corrections. And I told him, "This kid is guilty." "OK, what do you want to do?" "I want to keep him out of the system." So he said, "Well, find out where he's going, and call me. I'll have some people called and try to get him transferred up here. He'll be a long ways from home but he'll—you know who's in prison. It's the worst guys in the system. They're locked up there twenty-three hours a day. He can work as a plumber, a porter, or whatever. He can study. No pressure, no gangs, whatever." So I said, "Are you serious? That's great!" So I asked him [Darryl], "Do you want that?" And it seems like he does, so I've got to call my buddy and get him to put the wheels in progress. He'll do his time, but he'll do it not normally.

An amazing story of advocacy circulating the gym while I was doing fieldwork was Peter's nine-year attempt to get one of his amateur fighters out of prison. Raoul was accused of armed robbery and sentenced to seven to twenty-one years in prison, even though another person admitted to committing the crime. Not only did Peter hire several attorneys and persist when everyone believed there were no more options, but also he kept his boxer going while he was in prison, both emotionally and practically. He remembers:

> So I told him, "You have my home number, and you have carte blanche to call." And if I would have ever taped those calls—a guy, an innocent guy trying to maintain his sanity in the most awful conditions you can imagine. Fortunately for him, I did thirty-five years in the system, and I knew a lot of people. And wherever he would go, I would know some people, and I could call somebody and say, "Look, look after this kid for me because he's an innocent man." And they wouldn't question me. They wouldn't say "Aw, really? You found one?" Yeah. I had to retire from jail to find an innocent guy.

Mike, Harry, Peter, and other gym trainers spend a significant amount of time and money thinking through their fighters' needs, social circumstances, and psychological processes. This can be in small but crucial ways. When Mike is asked to nominate a fighter from his team to the Police Boxing Association (PBA), which travels around the world competing with other police leagues, he thinks the opportunity is important for Adrian because he has not traveled outside of New York and Pennsylvania. Though it is one nomination, it means a life-changing experience for Adrian, who visited Ireland twice and several states in the US. In addition to paying part of Leon's college tuition, Harry pays his utility and cell phone bills. Trainers do everything for fighters, from posting bail, paying gym dues, and babysitting children to picking them up when they are released from prison. Peter has buried a fighter who died without the resources to pay for a funeral.

The most meaningful role that trainers assume is as confidantes. Trainers spend tremendous amounts of time talking with and listening to their athletes. When Scott needs to bring his middle-aged mother across the US–Mexico border, he discusses with Mike, at length, the difficulty of the impending journey. After crossing into California, Mike is the first person Scott calls from a pay phone to say they are safe. Upon his return to New York, he brings Mike a bottle of tequila to celebrate. When Diego earns a high score on a practice GED test while confined on Rikers Island, and afterward when he passes the exam, he calls Mike from jail with excitement. And when Max's partner has a baby, Max endlessly discusses fatherhood with Mike: how to burp the baby, how to get vaccinations, and how to change diapers. Max calls Mike the father he never had, and appoints Mike as his son's godfather. Mike is also confidante to several fighters, who try to resist reentering the drug trade but find making ends meet impossible on minimum wage.

As trainers care for their boxers, they utilize the same trope of tough love and express the same commitment to individualism as they do in the ring. When applied in the social world, personal-responsibility narratives naturalize the inequality of social circumstances and refuse to allow excuses or complaints, demanding self-sufficiency instead. In particular, trainers look to work to solve problems and look to discipline to overcome disadvantage. When Max complains about the pressure of fatherhood and his lack of energy, it provokes a hail of criticisms from Mike, who tells me:

> I cursed him out three times yesterday and I gave him a long talk about discipline. Well, first of all I told him not to have a baby, and he had a baby. You have a baby, you have responsibility. Baby need Pampers, baby need milk, baby need Similac. Number two, you have to deal with the baby mother. Whether you like her or you don't like her, you still got to deal with her. Number three, you need to work now. He's bitching and moaning, "I'm tired. I don't want to work." Yeah, everybody—that's what everybody in the real world do. You wake up, you go to work, you try to get in your boxing and workout. You go home, you play with your baby. He's feeling the crunch of the real world. But

> before he was a teenager. He'd get up and hang out in the street and come into the gym and hang out in the gym for four hours and then go home. Now he can't do that, and it's a crunch on him and he gets whiney and I don't want to hear that shit. Be a man and do what you got to do.

"What you got to do" as a "man" can be decoded as the patriarchal expectation of breadwinning and heading the family. This imperative is significant because Mike knows that this possibility is almost occluded in the racialized postindustrial landscape of Brooklyn, where finding adequate work for men of color without high school degrees is extremely difficult, never mind for men like Max, who also are marked by a criminal record.[11] But the context of joblessness and mass incarceration is rarely integrated into Mike's mentoring. Despite his knowledge about it—indeed his life experience is shaped by it—Mike ignores it and instead demands that his amateur boxers fulfill the expectations of dominant masculinity through labor. Mike's sentiments belie the tension between the need for support, which is feminized as weakness, and the requirements of manhood, which demand self-sufficiency.

Mike takes a similar position with Adrian, a fighter who has a history of serious physical and psychological abuse. Mike will acknowledge that Adrian has suffered at the hands of parents, teachers, and major socializing institutions, but when talking about Adrian's future, he will focus only on Adrian's response. I worry to Mike that Adrian is, quite literally, starving, and Mike responds:

> But eh, look, that's life. Look, let me tell you something. I'm not the most handsome motherfucker. I'm short, I'm chubby, I got fake yellow teeth. I'm going fucking bald, I got bumps on the back of my neck, and I have no fucking money. So I say, "Well, I'm short, fat, bumps on the back of my neck, and I have no fucking money. But the other side: I'm smart. I'm charming. I make good fucking jokes, and I make people feel comfortable." I have to use my brain. I can't match muscle for muscle, look for look. So Adrian gotta understand that. Yeah, he don't have the talent, so your endurance got to be incredible. Your willpower gotta override this man's talent. And that might go farther. You gotta do dirty tricks. You gotta play mind games. . . . He gotta understand that. You gotta work with what God gave you. And that's that. You can't get jealous. Yeah, I wish I was six [foot] two and didn't have to sleep outside.

In Mike's assessment, hunger is part of life. It is not narrated as the product of anti-black racism and social inequality but rather a feature of everyday urban existence. And, as Mike suggests, the only response to that "fact" is individual: to adapt by drawing upon existing strengths and relying on "endurance."

Harry loses his patience with Kenny, who finds it disorienting when his father returns home after years in prison. Kenny and his siblings are raised by their grandmother when their mother's crack addiction interferes with consistent parenting. With his father's reappearance, Kenny is confused by the sudden interest in creating a nuclear family. After training one day, he discusses the discordance with Harry and later tells me that Harry has been supportive. Harry has told him to consider his father a "sperm donor" rather than a parent, which puts Kenny's mind at ease. However, when I talk with Harry about Kenny and ask if he is concerned about him, Harry is blunt, almost blaming Kenny for his psychological response to the collateral consequences of his father's imprisonment. Harry tells me, "[P]ut it this way: I could have used that excuse. You got to have power over that. Kenny got the talent, but he empty inside. You know? He can be a lot. He could do a lot, but he's empty inside."

As hinted in Mike and Harry's references to their own lives—best exemplified by experiences of homelessness, drug addiction, imprisonment, and fatherlessness—trainers construct and reference a hierarchy of suffering to deflect the suffering of the boxer with whom they are working to another person who is suffering or has suffered more. Trainers point to personal histories of deeper oppression than the pain at hand. When amateur fighters, or ethnographers for that matter, make claims about the unmet promises of US citizenship, they are referred to others who do not enjoy those same promises. Boxers who live in the US without documentation are common figures for this comparison. Scott is used by several trainers as an example of "heart" and "courage" in the midst of suffering. After he crosses the US–Mexico border with his mother, he cements his heroism and instruction potential in the eyes of many gym trainers. That he also works twelve-hour shifts in a minimum wage job without complaining enhances his status. Harry admires Scott's "heart":

> I would love to see Scott become a world champion because he has a hell of a story to tell. Because of how he left [to get his mother] and he came back, what he had to endure to get back here. He had to cross over the border and stuff like that. That's daring defeat when you do something like that. To get back under those circumstances, that's a guy who wants something out of life and who has a plan in life.

Trainers instruct their fighters to enact the same gendered, heteronormativity outside the ring as inside: focus on discipline and regimen; have courage and heart; be personally responsible; tackle any obstacles; if you perceive a barrier, there is no alternative except to overcome it; failure is simply not an option. Trainers utilize discourses of personal responsibility and freedom of choice, which serve as the bases of American capitalism and its corresponding Protestant work ethic.[12] Yet in the gym, they are reinforced in amateur athletes in a different form: through bodywork and social relationships.

These notions of suffering, sacrifice, determination, and will are deeply held among trainers, and they practice what they preach. When Mike became homeless, he never complained about his exhausting routine roaming the streets at night and coaching in the gym during the day. Instead he joked about his subsequent weight loss as "the homeless diet." He would not stay with anyone from the gym because he felt it was undignified: his task was to endure. Harry frequently discusses his own fight back from a serious crack addiction: prison, rehabilitation, relapse, and homelessness. Fighters rarely challenge their trainers because they know their trainers have suffered substantially. For every barrier Harry and Mike ask their fighters to overcome, it is probable that Mike and Harry have faced a similar barrier themselves. This lessens the social distance between mentor and mentored. Because of this minimal distance, trainers are more reputable and believable. The source of their authority is past experience, which gives them legitimacy in the eyes of their amateur boxers.

ANTI-BLACK RACISM, SOCIAL INJUSTICE, AND SOCIAL CRITIQUE

If trainers espouse tough love and prioritize individualism when they work with boxers, they present a different perspective when discussing their motivations for working as boxing trainers and the life chances of men of color in postindustrial New York. In these instances, trainers articulate critiques of anti-black racism and structural injustice and advance arguments about social rather than personal responsibility.

Harry's narrative of recovery from crack-cocaine use and a history of crime informs his athletic and social practices as he seeks to prevent young black men from making the mistakes he made. According to Harry's own account, he fell in with the wrong crowd as a young man in Bedford-Stuyvesant in the 1980s and embarked on a path of marijuana and cocaine use and then crack addiction. He turned to petty crime—low-level drug trading and robbery—to finance his drug use until he shot a family member in a Brooklyn social housing unit. While serving a multiple-year sentence in Attica Correctional Facility, he vowed to change his life and never to go back to prison. He kept to himself for the remainder of his term, studying for his GED, and then, when released, sought drug rehabilitation. He held various jobs during the day and returned to the sport in which he had excelled as a boy. This time he coached in his spare time rather than boxing himself. When he could afford it, he trained fighters full-time. On the process of becoming a trainer, he reflects, "One thing led to another, and I fell in love with the sport all over again but from a different perspective, from a different view, from a different angle. I said 'I can still make a difference.' "

When discussing his history, Harry locates his participation in crime and drug use in the socioeconomic context of the 1980s and 1990s. In particular, Harry argues that growing up in the racially segregated neighborhood of Bedford-Stuyvesant during the height of the crack-cocaine boom and living in deteriorating public housing shaped his opportunities. Though he considers it his responsibility to respond to the conditions of racial oppression, largely through self-help, rehabilitation, and labor, Harry believes in the importance of governmental and social responsibility and warns of the consequences of societal inaction. When talking about US public policy and white racism, Harry argues that the government has the responsibility to provide men with the means to support themselves with respect. He will point out the contradictions of completing a prison sentence and continually being penalized for past crimes. And he will analyze the minimum wage in the context of New York City rent prices, warning of the potential for race riots because of an inadequate affordable housing stock for residents of color. Harry's desire to make a difference, then, is shaped not only by his past but also by a vision of society in which the state and everyday people help each other more. Trainers fall into the latter category. When I ask if all trainers should give their amateur boxers the athletic, social, and psychological attention he devotes, given how taxing this can be on trainers, he does not waver. He responds, "Sure, because if everybody thought in those terms, you'd have better people."

Harry can become frustrated with the fighters with whom he works, but he will not give up on them. At one point, he develops problems with Kenny, who is lying to people in the gym by boasting a world championship. When Harry confronts Kenny about the fib, Kenny clarifies that, "*in my heart* I'm a champion." The aporia between Kenny's actual and existential championship annoys Harry. He stews over the incident for several days but still maintains his basic tenet of social responsibility: "I just can't close the door on people. To me, nobody closed the door on me [when addicted to crack]. There was always a door open no matter what."

Harry points to famed trainer George Washington from the Bed-Stuy Boxing Center as a role model and tries to emulate Washington's devotion, tenderness, and sense of family.[13] When Harry reflects on his relationship with Washington, he gets progressively more nostalgic and asks if I want to meet his mentor. We drop everything and immediately drive to the Bed-Stuy gym and play cards with a seventy-something Washington, who giggles when he cheats and whose eyes sparkle when Harry catches him. Washington's feigned deviousness and expectation—even joy—of being caught illuminate his unspoken bond with Harry. When chatting and joking with Washington, Harry looks happier than I have ever seen him. Despite the fact that Harry has boxers waiting to be trained and white-collar clients scheduled for lessons back at Gleason's Gym, we spend several leisurely hours with Washington; Harry seems unable to tear himself away. On our way home, Harry emotionally remarks that Washington has played an indescribable role in his life. When everyone else had given up on him, Washington did not. When Harry was addicted to crack and homeless and had nowhere to go, Washington always made him feel welcome at the gym. Washington was a steady and stable source of care and support in an otherwise unstable time. He always made Harry believe that he was more than his addiction and criminal record. Harry reflects, "It was like a father I never had. Always, always, he was always there for me and he always believed in me. When the times I didn't believe in myself, he never turned his back on me. Always there for me."[14]

When asked why he does not discuss systemic white racism, failed neoliberal social policy, and social inequality with his boxers, Harry explains that he worries that anger at racial injustice will produce "bitterness," which he considers a dead-end, self-destructive, and unruly emotion. The assumption undergirding Harry's concern is that critique can only end in bitterness and that there are no existing spaces—political, social, or otherwise—to actualize critique. His own battles with bitterness inform this apprehension,

> The world don't owe me anything, so what's the point walking around bitter? You know? Every decision you made, you made a conscious decision. You did it to yourself. You made your own decisions in life. You just have to learn to deal with it. Accept life for what it is. You understand what I'm sayin'? 'Cause

if I walked around bitter all the time, believe me nobody would want to be around me and nobody would want to deal with me.

And yet Harry's argument about the primacy of individual decision-making is contradictory because Harry does, in fact, believe that the world owes people certain things. His very work—physical and social—is an enactment of the conviction that the world owes his fighters—who have been demonized as a pathological cast of characters—drug dealers, hustlers, ex-cons, juvenile delinquents, and social outcasts—better opportunities. The care he received from Washington—and which shapes his work—performed that belief. But when training boxers, he falls back on the idea of self-help that he believes contributed to his success in drug rehabilitation. His tough love simultaneously occupies two contradictory positions: the idea that his athletes should strive in life and his anxiety about the consequences should they not succeed.

Mike did not face the same struggles with addiction or the periods of forced confinement as Harry, but as a black youth, Mike found his possibilities for a good education, decent employment, and escape from the poverty of his Crown Heights neighborhood were limited by institutional racism. Coming of age at the height of the crack boom, he was presented with economic opportunities in the drug trade, but after forays into this extralegal economy, Mike found the consequences of criminality unappealing. He turned instead to boxing and then the armed forces. While he is proud of his athletic and military accomplishments, Mike believes anti-black racism blocked avenues for social and economic mobility. His work at the gym attempts to provide young men with the knowledge and life chances to which he did not have access. He recounts:

Nobody navigated me. If somebody had navigated me, I'd probably be in Harvard somewhere. Street navigator. Yeah, that's what kids need. That's the perfect word. They want to do right, but they haven't been navigated. They don't know what to do. You know what I mean? You counsel them on more things than this boxing shit. They don't know what to do. Baby stuff, how you do the baby stuff. Things like—even how to get the baby circumcised when he little. You gotta counsel them on everything—where to get a job, what to do.

Mike's instruction attempts to provide his fighters with the "street navigation" he never had. He asserts that poor urban areas are so segregated that young men are not taught how to move out of them. They are not given basic information like how to apply to college, how to apply for a job, or even how to acquire basic documentation, like a passport. Society's biggest failure is not mentoring and providing young black men with the resources to leave the ghetto. His work as a trainer is motivated by a critique of racial oppression and a need in the generations after him. He undertakes his work because other institutions have relinquished their responsibilities:

> These kids get raised on the street, and they're not guided. Max is a smart guy, but he didn't know what to do. He had no guidance. "Where I go to get my GED?" "My girlfriend pregnant, where I go?" "Where's health care?" "How I fill out an application?" "How you sign up for a lease?" "What to wear on a job interview?" You know, everything. These guys just don't know. When they go do things kinda wrong and do a social faux pas, they get frustrated. They get in a corner. And most people—like almost my whole team is criminals. All of them went to jail at one period of time or another, and when you fill out an application, you're like ostracized. You did your fucking time, that's it. You can't get a job. You can't do this, you can't do that. Boxing is like, they embrace you.

To Mike, the gym is a makeshift institution for socialization and a place where men who are frustrated, excluded from full citizenship by criminal records or a lack of work papers, and unable to meet the expectations of dominant society can be supported and even embraced. Mike sees it as the last social space for homosocial bonding and where young men learn the rituals of masculinity:

> I think this the last place where men get trained by men. There used to be outlets—like the army. There ain't no outlets anymore. They not used to dealing with men. I don't care—if you're a single mother, you can't raise no man-child.

At times, like Harry, Mike can reveal hesitation about the roles he has taken on, especially the role of surrogate father. After he has yelled at Max, I ask Mike how Max responded. Mike explains:

> Well, I don't *make* him. He kind of listened. I mean, that's the kind of talk his father should have with him. I shouldn't have to have that fucking talk with him. All these kids have no fathers. The majority of these boxers don't have no father figure so I have to step in, and I've got to have these talks. They don't understand that when you get older, the choices you make affect you for

> fifteen to twenty years. When you're younger maybe you'll get reprimanded for it, but now the choices you make affect your ass. You get used to working. Yeah it's hard going to the gym and working full-time and taking care of your baby. But that's what you got yourself into. You have to get that discipline in mind.

Also like Harry, Mike retreats from acknowledging and critiquing the contexts of social and economic injury to demanding personal responsibility. Mike analyzes injustice at the social-structural level, but he still promotes a form of masculine individualism and, in particular, the transcendent power of labor. But unlike Harry, Mike does not draw upon self-help discourses. His belief in individualism comes from a careful political assessment of the postindustrial landscape and the recognition there are literally no other options. Anger at anti-black racism is justified, and bitterness at urban marginality is legitimate, but self-sufficiency and personal responsibility are still necessary to succeed. When I ask Mike why he demands such magnificent acts of will from his amateurs, he responds, "You can sit in the gym angry and depressed all you want. But it's not going to get you anywhere." Mike's work, then, enacts social convictions while accepting the reality of current social conditions as unalterable.

RECONSIDERING KINSHIP AND SOCIAL CAPITAL

Each day, when Peter's amateur boxers arrive at the gym, and again when they leave, they kiss him on the cheek. When I first started doing research at Gleason's, I found this surprising. After understanding the work that trainers undertake with amateur boxers, it became commonsensical. Through the physical and social demands of boxing, coaches and amateur boxers develop extremely close relationships. As Mike says, "I know more about them than they families." Trainers provide amateurs with emotional and material sustenance by encouraging, supporting, and loving their fighters. These impromptu relationships form out of mutual need and are imbrued with struggle, suffering, and intimacy.

The trainer-boxer relationship is so constitutive that it shapes almost every aspect of trainers and fighters' lives. Peter laments that his extra-gym relationships have languished because of his commitment to the sport. Similarly, the grueling gym schedules that Mike and Harry keep often foreclose possibilities for socializing and spending time with other people. Trainers sacrifice their own relationships outside the gym and instead adapt similar responsibilities as parents and kin inside the gym. Under these circumstances, intimacy in a community of men is legitimate.

Peter hints at the importance of the boxers in his life when he discusses the day Raoul was released from prison. To Peter, it was not simply the day his boxer got out of prison but the day he was reunited with the gem of his life:

> It was really such an emotional moment. We all cried. God, it was so emotional. And he was like—he couldn't believe it. If you ever see the tapes when we went out through the court's front door, he kissed the ground. And that was—if I never do anything in my life again, I often say to people—I've accomplished this, that, or another, no big deal. *That* to me is the jewel in my life.

Even though Raoul does not compete anymore, he stops by Gleason's regularly to check in with Peter:

> And, you see him here now, like a big Saint Bernard, there's real love between us. He knows that only a person that really loves you could go that mileage. So no matter what—he has problems because when your life is changed like that—and he doesn't fight anymore, but he still comes here because we can sit down and talk, and he can train. I always buff him back up.

Peter and Raoul are bonded as family. The practices of training amateur boxers entails more than a social critique of the institutional deficiencies of postindustrial New York; training engenders and enacts the practice of kinship.[15]

In *Antigone's Claim*, Judith Butler explores the possibilities for intimacy resulting from "idealized" kinship.[16] Rejecting structuralist models of family formation, which rely on "the fiction of bloodlines," Butler draws upon the work of feminist anthropologists who deny cross-cultural structural features, advancing a broad definition of familial arrangements that "organize the reproduction of material life." Butler uses the example of Antigone and the scholarship of David Schneider to suggest that kinship is not "a form of being but a form of doing." In other words, instead of understanding kinship as a position or a status (i.e., being born into a family), it could be understood as a set of practices.[17] Such a rearticulation offers the opportunity to conceptualize kinship in what Butler calls the "social organization of need."

Trainers educating their boxers embody Butler's idea; the relationship between trainers and boxers and the process of training demonstrate kinship based on action, on doing, on practices. These practices of intimacy improvised at Gleason's Gym are valuable and important socially for men—both young and old. Through tough love and bodywork, Harry, Mike, and other trainers tightly circumscribe overt expressions of tenderness but they also produce opportunities for care, identification, and intergenerational friendship. Trainers help young men develop dignity, respect, and status, and they usher their amateurs through life's transitions.[18] There is a cost to these relationships, of course; trainers demand sacrifice from their amateur fighters, and trainers compel asceticism as the price of their care. But given the dearth of employment opportunities in Brooklyn, these new types of relationships are natural outgrowths of postindustrialization.

Though the tough-love rhetoric that trainers use to train and care for amateur boxers is generally associated with neoliberal politics, when advanced in the gym, this particular iteration of personal responsibility can be considered a way of not letting people be defined by their tragedies.[19] When deployed by men who dedicate their lives to combating—literally and figuratively—oppression, trainers' demands for individual accountability and personal responsibility challenge the hegemonic practice of defining amateur boxers solely by their tragedies, by their "lack of's," or that to which they have not had access. In compelling their flock to sweat, to bleed, and to reach the next level, trainers reject a location disadvantage, and they challenge a defining feature of postindustrial subjectivity and the ideological relegation of men of color to the accepted dishonored archetypes—damaged fatherless men, deadbeat dads, deviants, hustlers, gangsters. Trainers cannot see their athletes as victims because of necessity. Instead, they imagine them as sources of power and greatness. While anti-black racism and the paucity of opportunities that amateur boxers experience remains a reality, trainers see them differently than neoliberal politicians and policymakers do. Trainers ask their fighters to imagine themselves outside of social injury and disenfranchisement and they encourage the young men under their stewardship to see their worth in different ways. They demand that they produce alternative mechanisms of measurement to evaluate their lives and the progress made with each day. The journey—their identity—is never final.

In this process, trainers arm young men with social capital that is imperative for survival in postindustrial New York City, and they foster the development of skills that are unavailable within other spaces. As many scholars have noted, social capital—strong social connections, dense social networks, transparent forms of social communication—are the prerequisites for success in the postindustrial economy. Social capital is one of the most important resources that middle- and upper-class parents give their children, further illuminating how the relationship between trainer and boxer is akin to family relationships. Based on their own experiences, gym trainers recognize how the denial of such capital constrains the opportunities and chances that are available to amateur boxers, as compared with their wealthier, whiter peers. Trainers thus structure the gym as a place where amateur boxers can learn the requisite skills, thereby acquiring the capital necessary for endurance not only in the ring but also in other aspects of their lives. Amateur boxers develop networks, connections, and channels of communication and find a place of support, all of which is necessary amid their struggle not only to bear the deleterious impact of New York's racialized postindustrial landscape but also to persevere. They find support and capital amid manifold obstacles and demands of silence at the first utterance of critique about inequality.

Chapter Four

PASSING TIME: THE EXPRESSIVE CULTURE OF EVERYDAY GYM LIFE

"In order to form a good Boxer, it is necessary to possess strength, art, courage, activity, and wind."

—A PUPIL BOTH OF HUMPHREYS AND MENDOZA, 1784

TUCKED AWAY IN THE BACK RIGHT CORNER OF GLEASON'S Gym stands Mike and Harry's corner, affectionately referred to as Mike and Harry's "office." Their quarters consist of two small square lopsided Formica tables, a scattering of broken plastic chairs, and three lockers overflowing with boxing equipment (sweat-soaked headgears, boxing gloves, jump ropes) and stocked with a supply of boxing necessities (rolls of duct tape, pots of petroleum jelly, water bottles). Upon arrival in this corner, one will find Mike, short and stout with the confident gait of a wrestler, and Harry, a former heavyweight with a stern expression interrupted episodically by flashes of a radiant smile, obsessively rearranging the items of their lockers. In running monologues, they mutter to no one in particular the tragedy of the cabinets: their endless attempts to achieve some semblance of order perpetually undercut by the lack of participation from their athletes. A cheeky boxer will mock the melodrama by suggesting the implementation of a formal policy requiring a borrower of equipment to sign a legal, notarized document promising safe return of the rented item to its designated shelf. No signature, no headgear. Another will brainstorm potential punishments for the infractions about which Harry and Mike complain: Would a stint on a chain gang teach the thoughtless perpetrator a lesson? The loss of a limb? Yet another will suggest that the "problem" of the locker is that of smell and not of organization. An eruption of laughter demonstrates the rebellious alliance of fighters against their trainers, but a sharp glance from the latter instantly cools the joking and encourages tending to the tasks at hand. Eyes will cast downward, smiles will fade, and the athletes will return to lacing their shoes, wrapping their hands, and putting on their gloves.

The period of time when boxers train is tightly circumscribed. Fighters have set workout routines, and the counting of the gym's timekeeping bell, which runs three minutes for a round, fifty seconds for rest, and ten seconds for a warning ("seconds out") and loops continuously, structures physical activities. For the most part, athletes do not deviate from this temporal organization to socialize. The brevity of the one-minute rest in between rounds makes it difficult to carry on or keep alive a thread of a conversation, and ideally, the rigor of pugilistic labor should discourage boxers from expending additional energy on talk. Trainers' watchful eyes, which follow their athletes' every move, even from a distance, silently command total focus on the body. Trainers are quick to reprimand miscreants who indulge in the luxury of chatting or joking when they are supposed to be working out.

This intense time, however, is only one part of the workday at Gleason's Gym. Gym regulars—trainers and boxers—pass hours pursuing social interests in addition to athletic endeavors. Because many trainers arrive at the gym between 6:00 a.m. and 8:00 a.m. and stay until late in the evening, they put in shifts of over twelve hours. They are not working this entire time. The ebb and flow of gym life provides them with periodic reprieve from their toil, which they use to eat, sleep, read, play games, and talk. Athletes, too, spend long stretches in the gym. Many male boxers are unemployed or not in school, so they have time to spend in the gym. "Gym rats" are fighters who are known for their habitual presence; they devote between six and eight hours to hanging out. Others stay between four and five hours. Regardless of the duration, most competitive pugilists spend time with their teammates and trainers before they box as they prepare for their workouts and after training as they recover. If training is devoted to work, this nontraining time is dedicated to social interaction.[1]

When gym regulars socialize, they draw upon expressive practices to interact. Expressive practices, such as conversation, joking, narrative, and argument, help people form solidarities, construct audiences, and articulate and negotiate value systems.[2] At Gleason's Gym, trainers and fighters use expressive practices to make sense of and provide their views on the world. Participating in discussions, debates, joking, and giving advice allows gym members to derive some of the social benefits of a workplace, such as the acquisition of social knowledge, inclusion in acts of deliberation, and the demonstration and maintenance of friendship. In a postindustrial landscape, where access to formal worksites is limited for many men, expressive practices foster the development of admired collective forms of identity, such as gender and work.

This chapter looks at how Gleason's regulars spend time in the urban gym when they are not engaged in athletic pursuits. It analyzes the features and functions of the gym's expressive culture and the norms embodied in it. I argue that rather than emphasizing individuality and individual initiative, as is done through boxing training and competition, expressive practices and relationships place social importance on the collective. Spending time together and communicating life experiences create group cooperation and cohesion. In other words, speech acts in the gym are not simply a performance of the self but also are a way that speakers organize themselves as a collective. This social organization creates one of the only spaces for sociality available to many boxers and trainers in postindustrial New York. The majority of amateur fighters and coaches do not socialize outside of the gym unless at a fight or watching an important championship at a trainer or teammate's home—though even this is rare—socializing overwhelmingly takes place within the gym. The time before and after training provides a space where boxers can relate to those who have similar experiences. There is support in coping with the daily exigencies of urban struggle, and networks are woven that boxers utilize when they need help. The social interaction of the gym is communal and the value of sharing time, experiences, and entertainment as well as engaging with others is idealized. The social interaction of the gym also fosters the production and expression of tender masculinities, by which boxers can self-disclose, demonstrate emotional vulnerability, and receive validation and support.

PASSING TIME AND THE FORMATION OF THE GROUP

Gym regulars pass a significant amount of time sitting around reading, talking, watching movies or old fights on portable DVD players, playing chess or dominos, or doing nothing at all. What is called in the gym "passing time" entails a certain amount of boredom, an unrushed pace of life, and few other obligations to meet. As people read magazines, newspapers, or books, they may look up and tell others who are reading, talking, or even napping about interesting excerpts. When people interact, the flow of conversation is undirected and unhurried, and few transitions are made between topics. A conversant will not think twice about interrupting someone who is reading or already engaged in a discussion. Similarly, if someone who has been reading shares part of his or her text, there is little obligation to continue talking after the passage has been delivered to the interlocutor. It is not considered rude to interrupt or to terminate a discussion at any point and without notice. Passing time, then, is about being in another's company and sharing the day rather than a telos.

Boxing is not a common topic of discussion when people pass time unless a particularly spectacular championship bout has been fought the preceding weekend. When I conducted fieldwork, I was surprised by how *little* people discussed the sport, instead talking about personal experiences and phenomena outside of the gym. Topics of conversation are current events, popular culture, and newspaper stories. Articles from the *New York Daily News*—the gym's newspaper of choice—movies, or television programs on popular stations such as Court TV, the Discovery Channel, and the Travel Channel are discussed at length. Stories that surround the uncommon and strange are much more popular than the practical or mundane.

A popular rhetorical strategy employed to engage others and unite them in conversation when the group is otherwise dispersed, fragmented, or disinterested is posing a question that the speaker knows is almost certainly unanswerable. This is intended to pique the interest of the audience, position the speaker as an authority on the subject, and create the need for further explanation. Asking an impossible question with little to no segue in order to capture the attention of a potential audience is one of Anthony's favorite techniques. Anthony does not socialize outside of the gym and does not consider himself a particularly social person. Though he says he never intends to pass as much time as he does at Gleason's, he is known for taking a great deal of time preparing to train and for sticking around long after his workout is over to discuss sports, politics, popular culture, or anything else that happens to be on his mind. It is almost a daily ritual to hear his trainer, Mike, yelling at Anthony to "get going!" and "stop wasting my time!" when he procrastinates starting his training by chatting. It is also a daily ritual to hear Mike and Anthony conversing for hours after Anthony has finished his athletic tasks.

One day, after completing his training, Anthony sits down in Mike and Harry's corner and looks through a photography book called *25 under*

25: Up-and-Coming American Photographers. One of the twenty-five artists featured is Bayete Ross Smith, who, on another occasion, has photographed Mike and several female boxers. Two of Ross Smith's pictures have made it into the collection, which now rests on a table for anyone to peruse. Publications left on the table are considered the communal property of Mike and Harry's office; readers can look through them at their leisure but are expected to ask before taking them out of the gym. With little else to interest him, Anthony flips through the book and past the photos of the women fighters. After scrutinizing one picture in particular for several minutes, he holds it up for me to see. The shot is of four black women seated in a row on a couch. They wear multicolored sequined tube tops, and two of them sport brightly colored cropped hair. I stare back at Anthony, unsure of what he is asking of me.

ANTHONY: What do you think that their nationality is? What would be your guess?
LUCIA: I have no idea. Let me see.

I look closer at the picture for clues and find none.

LUCIA: Anthony, how in the world would I know that?
ANTHONY: If they ain't Jamaican, I'm telling you.

Anthony's enticement is incredibly effective. He knows I am skeptical of quick visual racial categorizations like the one he has just performed and which we have debated at length on other occasions, so he succeeds in intriguing me as to how he has determined the nationality of the women in the photograph. I oblige his lure.

LUCIA: Why?
ANTHONY: 'Cause that's what they do! They think this is kind of sexy or cute.
LUCIA: This color hair?
ANTHONY: This *now-or-later* color hair. The only thing that [might] make them not be Jamaican—they might be from the South.
LUCIA: And how do you know *that*?
ANTHONY: They don't have super long nails on.
LUCIA: You're telling me that Jamaicans like long nails?
ANTHONY: They love them long nails.
LUCIA: So can you tell where someone is from if you meet a black woman?
ANTHONY: Mostly.

LUCIA: *How?*
ANTHONY: There are just certain things.

Registering my visible doubt, Anthony begins a lecture on the social functions of stereotypes. Some stereotypes, he argues, such as Jamaican women's penchant for dyeing their hair vivid colors, are based in truth.

ANTHONY: It's sort of like certain stereotypes are totally false. Some stereotypes are based on the truth. They are. Even though—let me tell you something—even though people get offended, they are based on the truth. Right? It was very hard for me to believe that Sam [another boxer in the gym] is Italian. He kind of has the demeanor of a Hispanic person. Or a Puerto Rican.
LUCIA: How?
ANTHONY: He seems very comfortable around, um, you know, other people.
LUCIA: Black men?
ANTHONY: Yeah!

Anthony goes on to argue that it is the task of the decoder to read certain behaviors and situations in order to determine whether or not drawing upon common stereotypes is appropriate. He learned to do such decoding while incarcerated. He asserts, "I've been in prison for a long time. Not that I've been in *forever* but I've seen it in there enough to see these things in people."

As part of his argument, Anthony uses another common speech practice in the gym: drawing on personal experience. Referencing life experience—in this case, the knowledge that he acquired when forcibly confined—and using it as evidence establish a speaker's right to speak about a topic and give the speaker legitimacy. Anthony uses his experiences in prison in an attempt to persuade me that he can distinguish valid stereotypes from unfounded ones. But Anthony is not satisfied with the mere assertion that he possesses the ability to perform complicated stereotypic sorting; he wants to show me. To do this, he sets up an experiment. Rehearsing his argument that Sam, a white boxer, is unusual in his comfort around male athletes of color, Anthony tells me that in prison he noticed that white men are anxious to prove their masculinity to black men. An inherent feeling of inferiority, he suspects, motivates their desire to appear strong, and he saw that they would go to great lengths to prove their toughness. Anthony sees this same tendency in the gym. He explains, "White men in the gym, they have this—I'm not saying that they're the only ones who have this because I've been around it for a long time in prison—but they had this thing where—how do I explain it? They got to puff their chest out a little further or hit the bag a little harder." He instructs me to look at a white man working on a heavy bag in front of us. He tutors me, "If you watch this guy—see this guy with the shorts? He's going to hit the bag real hard, and when he hit the bag real hard, he's going to see who's looking at him." When the man strikes the bag and stops to survey his audience, Anthony raises his eyebrows with a knowing smile, sits back in his chair, and rests his case.

To keep a conversation going and include everyone in it, discussants conduct informal polls, which make the discussion accessible and interesting to all, even when only one person may know about the subject. As he is getting ready to work out one morning, Anthony chats about a program on dog sacrifice in southern Africa that he had seen on the television the night before. This story brings together three popular topics of discussion: stories about unusual animals, international travel, and perceptions of racial and cultural difference. Anthony discusses how dogs are represented in this particular African region and why they are sacrificed once a year. As he talks, people listen in amazement and are eager to learn more. They ask questions, and, if he can, Anthony answers them. At the end of his narrative, Anthony takes an informal poll, asking the audience: "What do you think the most prized part of the animal is? What do you think the best part of the animal to eat is?" People sit stumped. After thinking hard for a moment, Max giggles and shouts out, "its balls!" Others consult with one another and earnestly submit their answers: "Could it be the leg?" "Would it be the tail?" Anthony dramatically starts to leave the intrigued group by sauntering off to start his workout. But just before reaching the mirrors, where he will shadowbox, he pauses and looks back: "The nose," he answers. "The nose is the most prized part of the dog. Only special people get to eat the nose." He turns back around again, abandoning his students in stunned silence.

Speakers like Anthony organize the group verbally.[3] Though only Anthony knew about dog sacrifice, taking an informal survey allowed him to involve everyone in the activity. And it created the conditions for more discussions about similar topics. Long after Anthony went off to exercise, the group chatted about unusual animal stories they had recently heard: the "falcon" that abducted a Chihuahua in Bryant Park the previous summer; the forty-nine-foot python—the largest snake ever reported—recently discovered in Indonesia; the Bengali tiger found living in a Harlem apartment.[4] Through these conversations, gym regulars behave as a group and begin to understand themselves as such. Though the sport of boxing is highly individualized, the gym supports periods of time when and provides social space in which people can use expressive practices to participate in a meaning-making collective. For this collective, the ideal of community supersedes the inventiveness of a particular exchange or conversation.[5] The group is paramount, more important than any speaker or the content being discussed.

As people pass time in the gym, they drift in and out of conversation at leisure. If there is a discussion going on, people can enter and leave it according to their interests, schedules, or energy levels. It is not considered impolitic to change the topic without warning, though it can be experienced as annoying. Multiple conversations are held at once, requiring speakers to juggle more than one line of thought, and it is not perceived as rude to interrupt. One morning, several discussions among three boxers—Anthony, Lily, Sean—Harry, and me are maintained. At any given point, only two or three people are involved, but the configuration changes with no announcement or pause. Though I note the various speaking arrangements below, in real time there is no lapse between when people come in and out of the conversation.

Anthony sits lacing his shoes and wrapping his hands in preparation for his workout while Lily, who has just completed her workout, jumps from leg to leg in an effort to cool down. The conversation begins when Anthony, who has just returned from England where he filmed a commercial with Mike Tyson, expresses disbelief in the exchange rate. He raises the issue with Lily, who is British, and with me, who has lived in the UK.

Anthony, Lily, and I brainstorm.

LUCIA: You got a standard exchange rate.

ANTHONY: *Are you kidding?* I gave them 150 dollars and they gave me 85 pounds.

LUCIA: That's standard.

LILY: Do you remember what the exchange rate was?

ANTHONY: I got a receipt. I got like *three* receipts. On that regular receipt it *looks* like the math makes sense but . . .

LILY: Well . . . we were getting two dollars for every pound.

LUCIA: It was like 1.5 for me—someone got Dunkin' Donuts!

ANTHONY: It must be you.

LUCIA: It wasn't. I did get some yesterday in Cranston.

ANTHONY: I was sure that was yours!

LILY: I got the cutest surfing outfit yesterday at Old Navy. *So cool.* I'm going to look the part even though I'll be flat on my ass because I can't surf.

ANTHONY: You're going surfing? Florida!

LUCIA: You should talk to Ryan [my friend]. He surfs.

LILY: I just want to stand with a board by the water.

LUCIA: That's pretty much what Ryan does.

ANTHONY: [*laughs*] She said, "That's pretty much what he does."

LILY: I got these really cool board shorts and a cute T-shirt. So cute! Fourteen dollars.

Anthony turns to Lily to engage her directly. They break off the conversation as Sean, who is shadowboxing by the table in an effort to socialize and delay his workout, starts talking with me.

ANTHONY: Where in Florida?

LILY: Huh?

ANTHONY: Where in Florida?

LILY: Fort Lauderdale.

ANTHONY: I used to live in Florida.

LILY: Huh?

ANTHONY: I used to live in Florida.

LILY: Ricardo [Lily's husband] wants to go scuba diving because he can't swim on top of the water. Do you have that problem, Anthony? He tells me that it's a black thing. Black people can't swim on top of the water because their bone density is heavier than white people.

ANTHONY: You know what my problem is? I can't swim for long because of my nose. I have breathing problems. Breathing out of my mouth causes that problem. That whole sinus thing. That'd be my problem.

Sean starts talking with me.

SEAN: I saw *Troy*. It was so bad. *So bad.*

LUCIA: It's true.

SEAN: There were like two good fighting scenes. And it was so bad. The whole thing was about Brad Pitt. What the fuck? I was *embarrassed* about that film.

Harry, with advice to give, interrupts Lily and begins a discussion with Anthony about his problems swimming.

HARRY: You have good form, Tony?

ANTHONY: What do you mean "form"?

HARRY: You turn your head to the side and take air and then turn your head to the other side and take air?

ANTHONY: That's what I *try* to do.

HARRY: Yeah. But the other way is not correct.

ANTHONY: So what you're telling me is don't take a breath every stroke?

HARRY: Yeah, you can't be breathin' every time. You making yourself work harder.

ANTHONY: OK.

Unable to resist joining the conversation because he recently has read a review of *Troy* in the paper, Anthony abruptly ends the discussion with Harry and joins my conversation with Sean. When the gendered dimension of the conversation interests Lily, she joins in.

SEAN: That movie was bullshit.

ANTHONY: It was *bullshit*?

SEAN: I didn't pay that money to see your chest puffed out.

LILY: You don't say that when Angelina Jolie sticks her titties out in *Tomb Raider*.

SEAN: That's different.

ANTHONY: In the newspaper it said "Brad Pitt nails the part and that's what makes this movie so great." That's what they said.

Not to be left out, Harry rejoins the conversation but directs it away from the movie *Troy*. In a non sequitur, he tells Anthony and me about his upcoming trip to Las Vegas.

HARRY: De La Hoya fight June 5th. We be out there June 4th. I'm tryin' to stay.

LUCIA: That's when they're announcing too.

HARRY: What?

LUCIA: That's when they're announcing the reality show.

HARRY: *Last Man Standing*? Who?

LUCIA: What everyone was applying for. *The Next Great Champ*, maybe? They're announcing that at the fight.

ANTHONY: Him and Bernard gonna fight that night, right?

LUCIA: But not each other.

ANTHONY: Yeah, I know that.

These dialogues can be disorienting to read because of the constant interruptions. The conversation holds together a number of threads; the topics are scattered, people intrude, and not everyone knows what is going on all the time. No one really comes to the table with anything in particular to discuss but rather the exchange is freely associated. Bourgeois prohibitions on interrupting another speaker are not enforced or even considered. In fact, constant interruptions signify strong communication and a level of excitement in the range of topics being discussed.[6] This expression of passing time with others is significant *because* it is not marked—it is mundane, unremarkable, even frivolous. However, the discourse is textured and various, its participants consider it meaningful, and solidarity is constructed in its interstices. In the conversation above, people show *what* they know about those with whom they are talking—their habits, their preferences, their likes, and their dislikes. Lily and I know Anthony has visited London, is troubled by the exchange rate he received, and we talk about whether or not a mistake has been made. Ever the boxing trainer and obsessively dedicated to imparting knowledge, Harry is attentive to Anthony's breathing problems when he swims and tries to suggest ways to improve the form of his freestyle. This leads Lily, a white woman, to wonder if black men, such as Anthony, have the problems swimming that her husband Ricardo, who is also black, has. She asks Anthony about his experiences to ascertain whether or not Ricardo's swimming difficulties are a function of his perceptions of racial difference. Anthony is interested in Lily's upcoming trip to Florida because he has lived there. He nods to my known love of Dunkin' Donuts, while Sean alludes to the fact that days before, I had voiced outrage over the quality of the movie *Troy*.

More important, in the discussions above, people self-reference *that* they know each other. These references are articulated in a way that is never explicit but that is understood and meaningful. They are based on knowledge of gym regulars, and they show individuals that they are registered as part of the group. Conversation acknowledges the presence of others and each person is acknowledged as contributing.[7]

What begins as a light-hearted conversation can develop into a serious group debate. In the case of dog sacrifice, Anthony was the only person who had seen the program, which positioned him as the resident expert. Sometimes several people have read the story, seen the TV show, or have knowledge about the topic. In these cases, there are likely to be multiple perspectives, which can be contested at length. Early one morning, a discussion on headhunting in the Philippines generates heated deliberation. On one side are people who understand headhunting as secular intimidation through unpredictable acts of violence, and on the other are people who think that headhunting is a religious practice that emerges out of a sacred belief system. The dispute is eventually terminated when Mike—who, incidentally, has been out-argued—decides his athletes need to begin their workouts. Had the agonistic practice begun after his team's training or had Mike's points been considered more seriously, the debate could have continued for longer.

During the headhunting debate, it appeared that gym members argued points that they actually believed, but this is not always the case. In some debates, people will take positions that it is clear they do not accept as true simply to argue, piss someone off, or demonstrate solidarity with another individual. Debaters also can be inconsistent, jumping from side to side, depending on who has made a compelling or, more often, a humorous point. In a debate, then, participating in and sharing the experience of deliberation, or passing the time, is more important than winning it.[8] The rhetorical back-and-forth or competitive dimension of the debate, which has some features of the physical spar, presents itself in a different form. People suspect they will not persuade others of their point of view so the outcome is not important: The process rather than the result is valued. The arguments gym goers make help the group develop a sense of unity. To be sure, people do give their personal perspectives, distinguish themselves, and develop senses of individual status. But as they make their points, they collaborate to construct what linguist Julie Lindquist calls a "coherent text" and "assurance of collective identity."[9] This collective identity creates a supportive and communal space within the gym.

The expressive acts of passing time also have the quick manipulation of language at their core, which is integral to the pleasurable atmosphere of the gym. And anyone can join in the conversation at any point. Whereas training involves a rigid hierarchy, in conversation, joking, and debate, trainers do not dominate or have special speaking positions. Though some speakers are more savvy or quick-witted than others and have the upper hand verbally, the amount of time someone has spent at Gleason's Gym does not privilege anyone; provided new arrivals are respectful, they are as accepted as discussants who have visited the gym for a long time. Members are admired if they can keep up with the rhetorical features of the speech act or can narrate an interesting story. The form of these expressive practices, then, is more important than their subject matter: form expresses sociality, solidarity, and regularity.

HUMOR AND JOKING: FRIENDSHIP AND THE GYM'S SOCIAL ORDER

Joking is an important expressive practice by which individuals contribute to and participate in the group. Nonsense and joking are social barometers that gauge the intensity of gym regulars' bonds; the ability to tease and be teased indexes how important people are to one another and how comfortable they are with being ribbed. In other words, joking measures the strength of the group.[10] One afternoon, Ricardo, who is known for both his quick wit and his fondness for being clever, and I sit in Mike and Harry's corner watching people work out. After Omar completes his training for the day, he bounds into our corner to chat. He is wearing a *Kreyolfest* T-shirt from 2003, the souvenir of a yearly concert of Haitian and other Caribbean artists in Wingate Park, Brooklyn, run by the *Haitian Times*. Omar's shirt bears the newspaper's logo and the location and date of the event, but Omar seems to have forgotten that this information is advertised on his attire. It catches the attention of Ricardo.

RICARDO: The *Haitian Times*. You Haitian?
OMAR: On my mother's brother's sister's side.
RICARDO: What that mean?
OMAR: I don't know.

The three of us laugh.

OMAR: No, I went to the thing—
RICARDO: The riots?
OMAR: What?

Ricardo laughs.

OMAR: Oh! No, I went to the concerts at Wingate in—
R. AND LUCIA: 2003?

Ricardo and I laugh.

OMAR: Last year.

Everyone laughs.

Omar happens to walk into a corner of the gym where Ricardo and I are sitting bored and waiting for someone with whom to joke. Because Omar does not realize where our questions are coming from or how we possess the information we have, he becomes the unwitting subject of our light-hearted teasing. But this does not throw Omar; he does not miss a beat and takes our joking in high spirit. He even turns the table back on us by using to his advantage the same nonsense we have deployed against him.[11] When asked by Ricardo if he is Haitian, which must have seemed like an odd inquiry since it is quite well-known in the gym that Omar strongly self-identifies as a Sunni Muslim, Omar responds with an equally disorienting answer: "On my mother's brother's sister's side." Omar befuddles Ricardo and me, even forcing Ricardo to concede: "What that mean?" By the end of the exchange everyone has been confused at some point. There are no introductions or transitions, but the three of us agree to participate in the nonsense and to appreciate it. The banter is pleasurable because it is humorous, because we pretend that it makes sense, and because of the unexpectedness of its discontinuities.

The discontinuities in particular are enjoyable. In the midst of the joking are sharp references to serious topics. Our exchange takes place in mid-March 2004, just weeks after Jean-Bertrand Aristide is removed as president of Haiti. When Ricardo asks if Omar has been to "the riots," he is referring to Haiti's resulting political unrest. But as quickly as the comment is made, it is gone, leaving Omar and me perplexed and Ricardo to chuckle to himself at his adroit and unappreciated commentary. Folklorist Roger Abrahams suggests that one of the features of joking is that it "presents nonsense as if it were sense, putting together dialogue and song in a continuous fashion but without the usual logic that determines continuities." Such nonsense also produces future possibilities; it creates opportunities for the creation and reinforcement of friendship.[12]

The exchange among Ricardo, Omar, and me did not embarrass anyone, but the attempt to discomfit someone can be part of the gym's culture of joking. Rather than manifesting as malice, embarrassment is controlled and ordered by casting it as play.[13] One afternoon, Harry puts Wells and Lawrence in the ring to spar. Wells has just returned from a long hiatus from Harry's tutelage, and sending him to spar with Lawrence, one of the most talented fighters in the gym, serves as a faux punishment. With little else to do with Wells because he is so out of shape, Harry pretends to give Wells an object lesson by instructing him to work with someone who is far superior in ability and preparation. Spars—and the elements of pugilistic training in general—are sacred rituals and the proprietary realm of the trainer. I witnessed only a handful of instances when people played and joked during or interfered with spars. Harry, in particular, is rigid and does not abide by anything but total focus in the ring. In this case, though Harry attempts to encourage the discipline of a typical spar, as his boxers rebel and the practice degenerates into play, he cannot contain his amusement. Despite himself, he suspends his rules and teases Wells, good-naturedly trying to humiliate him in front of a large crowd, who wonders why Wells is in the ring on his first day back training in the first place.

When the spar begins, Harry instructs Wells to throw various punches as he would in any other spar. However, determining that a rigorous exercise is out of the question, Wells and Lawrence ignore their coach and fool around, batting each other's gloves with fake punches and pretending to take cheap shots. Every few seconds, they stop, drop their gloves, and bend at their waists in laughter. Harry, who has not given up on the athletic activity, laughs from time to time, but struggles to regain his composure, asking the duo "What are you doing?" For brief periods of time, Harry succeeds in cajoling Wells and Lawrence to put in a minimal amount of effort; Lawrence even turns southpaw at one point to confuse Wells.[14] But when the timekeeping bell rings, halting the activity for one minute, Wells directly challenges Harry and the spar disintegrates.

HARRY: Can I ask you a question?

WELLS: Yeah.

HARRY: The man about ten inches taller than you, what happened to the waist? What happened to the body?

WELLS: Take my place, Harry!

Talking back to a trainer is taboo. The crowd, sensing deviance and growing larger by the minute, erupts in laughter. Not to be outdone, Harry quickly retorts.

HARRY: You saying that because Lucia is here.

LUCIA: If it was for my benefit, it was pretty funny. But I think it *is* a good idea.

The crowd giggles and more trainers gather around. They see an opportunity to participate and taunt Wells.

CROWD: Wells is a bum.

HARRY: Huh? I *know* Wells a bum. He gotta lot of nerve to say that. In fact, if you can't represent, take that Bed-Stuy shirt off.

The crowd lets out a collective "oh!"

HARRY: And tell it like it is. That's right. If you can't represent, take that Bed-Stuy shirt off. Bed-Stuy do or die! You dying out there. You ain't doing.

Harry laughs but when the seconds-out bell rings, he tries to instill order for the last time. Wells and Lawrence showboat—perform in the ring for their audience—and the crowd chuckles. Sensing he has lost control, Harry throws up his hands and laughs. Ed, a trainer, then holds Wells by his shirt on the ropes so that he is incapable of defending himself or moving around the ring to escape punches. The crowd laughs, and without warning, changes allegiance and cheers for Wells. In total exhaustion and desperate, Wells pulls Lawrence down to the floor of the ring and they roll around. Harry draws the spar to a conclusion and reassures Wells, "You know we love you, Wells." With a deadpan, Lawrence thanks Wells for the "work." With the voice of a reporter and my hand as a fake microphone, I put my fist under Harry's chin and ask him for his assessment of the athletic activity.

LUCIA: What do you think about that spar, coach?

Harry smiles.

HARRY: Excellent work. The best I ever seen.

Harry attempts to embarrass Wells by repeatedly trying to emasculate him. He calls out Wells's height, which could be hurtful as Wells is short by conventional gender standards, standing somewhere around 5'6" (though not the 10 inches that Harry had alleged in the spar). Harry agrees with another trainer who calls Wells a bum, suggesting Wells has not accomplished anything, despite the fact that Wells is a *New York Daily News* Golden Gloves champion, and this is his first day back in the gym after a period away and not a fair time to gauge athletic ability. In fact, most gym regulars would consider Wells a pretty good sport to even get into the ring with Lawrence when Wells has done absolutely no aerobic preparation. Instead, Harry cuts Wells no verbal slack and continuously chides him as if he were participating in a real spar. He berates Wells as not fit to wear a Bed-Stuy T-shirt, a symbol of masculine pride for boxers who have roots in the neighborhood gym and community in general. The Bed-Stuy gym is also where Harry and Wells met, so calling into question Wells's right to wear a shirt that bears the Bed-Stuy name implicitly calls into question Harry's devotion to Wells, their bond as trainer and boxer, and the history of their relationship. Harry also casts doubt on Wells's character: Harry's pronouncement that Wells is not worthy of representing Bed-Stuy is a direct challenge to Wells's toughness and respectability, which are admired identities for men in the gym. To add insult to injury, when Wells attempts to defend himself by suggesting Harry himself get in the ring, Harry dismisses his defense as male bravado designed to impress a female spectator, one of the least important people in the gym hierarchy. It is a gesture designed to humiliate.

The fickle crowd participates in Harry's teasing. Jeering and yelling during a spar is rare. Gleason's rules—posted prominently on the wall of the gym—prohibit screaming or even talking during a spar; onlookers are allowed to watch the event but outside interference is not permitted. Only a trainer and his boxer talk during a spar. And yet during this spar, the crowd not only taunts Wells but also intermittently cheers for his opponent, who is the stronger of the two fighters. When Wells is cracked, the crowd expresses titillation rather than concern about a dangerous mismatch. Ed breaks the rule of noninterference by physically holding Wells on the ropes, thereby giving Lawrence free license to take body and head shots with no possibility of Wells defending himself. (Lawrence, who is incidentally Wells's teammate, declines to take these punches.) Harry, who should be Wells's most vocal advocate, sides with the crowd, agreeing with their insults.

Wells responds by challenging the conventions of the spar with exaggeration. He boldly answers back to his trainer and he plays with Lawrence, gently striking him, missing punches on purpose, and pulling him to the floor in absurdity, maneuvers that would never be tolerated in a serious spar. Lawrence conspires with Wells's performance by going along with it and then by thanking him for the work at the spar's conclusion. Harry's laughter and assessment that this is the "best work" he's ever seen condones Wells and Lawrence's playfulness.

Together Wells and Harry momentarily reverse the social order of the gym. They transgress by engaging in practices that are not allowed in a spar and by turning it into play.[15] Through humor, they connect and interact with each other in a new way that reinforces their friendship. Their theatrics are pleasurable to each other and to spectators, who are not accustomed to seeing a spar invested with so much amusement. This "play" spar also references and complements the rigorous spars that Wells has undertaken and will undertake in the future under Harry's guidance. The use of humor welcomes Wells back to the gym and is a way for Harry and Wells to deepen their bond[16] and restructure the social order. Abrahams writes, "The importance of license is that it permits a playful restructuring of the world. The recognized community order of things, actions, and especially interactions has a deeply felt sense of logic to it, simply because it *is* ordered and provides comfort and control to those who share this perspective."[17]

Not all teasing is as enjoyable or lighthearted as Wells's mock spar. In addition to providing a fun atmosphere and reversing the social order, joking is also used to uphold the social order. Joking promotes the values of the gym and is used by members to teach one another about the norms to follow.[18] When joking is used to instruct or give a lesson, it can be sharp and pointed. When Harry trains me, for example, he likes to ridicule my "chicken legs." Usually I could take Harry's comments in stride but there were days when his attention to my bowlegs made me sensitive. I would try to coolly shrug off his quips, but my hurt was transparent. Harry was never deterred, nor was his joking purposeless. His attention was intended to enforce a social ideal: his determination to target a physical attribute about which I was embarrassed attempted to inure me to negative comments about an imperfection and to encourage my acceptance. Through his incessant teasing, Harry conveyed an operating principle of the gym: the importance of not being defined by a flaw, a shortcoming, or a failure. This is the primary trope of boxing training: a situation, predicament, characteristic, or experience may be imperfect—or even troublesome—but it cannot be a defining feature. As discussed at length in chapter 3, training demands that a boxer overcome hardship and keep on fighting no matter what. Joking that upholds the social order is a *mise en abyme* for the training ideology: it shows the recipient that he or she should not be deterred or demoralized by a weakness or a deficiency. Harry's making fun of my bowlegs taught me not to allow anyone else to shape my relationship to my body, my self-value, or my reality.

In this case, joking was intended to change my feelings about myself. In other cases, joking can be a call to action. When one trainer who cannot read is mocked mercilessly by a group of trainers for not being literate, he is brought to tears. A short time later, he enrolls in literacy instruction. For this trainer, communal pressure precipitated a change in behavior that was more consistent with the values of the gym: the ability to read and respect for being well-read. Though the act was cruel and took an emotional toll on the gym member, the joking was a moral check on someone who violated Gleason's social principles. Sharp teasing articulated the urban gym's ideals and served as a way to enforce the social importance of reading and writing through social control.[19]

Almost all gym members find the incessant joking exhausting at times. Harry calls the gym a "fishbowl" and a "house of glass" because of how interested regulars can be in others' business, especially their disadvantages and difficulties, and because of how people believe they have the right to address such difficulties and the authority to provide advice. Mike would routinely leave the gym for hours at midday in order to escape the gym's claustrophobic social scene. Jokes, as harsh as they can be, ensure a particular social order as much as they challenge one and can be both pleasurable and suffocating.[20]

"SPEAKING MY MIND"

Other discussions are more focused and intentional than banter, deliberation, and joking. In these situations, there is less prolonged enticement into the conversation, but rather a speaker will dive right into the topic he or she wishes to discuss. Conversations may not stay completely on course, veering slightly, but the associations are tightly connected. That is, conversations do not jump from unrelated topic to unrelated topic but rather transition from one subject to a related one. Anthony says that talking with others before and after his workouts allows him to "speak my mind," something that he likes because he has few other opportunities to do so. He can get thoughts and ideas off his chest and discuss many of the topics and subjects he investigates through reading and watching TV programs when he is not in the gym. This allows him to link his life outside the gym with his life inside the gym. As explicated in chapter 2, many amateur boxers live cloistered lives. The regimentation of pugilistic training necessitates some form of self-imposed seclusion. But for men who have spent time in prison and do not want to return there, sequestering themselves helps them steer clear of old social networks, avoid reengaging crime, and avert technical parole violations, infractions that can result in re-incarceration. The gym provides a forum for men who rarely engage in social activities outside its confines. At Gleason's Gym members can discuss topics and feelings that are important to them largely in the company of others.

A talk between Mike and Anthony about Ronald Reagan is a good instance of the ways that gym regulars use expressive practices to speak their minds. Reagan's death prompts intense discussion not only between Mike and Anthony but also among many gym regulars because people simultaneously are fascinated by the publicity and frustrated by the celebration of Reagan's presidency, in particular his public policies. As residents of communities who were affected by many of Reagan's decisions, especially the retrenchment of social-welfare programs and the inauguration of repressive anticrime practices in urban areas, they are surprised that commentators and the general public laud his methods of economizing. Anthony enters the gym one morning and immediately reports to Mike that he saw "your boy" Ronald Reagan on the television that morning. Just before Anthony had arrived, Mike already had voiced to others his annoyance at the press' representation of Reagan as a good president. One politician's anti-black racism then leads to other commentaries about the bad decisions of city politics and other expressions of white racism.

ANTHONY: You know, they're taking a lot of junior high school children to see the casket. A bunch of teenagers were there. It was literally like the whole state of California went to see Ronald Reagan's casket.

MIKE: You upset?

ANTHONY: I wasn't upset. It's just so many *times*.

MIKE: I'm upset. I'm upset about Ronald Reagan.

ANTHONY: They said "It's gonna be ninety degrees today, and *here's the people watching Ronald Reagan!*" You know? "O.J. had an interview with Katie Couric, and *here goes the people seeing Ronald Reagan!*"

MIKE: I'm gonna get on a bus and shoot again.

LUCIA: Again!

ANTHONY: Again.

LUCIA: To impress Jodie Foster?

MIKE: Angelina Jolie.

ANTHONY: Mike! No lie. This one Mexican lady—you can glance at her and say, "Oh she's Mexican," you know what I mean? There was no doubt about it she was Mexican—she was crying. She couldn't even walk. Over the casket. I mean, *come on*!

MIKE: Same Reagan who cut out all the summer youth programs in the 'hood. Same Ronald Reagan who had minimum wage at three dollars an hour. Same Ronald Reagan who cut the fucking welfare bill. Same Ronald Fucking Reagan who cut the school lunches. My mother couldn't find an apartment, but he was spending millions and millions of dollars on the Star Wars program. What? What happened to that? I mean *billions*!

ANTHONY: Mike, tell me why your guy Bloomberg is going to stop Mr. Softee?

MIKE: And what's up with that?

ANTHONY: That's history. That is the culture of this damn city. All you see is the kids running to him.

Michael, an amateur fighter, arrives looking depressed.

ANTHONY: What's good Michael?

LUCIA: Hi Michael. Are you all right?

He solemnly nods.

MIKE: I think he's sad that Ronald Reagan died.

ANTHONY: Damn. "Conservative Republican"? What that mean? How do you do that? A Republican *and* Conservative?

MIKE: What about the millions of dollars in cocaine that was funded so you could have your war? "I don't recall."

ANTHONY: "I don't recall!" Everything was "I don't recall!" Right? Like ten questions in a row and he didn't know. Early signs. "Let me sleep on that."

MIKE: He set the framework for Bush.

ANTHONY: Oh, yeah. Yeah.

MIKE: I want to know where the billions for Star Wars went.

ANTHONY: Mike, it was so funny. Then they have Katie and O.J. and she's basically telling him "We know you did it." You know? "So what do your kids think about it?"

MIKE: What did he say? "What if I cut your throat right now, bitch?"

ANTHONY: And you know, O.J. could run for president. He's a good talker. He was swift. He was swift, Mike. She would ask him a question, and he was right there. *Boom.*

LUCIA: Do you think he did it?

ANTHONY: I don't think he did it physically, but I think he knew something about it because psychologically you don't run.

MIKE: I ain't talking no more if you think he did it.

ANTHONY: Oh, that's my boy, O.J.!

MIKE: It's impossible. How you gonna decapitate somebody and you don't have one speck of blood on a white Bronco? If you can't explain that one. No DNA. No blood. No physical evidence? You know what I mean?

ANTHONY: No he didn't do it physically.

MIKE: *They* said he did it physically.

ANTHONY: Yeah, they did say that. But he did know something. Even if he didn't pay for somebody to do it, he knew something. The woman was a coke addict. And it could have been somebody who she owed money to.

MIKE: That's right!

ANTHONY: She was using O.J. money to get high. So he probably knew something was gonna happen to her and that's why he ran. 'Cause you don't run for no reason. You don't do it.

The conversation then turns to Scott Peterson's attempted escape to Mexico and the psychology of fleeing a criminal investigation. As the subject of a criminal investigation in the past, Anthony believes he has situated knowledge about when a suspect feels compelled to flee and when one does not. In this case, the former implies guilt.

Both Anthony and Mike are bothered by the media hype about Ronald Reagan's death and communicate that frustration. They work to explicate specifically the features of the publicity that they find so exasperating, such as the representation of Reagan as a good president when clearly they feel he was not. They then give their political perspectives on and personal experiences with the trade-offs Reagan made between the social welfare of poor urban residents, like Mike's mother, and Cold War military policy. They provide their understandings of and experiences with anti-black racism in public policy. Their commentary leads to another instance of anti-black racism in the US criminal justice system: O. J. Simpson's murder trial. "Speaking my mind" in this example involves Mike and Anthony's interpretation of racialized political and social structures: from presidential policies to the criminal justice system.

The criminal justice connection is not irrelevant. It is a frequent topic of discussion in the gym. Just as sociologist Phil Brown talks about the uses of "popular epidemiology," Anthony and Mike create what could be called popular legal knowledge.[21] Because many amateur boxers and trainers have been through New York City's court systems and have experience with the numerous configurations of postindustrial forced confinement, they are acquainted with its codes and practices. Some spent time reviewing their cases while in prison and have highly specialized knowledge of the penalties and psychologies of crime. Above, Anthony and Mike talk about O.J. Simpson and then Scott Peterson and the psychology of guilt. In doing so, they articulate their popular legal knowledge. This construction of popular legal knowledge—like the other forms of knowledge amateur boxers and trainers possess—privileges lived experience over theory or even more formally acquired knowledge as evidence.[22] And it serves as a way to assert authority.[23]Through these conversations, participants become social critics.[24]

In the example above, "speaking my mind" involves two people sharing commentaries on current events, political leaders, and anti-black racism. It is more focused and intentional than what in the gym is called passing time. It also can be more personal. "Speaking my mind" may involve self-disclosure and sharing personal problems. It can entail discussing private issues, seeking advice from others, and giving honest counsel. This advice solicitation and donation manifests itself around a number of aspects of boxers' lives. One of the most prevalent is romantic partnership. Men will frequently talk about the problems they have with their girlfriends and wives and ask for opinions from others about how to deal with a particular dilemma.[25] Teammates will listen and give their opinions. In these discussions, there is no shame in expressing sadness, frustration, fear, and anxiety about relationships, in sharing feelings of masculine inferiority, and asking others for opinions. Because of this openness, guidance and comments are often tender. People pay attention to each other, lending support in the process.

One morning before training, a boxer who is distraught discusses his disappointment with himself for harboring violent impulses when he verbally fights with his partner. Though he has worked hard to develop strategies for controlling his aggression, he still gets angry enough to scare himself and his wife. After reciting the techniques that he utilizes to diffuse his anger, he asks his teammates if there are others that he has not considered. Though no one can offer alternatives, the men of Mike and Harry's corner listen to his concerns without judgment. They commend him for implementing the strategies that he has identified, and they urge him not to give up. They express confidence that with regular use of the techniques, over time, his aggression will lessen. By staying committed to nonviolence, they argue, this boxer will be able to gain control of his rage.

On another occasion, Adrian, who self-defines as a "loner" and who has never had a romantic relationship, talks openly about the humiliation of having connected with a woman but being unable to act on his feelings. He likes her but cannot afford to call her, take her out, or buy her things, which he believes would be his responsibility as a significant other. He has no job, and without one, he feels he is not "established enough" to begin a relationship. With no job prospects, he worries that he will never be. This dishonor saddens him and makes him feel inadequate. He is trapped and unsure about what to do. After listening to Adrian, his teammates ask several questions to fully assess the situation. Max wonders: does he feel a low sense of self-worth in general? Anthony asks: does he consider himself overly concerned with how others perceive him, even outside romantic relationships? Adrian is unable to find answers to their questions, but this does not thwart the teammates' support. They advise him not to conflate money with the ability to act on romantic impulses and especially not to let money dictate his level of pride in himself and his feelings about himself. Anthony and Max suggest that he take some time to develop respect for himself and to learn not to let others determine his sense of value.

Listening to people's problems and giving advice are common features of peer relations in the public and private spheres. But that such vulnerability can be expressed in a space dedicated to ritual violence and hyper masculinity is noteworthy. This form of "speaking my mind"—that which surrounds personal problems—allows men to develop and enact a form of tender masculinity. This sensitive and connected form of masculinity departs from the representations of black men in the popular imagination, especially the popular press, as pathological, detached, and hard. bell hooks argues that denying black men dignified opportunities for the wage while providing black women with service economy jobs creates an injurious emasculation.[26] Instead of work, men of color have the streets and hip-hop culture. She argues, "Contrary to the notion that black males are lured by the streets, mass media in patriarchal culture has already prepared them to seek themselves in the streets, to find their manhood in the streets, by the time they are six years old. . . . This media teaches young black males that the patriarchal man is a predator, that only the strong and the violent survive."[27] Today, men of color garner attention for failure—for their lack of work, lack of education, and involvement in the prison-industrial complex. Negative stereotypes enliven commonsensical understandings of black men's structural positions and "overdetermine the identities black males are allowed to fashion for themselves."[28] As the therapist Terrance Real instructs, "Instead of cultivating intimacy . . . we teach boys and girls, in complementary ways, to bury their deepest selves, to stop speaking, or attending to, the truth, to hold in mistrust, or even disdain, the state of closeness we all, by our natures, most crave."[29]

In the gym, however, men cultivate intimacy with each other and fashion alternative identities, which are based on closeness and connectedness with other men. Tender masculinity allows them to express their deepest and most vulnerable worries, and they overwhelmingly are met with validation and support. While the acknowledgment and discussion of such openness, even exposure, generally is considered feminine and a feature of women's relationships, in the gym it is viewed as a legitimate aspect of men's social relations. Gym regulars cannot always help one another, but there is comfort in listening to difficulties and in the recognition of struggle. The creation of such a space in which men can become close and lean on one another is a meaningful alternative to "the streets," "hip-hop culture," and the displacement of social-structural inadequacies onto individual failure and pathology. Further, as noted before, it is important to a group of men who, in a postindustrial landscape, have few other outlets for discussing their trials and tribulations.

THE IDEAL OF THE COLLECTIVE AND SHARING IN POSTINDUSTRIAL NEW YORK

In Mike and Harry's corner, boxers are accepted no matter what their histories and experiences may be. Those who do not want criminal futures face a challenge transitioning from illegal and extralegal economies to wage labor and other forms of lawful employment, if available, or to chronic under- and unemployment. At Gleason's Gym, trainers and fighters are surrounded by others who have made similar decisions and have undergone similar transitions with success. Their peers can understand the difficulties and frustrations inherent to this change and can offer advice. Those who have been incarcerated are not socially ostracized, and those with troubled backgrounds are not discriminated against; rather, they are supported by the gym management, trainers, and fighters. Experiences such as spending time in prison and being unemployed are speakable and not taboo. Max is known as a gym rat because he spends hours in the gym, predominately with his trainer, to avoid his neighborhood and the temptation to reengage in criminal labor. After years in custodial supervision and with a baby on the way, Max wants to cease any criminality. When I ask him about the gym, he responds:

> I feel with a passion that everyone who is in there, they help me. They see that I'm a good kid. This is the first time that someone is trying for me instead of looking at my past and saying, "No, I'm not going to help him." Here they know I'm a good kid and know that I'm trying. . . . They help me.

In postindustrial Brooklyn, the sociality of the urban gym helps boxers and their trainers create peer relationships, form friendships, and build the forms of collective identity that Paul Willis warns are threatened when wage labor is lost.[30] Training together and socializing together help men see themselves as men and as a group; they create solidarity and weave networks. The sociality of passing time, joking, and "speaking my mind" shapes the worksite of the gym. It is a crucial component to the work of training because it complements the rigorous bodily and professional aspect with opportunities for social interaction. As it is primarily segregated by gender, it provides means for homosocial bonding and for the production and expression of what I have called tender masculinity.

Certain social values are articulated in the time before and after training through the gym's expressive culture. Though they respect their trainers, boxers stand on the same ground as their coaches; unlike in training sessions, when engaging expressive practices, social equality is promoted. Also, as in the ring, speakers are admired for how they conduct themselves rather than for their histories. Boxers earn recognition, develop self-worth from both figures of authority and their peers, and form groups. Forms of linguistic play allow men to exercise parts of their lives and of their beings that are not recognized in the world outside of the gym. Whereas boxing is a largely individual endeavor and involves atomized individual athletic activities, the social interaction of the gym is communal. The value of sharing time, experiences, and entertainment, as well as engaging with others, is idealized.

Passing time, joking, and "speaking my mind," as well as the tender masculinity gym regulars facilitate, give men interpretive power that allows them to take the racial exclusion and urban marginality of the outside world and turn it into something different. When boxers are subjected to the vicissitudes of postindustrial Brooklyn's racial and class hierarchies, they come to the boxing gym and discuss the particularities of their subject positions. In apposition to the "just do it" orientation of training, "speaking my mind" gives speakers interpretive control. Speakers use this space to talk about public and private problems that are relevant to their experiences. It is an intervention into the social world, a way of engaging, through dialogue with each other, mainstream public discourse that otherwise lends no ear to their voices. With its focus on sociality, collectivity, and social support, it complements the individual pursuits of training practices.

Chapter Five

THE CHANGING POLITICS OF GENDER

> The science has also its enemies, and perhaps of a more formidable nature, in the fair sex; for what has love to do with war—"To play with mammets and to tilt with lips," is their motto. Yet I do not despair of finding advocates among the ladies. Minerva presided over war, and, if we credit the poets, kept even Mars in awe. But I do not bring a solitary instance in my favour, I will call a whole nation to my aid; the Amazons, renowned for warlike achievements, were women. Less ancient times have produced a maiden, whose arm has thinned the ranks of the bravest Englishmen, for who can doubt the truth of a history, so well authenticated as that of Joan D'Arc, the Maid of Orleans? Have we not seen in our own time a Madame D'Eon invested with military command? And is there not at this moment a lady, who has rid her own matches at Newmarket, and drives a tennis-ball with a dexterity and vigor that would do honor to the most skilful and brawny arm in the kingdom?
>
> —THOMAS FEWTRELL, 1790

DON'T BACK UP.

Don't back up.

Please don't back up.

I repeat this phrase silently to myself, prying my eyes open when I realize I have shut them tightly in anxiety. One of the most important rules of boxing is not to back straight up, and Maya has just done this twice in the current round, getting hit brutally in the face as a punishment. Luckily, it is Maya's only apparent weakness, and not a second later, a fan in the audience verbalizes my unspoken plea, and Maya rectifies her mistake. She moves forward with renewed energy, as if empowered by her corrective. I exhale loudly and pledge to keep my eyes open.

It is 7:30 p.m. on a frigid Thursday night in January, and I am at Maya's professional debut at the Paradise Theater in the South Bronx. I have come to support her—to cheer and wave her birth country's Trinidadian flag—as she transitions from amateur boxer to professional fighter. But I am having difficulty focusing on the tasks at hand because I hardly recognize the athlete in the ring. Since I last saw her, Maya's five-foot-three frame has lost thirty pounds, and whatever small amount of fat that remained has been eaten up by muscle. Two years ago, she had little interest in competition, instead training sporadically and concerned about losing too much weight. With no offense to me, she told me she did not want to get skinny like a "white bitch." Her goal was to get healthy and maybe learn to eat better. Since then Maya has won almost every national and international amateur tournament she has entered, frequently by knockout.

At the weigh-in the day before, I cannot help but mention to Maya my surprise by her change, to which she quickly retorts, "What? That I look like a crack whore?" She is trying to make weight, and she is hungry and I am holding the chicken and avocado dish that she will devour seconds after stepping off the scale. Still, the flippancy with which she dismisses my comment and, by extension, her talent, hard work, and experience baffles me. Mike, her trainer, laughs at my incredulity but eventually grants me: "She look different, right?"

But it is not Maya's corporeal transformation that amazes me most. I have spent enough time in gyms to see bodies change rapidly and dramatically. What takes me aback is that Maya appears to be a different person. The calm and grace with which she enters the ring foreshadows her almost total domination of the fight. In the bout, she performs a calculated precision—evidence of her talent—and battles with confidence, moving around the ring with agility. Though her coach has trained her to "fight like a man"—taking more body than headshots—Maya does not *act* like a man and forgoes the stare-downs, showboating, and trash talking typical of men's matches in favor of an amicable and respectful gamesmanship. Goose bumps cover my arms as I see expressions of her self-assurance, especially when she cuts off her opponent at almost every turn and when she allows a humble smile to stretch across her face after the fight. She is declared winner by unanimous decision.

Over the past thirty years, women like Maya have joined boxing gyms in large numbers to train and participate in local, state, national, and international competitions. In doing so, they have staked claims to undertake pugilistic exercises and join pugilistic spaces, historically masculine domains. These claims have not been made without struggle or contradiction. They have been accompanied, on the one hand, by the need to revise conventional gender expectations and, on the other, by the need to gain acceptance—or at least tolerance—from a skeptical male gym community. At odds are hegemonic codes of femininity that regard building muscle, hitting, grunting, sweating, and even cultivating a boxer's hunched stance as uncouth and unladylike and the necessities of those same practices to succeed in the ring. Women desire gender identities that are less resolute than the identities men crave, if only because women's involvement in the sport is so new that there are few models on which—or against which—women can mold themselves. Many female fighters recognize that the first generation of competitive women boxers—Christy Martin, Mia St. John, and Laila Ali—expressed ambivalent relationships to their femininity and know that this ambivalence was exploited by male commentators and fans as a way to dismiss the legitimacy of women's boxing, relegating it to a "gimmick" or "sideshow."[1]

This chapter looks at how women have fought for a place in the urban gym, where men categorize and name them and obsessively assess their standing. It analyzes some of the identities women create and how they negotiate developing enough—but not too much—strength as to maintain femininity and taking some—but not too much—control of their bodies in order to form an effective comportment. I argue that to reconcile contradictory demands, the identities women develop are flexible and situational, and that they are able to corporeally shape-shift according to the contextual demands of the gym community.

This chapter also examines how men have responded to women's integration into the urban gym. Women's participation has generated unease among the men of Gleason's, who often argue against women pugilists in the abstract but may respect a particular individual female boxer for her devotion or talent. I contend that to deal with this gendered discomfort, even outright hostility, women have formed supportive strategies and subcultures of belonging. They care for each other through pep talks in the locker room, cheering at competitions, and encouragement on social networking sites. Within their teams, they form deep friendships and gain affirmation. In other words, through their supplemental position, women have challenged the practices of masculine ritual and softened the long-standing prohibition of women in the sport, though frequently at great expense.[2]

"YOU ABSOLUTELY CAN'T HAVE A WOMAN IN THIS GYM": A SHORT HISTORY OF GENDER EXCLUSION

In the 1970s and early 1980s, women asked Gleason's owners to be allowed to train at the gym, but Ira Becker, Bruce Silverglade's co-owner at the time, was adamantly opposed to women's participation in the sport. Silverglade remembers, "My partner was an old cranky guy who just always said, 'No women. You absolutely can't have a woman in this gym.' I had this view from growing up and my background that he was my elder, so go with it. It was a 50/50 partnership but it was *his* gym and I came into *his* gym and he was the older guy." Eventually, the gym's precarious financial situation made forfeiting the potential income from women's memberships irrational. Silverglade recounts:

> Before my partner passed away, I worked very hard on convincing him that women should be allowed to train at the gym. And the way I did it was very simple. I said, "Ira, when I go to the bank in the morning and I make my deposit, they don't ask me, 'Did that money [come] from a woman or a man?' And half the world is women! So why are we cutting ourselves off?" And again, it was in the late '70s and early '80s, and there were money crunches. So we needed the money. So finally, he said "You're right." And that's how we started.

In 1983, Gleason's Gym opened its doors to women.

Though women were permitted to train to box at Gleason's Gym in the mid-1980s, it was another decade before they were granted the right to compete in amateur bouts. Citing safety and medical concerns, United States Amateur Boxing, Inc. (USA Boxing), the national sanctioning body, refused to recognize female athletes. It took several rounds of litigation to secure women's membership in the organization and the attendant entitlement to fight. In Massachusetts, Gail Grandchamp spent eight years in the court system battling USA Boxing and the New England Amateur Athletic Union for permission to compete as an amateur. In April 1992, the state Superior Court ruled that it was illegal to deny inclusion in USA Boxing based on gender. By the time of the ruling, however, Grandchamp was thirty-six, making her one year too old to compete as an amateur.[3] In Washington State in 1993, after requesting and being denied an application to fight in the Pacific Northwest Amateur Boxing Association,[4] Dallas Malloy sued USA Boxing for gender discrimination in federal court, pointing specifically to a bylaw that prohibited women's memberships.[5] Malloy

A female fighter prepares for a round on the heavy bag. Photograph courtesy of the athlete.

won the case, and by the end of 1993, USA Boxing had created rules and regulations for a women's program.[6]

In New York City, USA Boxing Metro, the local division of USA Boxing, denied women formal participation until March 1995. Aware of the Washington ruling, Dee Hamaguchi, a boxer from Gleason's Gym, asked to compete in the 1994 *New York Daily News* Golden Gloves. After being refused, she submitted an application anyway, using only her first initial. When she called the *Daily News* to inquire about her status, she was told that she was the only woman to enter and that there was no competition.[7] This technically made her eligible for a victory by "walkover," but she was not awarded the distinction.[8] She also was deemed ineligible for competition because she did not have a minimum of five prior amateur bouts. Hamaguchi consulted the American Civil Liberties Union (ACLU), who thought the five-fight prerequisite was a form of discrimination and threatened a lawsuit. The *New York Daily News* Golden Gloves opened the tournament to women the following year. In 1995, Hamaguchi and thirty other women fought in the Gloves.[9] Today, according to USA Boxing, three thousand women are registered with the organization, and female boxing was included as a competitive sport in the 2012 Olympic Games in London.[10]

FIGHTING WOMEN

More than three hundred women train at Gleason's Gym.[11] Demographically, they differ significantly from the male boxers of the gym. Women fighters are more diverse ethnoracially, self-identifying as white, black, Latina, Asian American, and African Caribbean and emigrating from countries such as Germany, Hungary, Sweden, Ireland, and the Dominican Republic and from US territories such as Puerto Rico. They tend to be older than male amateurs; they range in age from eighteen to thirty-five, with the majority clustered in the middle. They are predominately middle class and, to a lesser extent, working class, and they are highly educated. They work as teachers, writers, artists, public relations specialists, nurses, administrative assistants, firefighters, and police officers or are college students. Most do not have children. Not surprisingly, because of their class position, female fighters have much less interaction with the social institutions—public housing, prison, welfare—that affect male amateur boxers. Most women have participated in high school or college athletics, playing competitive softball, basketball, soccer, gymnastics, track and field, and swimming. They often come to Gleason's Gym from health clubs after taking boxing lessons or classes, or they are neighborhood residents looking for a place to work out in the area and join as paying athletes. Caitlin began boxing because she wanted an interesting way to exercise; Danielle sought "to get in shape." Jennifer and Maya wanted to lose weight.

According to Mike, "ghetto girls," as he calls them, or women of color from low-income neighborhoods, do not join Gleason's Gym because memberships and training fees are cost prohibitive. When Mike begins to work (for free) with Josie, a fifteen-year-old foster child with a criminal record, a mother who uses crack cocaine, and an incarcerated father, he is quick to point out that Josie is an anomaly. But low-income men of color find ways to pay for their memberships and coaching, so it is unlikely that fees alone preclude the involvement of so-called "ghetto girls." More likely is that women do not know that boxing gyms are accessible to them, and without this knowledge, do not seek out the sport as men do. Even more likely is that there is an established tradition with networks for free training male amateur boxers, but not for female boxers. Trainers work with men for no cost to express their political consciousness and potentially to recoup their investment when male amateur fighters turn professional and are paid for their bouts. Because trainers do not have the same level of commitment to mediating the social and economic circumstances of low-income women and because there is little to no money in women's professional fighting, trainers do not have the same investment in female boxing. Coupled with the discomfort many trainers have about female boxing in general, women have less access to free or subsidized training. However, during my fieldwork, there was increasing diversity by class. Though the gym still drew primarily middle- and working-class women, more and more low-income women and low-income women of color were joining the gym, negotiating affordable prices with trainers for lessons.

Women may come from diverse backgrounds, but they seek a similar transformation from boxing, whether through general fitness, rigorous training, or competition: empowerment through the production of new identities. And they choose pugilism rather than other forms of exercise—such as working out in regular gyms, yoga, spinning, etc., which are more normative for women—to produce these identities. These identities entail the assertion of novel forms of control and the development of different relationships to their bodies. Many women have histories of physical and psychological suffering. There is an irony in seeking solace from violence in a violent sport. But for these women, boxing is a corporeal reclamation, a way of taking back one's body and feeling empowered. For some, the social injury of violent romantic partnerships motivates them to take up the sport. When asked why she started boxing, Joanne answers, "I was in a very abusive relationship. I was in a very unhealthy situation. It started being emotionally abusive and then it became physically abusive."

Another female boxer echoes, "I started martial arts for self-defense." One pugilist began fighting after being stalked by a stranger in her neighborhood while another joined the gym to work out her associations with violence after growing up in a household with domestic abuse. Some women box to recover from the trauma of rape.

Other women have struggled with eating disorders, unhealthy exercise habits, and high-risk lifestyles, such as heavy drinking, smoking, and drug use. Joanne says that before boxing she had a negative self-image of her eating habits, which consisted of consuming food to cope with depression. She remembers, "Every time I would eat I would hate myself for it. I thought I was the ugliest thing walking." Caitlin considered herself problematically addicted to working out and thought the monitoring of a trainer would help her. And Danielle recollects, "Originally it was like, 'I want to get in really good shape.' That actually goes with body image stuff." But boxing changed Danielle's connection to her body. Now she loves her body for what it can do: not how it looks but how it works. She reflects:

> And this [boxing] has totally changed my view of my body in a great way, which, you know, was "I really want to get in shape so I look good" and now it's like my body works well. Even the syntax of it, saying "I want to lose weight" [versus] "I want to make weight." There's a different kind of way of looking at it. I am very much in my body.

Though women may join the gym for recreational purposes, unlike male white-collar clients, they often transition to competitive fighting. Mike says that women listen to instruction better than men and execute verbal commands without complaining. Trainer Alejandro thinks that women take criticism better than white-collar clients. Without a particular macho image to live up to and unlike the recreational male boxer, women's training is rigorous. The practice of sparring, in particular, opens up the possibility of competition. Once female athletes have sparred, they realize they are capable of competing. Danielle recollects, "We just kind of progressed, and I was able to spar. And sparring changed everything." Within a week of sparring, she knew she wanted to fight competitively. Caitlin thought, "You know, I'm doing this now [sparring], I might as well see what it's [competing] like." Pugilists such as Danielle and Caitlin exist in between amateur fighters and white-collar clients; they sign up to be recreational athletes, but they switch to competitive amateur boxers.

PRACTICES OF PERMISSION: NEGOTIATING VIOLENCE

Once female athletes decide to box, the process of learning to compete requires they revise their understandings of aggression and physical force. Many women are ambivalent about harming their opponents, believing that they cannot initiate violence. This is a gendered phenomenon, which is represented by women as innate or inherent. The operating assumption is that women should not, as a rule, be the aggressors. Defending oneself is acceptable, but leading off, a move considered skillful and desirable among male boxers, is difficult for women to practice. Despite Maya's numerous wins, she still expresses anxiety about using her physical power. She says, "Naturally, on the outside, I don't like to hit people. So I probably wouldn't hit somebody first. I don't know if my mentality is going to change but that's how I feel." Apprehension about aggression can be grounded in the idea that women naturally are weaker than men and that making the first move takes advantage of this physical inferiority. For Danielle, this uneasiness manifests itself as a hesitancy to hit women but not men, as though men can handle violence better than women. After years of competing as an amateur and winning the Golden Gloves twice, she admits, "I still have reservations about hitting women. No problem hitting men. Like, honestly, I really don't. That's fine. I'll go all out. But I always—there's *always*—like the first round with a woman, always I'm holding back." Joanne concedes that being able to hit a woman was a process to which it took time to adjust. She argues, "You have to learn with boxing. I had to learn to hit somebody hard. And I couldn't at times." In her first spar, Jennifer couldn't throw a punch for fear of landing it. She remembers, "Oh my God, I couldn't even do a round." And yet it isn't only physical aggression that makes women uncomfortable; conflict in general can be hard to overcome. Of hitting women, Caitlin thinks:

> It's because I hate conflict. I hate it. I avoid it at all cost. At all cost. I mean, it's sort of like, any debate about anything—well, debate is one thing but an argument—I'd rather just be like, "You know what? You're right. It's fine." So in a way, this is total conflict but, like, it's not personal. So maybe it's like a way to get something out. I mean, that's part of the reason I did it too. Maybe I can be more assertive.

When women do hurt—or even just hit—their opponents, they can feel bad, apologize, or even request the spar or fight be stopped. In other words, when women succeed in meeting the sport's goals, they feel psychologically and emotionally torn. This extends for women across class and race. One afternoon, when sparring with Joanne, Jennifer lands a hard punch on Joanne's lip. Joanne starts bleeding heavily, which troubles Jennifer to the point that she stops throwing punches, pleading with her trainer to end the exercise and exclaiming with distress to the crowd of onlookers, "She's bleeding!" After her trainer tells her to take advantage of Joanne's injury and "go after her," Jennifer still can't deliver a punch. She tells me afterward, "I just couldn't hit her when she was bleeding. I just had a hard time. When somebody makes me bleed, I go crazy. It's probably 'cause I know her and it's not—I mean, we're fighting but it's not a *fight* fight. We're just practicing. I feel like if you're practicing you shouldn't bleed to death." The subtext of Jennifer's anxiety is that she has the power to hurt her opponent irrevocably and that she does not want to do this. The exaggeration about "bleeding to death" also suggests that women experience the injuries of the spar or fight as inherently dangerous and as having more consequences than men do. The spar eventually resumes when Joanne reassures Jennifer that she is all right and even encourages her to "Hit me! Hit me!" Joanne is fully aware that she must give Jennifer permission to continue the spar. She later reflects, "I had to tell Jennifer it's OK to hit me 'cause I'm gonna hit you [Jennifer]. And I'm pissed that you made me bleed." Still, Joanne acknowledges the difficulty of Jennifer's position, having been in similar situations herself. She says, "There were times when I'd feel bad [hitting someone hard]."

When Gabriela spars with Lawrence, a male amateur boxer, who simultaneously instructs her (even though he has not been tasked with this responsibility), she lands a punch and apologizes repeatedly. After the spar, Gabriela tells me that she is contrite when she hits people but she doesn't understand why. In school, she took a course on female leadership in which her professor noted that women tend to apologize when they do well. Gabriela sees the same pattern in boxing and wonders why she feels remorseful when she is successful in a spar. The first time Layla sparred, she gave her partner a bloody nose, which she experienced as highly disturbing; she recollects, "That really upset me." To cope with her worry about drawing blood again, she began to target parts of her opponent's body that could not be injured. She continues, "I noticed—one of my problems now is that I either deliberately hit their glove or I hit part of their face that's blocked." Karen held similar trepidations about harmful physical contact. She recalls, "The first time I hit somebody I was very shocked, and I was afraid that I hurt him."

As Joanne's urgings, Gabriela's apologies, and Layla's cautious targeting suggest, women respond to the inhibition of throwing the first punch by developing strategies to give themselves and each other permission to fight. In other words, because female boxers believe they cannot hit first, they find ways to manufacture a reason. One practice women use to earn such permission is to hold back and intentionally be punched first or to fake out an opponent so the opponent thinks she is going to be punched. Maya uses this strategy. She explains, "I prefer that you hit me first, then I know I have a reason to hit you. Even if you don't hit the person first, you go to swing at them to make them *feel* that you're going to hit them so then they have the reason." Faking someone out places a boxer like Maya in a defensive posture, which she considers a legitimate gender position because she cannot be blamed or held responsible for any resulting aggression, however artificially constructed.

Another practice is to shift responsibility for the initiation of violence to a third party. Trainers serve this function. Because boxers are socialized to execute their trainers' every command, they have little room to protest. When a trainer tells his fighter to enact violent behavior, the boxer cannot or should not disobey. This helps women transfer anxiety about brutality to another person—in this case, their coaches—because they are merely following nonnegotiable directives. In the spar between Joanne and Jennifer, Joanne abides by her trainer's orders, which leads her to throw a series of hooks at Jennifer. This places Jennifer in a defensive position, allowing her to feel that she has the right to fight back, ending her hitting paralysis. Joanne explains, "I just had a sparring session with Jennifer, and I had to step it up a little bit because—I do what Raphael [her trainer] tells me. She didn't even hit me that hard. But until I started catching her with my hooks, she started stepping it up because she had to." Raphael's instruction gave both Joanne and Jennifer psychological authorization to throw hard punches at each other. In this case, a man had to grant the women permission to be aggressive even in the midst of discomfort with that very aggression.

Yet another practice is the creation of a fictive space that has different rules and boundaries than the gendered system outside of it. In this space, women possess the right to hit *a priori.* Danielle constructs for herself a "bubble" in which she is free to initiate violence. She explains, "In competition I enter into this weird jelly bubble where I have no idea how much impact I'm making on my, on the opponent. I'm so nervous, it's insane. And I just feel totally weakened. Totally weakened." Danielle's creation of the jelly bubble is a response to her fear of hurting someone and of losing control. She continues "And I think that for a while it was fear of getting out of control. It wasn't fear of getting hit because I'm actually not afraid to get hit. I've been able to isolate that that's a fear I don't have." Instead, Danielle experiences dread about "aggression being witnessed," which she links to gender. "Maybe as a woman we're not supposed to be—not to get too messy or too out of control or too sweaty. That comes up a lot for me. And then I have to work through that because that's something that's keeping me from what's really happening." Entering the jelly bubble provides Danielle with room where she can be violent without apology and where the fear of getting messy or out of control does not exist. She reflects, "So recently I've kind of been able to access that, be like 'OK, it's OK to be aggressive. I *do* want to win. I *do* want to beat this person.' I have to allow myself to feel that. And just—it's [boxing] so regulated that I'm not going to lose control and, you know, like kill someone. So I can just let it all go. And if I can really find that place in me, then I can have confidence in myself." Again, the logical extension of many women's fear is death—of actually killing an opponent. This is a sentiment that is never raised in discussions with male boxers despite a long history of ring deaths.

Once these practices of permission are performed, women do not have difficulty continuing the fight. That is, meting out the initial physical contact is the only barrier to the bout. Danielle says, "If I'm in there—when I get in the ring now and spar—I'm not thinking 'I want to dominate and beat the shit out of this other person.'" That is, she doesn't generate aggression immediately. But though it is not instinctual, she can create it. She continues, "I can draw it up. When I was sparring with Elizabeth and I was catching every right hand, I was doing badly. [She thinks] 'Wait a second. That was terrible sparring.' But the last round I was like, 'OK, I have to, like, beat the shit out of her now.'" Joanne explains, "Let me tell you something, when that other person throws a shot at you? You're like, 'You know what? Screw this. I gotta throw back.'" Joanne's quote not only demonstrates that women can overcome inhibition but also that inhibition is the *de facto* position. Once the self-justification is made and violence is initiated, women can continue with the fight. Because women must become comfortable with aggression in order to feel empowered, overcoming inhibition is a crucial first step to developing new types of identities. It is important to note that the fear of violence the female boxers harbor is not about *getting* hurt; it is about hurting others.

GENDERED SITUATIONS: "DIESEL FIGHTERS," "GYM HOS," AND "SKANKY FEMALES"

As female pugilists challenge norms, negotiate relationships to violence, and learn the skills of the sport, they also fight for space in a gym where men categorize and name them and obsessively assess their legitimacy.

A woman boxer competes in a professional bout. Photograph courtesy of the athlete.

Male trainers' and male fighters' responses to women inhabiting Gleason's fall along a spectrum, with strong support at one end and outright hostility at the other. At the very least, women's memberships have altered the gym environment. The requirement that trainers and every member sign a sexual harassment waiver has created a restrictive interactive structure that places limitations on the type of language considered appropriate. Mike frequently forgets that there are women in the gym. When he accidently uses words like "pussy," he watches the eyes of the women with whom he is working widen in shock. Other men express sexism, if not misogyny, outright. Anthony, an amateur fighter who supports women's boxing, can tell that men around the gym "have issues with women." He hears "bitch" uttered regularly and thinks that some men in the gym "hate women." Others still believe that women have no place in the gym. In a discussion about the brutality of boxing, Harry asserts that he doesn't think women should box at all. When I ask why, he contends that all boxers can get really hurt and that boxing is "inherently" not a sport for women. According to Harry, if you look at the history of the world, when there is "bad or brutality, it's usually men who are doing it." This is not to say that women cannot inflict brutality, but that usually it is men. To Harry, this makes women's fighting unnatural. Interestingly, Harry's position is consistent with the implicit understandings of many female boxers themselves.

To sort through the presence of female boxers in the gym and to process the meanings of their participation in the sport, male boxers and trainers have constructed a social hierarchy. There are several groups into which men triage women who come into Gleason's Gym: "diesel fighters," "gym hos," and "skanky females." "Diesel fighters" are considered the most legitimate of all female boxers because they most closely resemble male boxers. Diesel fighters exercise hard, compete, win tournaments, and are capable of convincing some skeptics that women have the potential to box seriously. They are trained and fight in the ring "like men." Since women are commonly dismissed as "headhunters"—meaning that they opt for jabs to their opponents' heads rather than taking more challenging and risky punches to their opponents' bodies—diesel fighters are respected for emulating a masculine fight style. Mimicking the training and fight practices of men means that women violate the codes, norms, and performances of a heteronormative dual-gender system. This relegates women outside the hegemonic gender order and into a gray area where they are perceived as having ambiguous gender identities. In other words, diesel fighters may be respected for their devotion to the sport, but they must shed their femininity.

One morning, Mike puts one of his female boxers in the ring to spar with Michael, an amateur boxer. Max, also an amateur fighter, finds the spar funny and jokes about the absurdity of the woman in the spar. But Mike, an advocate of women's boxing, tells Max that contrary to his assumptions, there *are* successful female fighters. One woman from Gleason's Gym, for example, who was 130 pounds, was as strong as most of Mike's male boxers of the same weight. Because of her strength, the gym considered this boxer to be "sort of a woman and sort of a man. She was a bit of both." And "she could lift men." Though Mike did not have the language to precisely describe this athlete, her muscle and power placed her outside understood gender paradigms.

Not only do diesel fighters demonstrate ambiguous gender identities, but also they actively discard aspects of their sexuality in order to gain respect. They make careful decisions when choosing their clothing: Diesel females wear baggy attire rather than tight-fitting garb as not to expose the contours of their body. They make particular decisions about the patterns of social interaction they engage: They are not overly social and tend to talk primarily with their trainers and their teammates to avoid being deemed "social butterflies" or, worse, accused of flirting. And they manage their bodies in specific ways: at informal competitions, such as "smokers," where only male locker-rooms are provided, diesel fighters will change alongside male boxers without protest or comment. This no-nonsense willingness with which women expose or conceal their bodies in the presence of their male teammates as they change from street clothes to fighting gear desexualizes both the women and the context.

The recasting of femininity and desexualizing by the men and women of the gym helps men make sense of the talent or strength of female boxers, who, in a dominant gender hierarchy, should not possess or display such strength. Men degender and desexualize women and women degender and desexualize themselves in order to make female fighting comprehensible and socially safe.

Christine, for example, is accepted in the gym as legitimate because her background of exceptional athleticism and because her discipline make her discernible "as a man." A firefighter by profession, Christine had long trained and sparred with male police officers at the police academy. When she entered the Golden Gloves, she joined Gleason's to spar with other women. Though she went largely unnoticed at first, after winning the first round of the Golden Gloves, the gym community took her seriously, and Harry, who had given her tips here and there, took her on as his fighter. Harry is opposed to female boxing in the abstract but agreed to work with Christine because he saw in her an unusual determination to endure the most intense training: she had worked as a firefighter as well as completed coast guard training and two weeks at boot camp, finding none of such training difficult. Her penchant for extreme regimentation before boxing served as a validating force in Harry's eyes.

Like diesel fighters, "gym hos" seek empowerment through boxing, but they train episodically rather than consistently and are considered too social for inclusion in the gym community. The men may humor and socialize with them, but they are not considered genuine athletes. Kelly is categorized as a gym ho because she jokes with her team at the expense of her workouts, talks too much to people in the gym, and is a "drama queen," yelling, complaining, or laughing loudly. The perception is that Kelly's primary purpose in visiting Gleason's Gym is social and not athletic, even though the behaviors she is condemned for are perceived as perfectly normal for male boxers.

Gym hos also are penalized for their choice of clothing; they wear tight-fitting attire instead of the baggy gear that characterizes most gym uniforms, breaking the codes of sexuality. Mike contends that too many women come into the gym wearing body-hugging clothes expecting to be respected. Kelly also is deemed a gym ho because she dresses inappropriately. One afternoon, Mike instructs her to pull her shirt down and reprimands her for wearing pants that are skin-tight. He scolds, "Your pussy is hanging out." Kelly assumes that he is joking until Mike explains he can see the outline of her vagina. She then asks "for real?" and immediately pulls down her shirt. Another woman's clothes provoke such outrage among a group of trainers that one suggests taking a picture of her pants and posting the shot on cameltoe.com, a website dedicated to posting pictures of women with prominent vaginal lips. During discussions about women's boxing with male athletes and trainers, I was repeatedly asked questions such as "What do these women think this place is? " and "What are women thinking by showing up in clothing like that?" They expressed disbelief that female athletes do not understand the norms of a boxing gym. Without this knowledge, they are considered illegitimate members. Women athletes also are considered inappropriate distractions to the important training men undertake. When I ask Mike why it is women's responsibility to tailor their clothing to meet men's standards, he naturalizes the male gaze that objectifies women and tells me that "men are men" and that it is human nature to look at women sexually. Gym hos are the opposite of being "like men": The men of the gym are literally obsessed with their genitalia.

Women have internalized some of the gym's gender expectations. I ask Layla if she feels comfortable at Gleason's and she answers:

> If you cover up a little, I really don't think it makes a difference. I don't think that's [her comfort in the gym] because I'm married and I'm always there with him [her husband]. That's why I'm always surprised when I see Hilary [Swank, who trained at Gleason's Gym in preparation for her role in the movie *Million Dollar Baby*] and the way she dresses. I notice the way the guys watch her and I wonder—I think to myself, even if I felt comfortable in that clothing, I wouldn't feel comfortable in that clothing in that environment. And then I get mad because I think that she's actually distracting the guys when they need to work.

Layla sees it as women's responsibility to dress in a nonsexual way. She also prioritizes men over women as the group that needs to work out without "distraction." And though she dismisses the idea that her place in the gym is authorized by her marriage and role as a wife, it is subtext. It signifies that sexuality plays a role in the construction of the gym's hierarchy.

Once the label of "gym ho" has been assigned, it is difficult to cast off. However, in my time at Gleason's, some women initially designated as such were able to prove themselves as serious athletes and transform into diesel fighters. Jennifer used to wear tight-fitting clothes and frequently socialized. She even became romantically involved with a fighter, a grave gym taboo for women (though not for men). But over time, Mike says she was "bit by the boxing bug" and began to train rigorously and compete. Because of this, she earned respect and diesel fighter status.

The last category of women—"skanky females"—do not train at all but visit the gym to watch men exercise and spar. Though there is a long history of men, such as newspaper writers, managers, promoters, matchmakers, and boxing aficionados, visiting the gym, when women do the same, they are dismissed and disrespected. Rather than being perceived as having a genuine interest in the sport, men believe that women are merely searching for prizefighters to marry and, by extension, become wealthy. In a discussion about how Gleason's Gym has changed over the past five years, Lawrence references the altered dynamics of both gender and class. He takes his thumb and moves it from up to down and laments, "It never used to be like this. It's corporate now. Women. A lot of women don't want to work out, they want a man." Even diesel fighters are suspect to Lawrence. He continues, "And the others, the serious boxers, even make it difficult to get a workout done. You just don't want the distraction. You come to the gym to get away from women and to focus. Women make it difficult to focus." Mike reprimands his fighters when they allow significant others to go to the gym. Considered skanky females, romantic partners are one part of the trinity Mike tries to prohibit: women, drugs, and drinking. When Max's pregnant girlfriend arrives at the gym, Mike screams, "What are you doing? Why are you bringing women around to show your skills? Whatever you want to do outside the gym is fine but when you're in the gym, you focus on boxing." Mike continues his tirade until Max apologizes and promises not to invite his partner to Gleason's again.

Skanky females are understood as making the lives of men more difficult by getting in the way of their goals. In addition to serving as a distraction in the gym, Mike thinks that Max's girlfriend wants to "trap" him with a child. When Max went away to school, his girlfriend wanted him to return to New York instead of obtaining his degree. To Mike, since no one in her family had ever been to college or graduated from high school, they fail to understand the value of education or the way to be "upwardly mobile," something that Mike thinks the boxing gym teaches young men. The woman in his boxer's life is "a problem." Similarly, Harry worries when a woman comes to the gym to watch Leon train. That Leon extended the invitation to a love interest means that his mind is not on the "right path" or "staying focused." According to Harry, women have no place in Leon's life, as a relationship cannot benefit him in any way. He tells me that Leon needs to "stop putting his mind into stuff that can't do anything for him." He continues, "Right now he's thinking about girls, girls, girls. And I say 'Leon, they're gonna be there. They're not going anywhere. Even if you a bum, you'll have a bum girl, but you're gonna have one. Women are always gonna to be here. They're gonna outlive us. Believe me because that's the last thing that need to be on your mind."

Several assumptions about women's boxing animate the gym's gender hierarchy. The first is that men of the gym are the worthy arbiters of determining a woman's motivations, level of talent, and social behavior. Men and only men have the knowledge, expertise, and experience to categorize a woman. Once they label a female boxer, the name is likely to stick and be taken up by other male members of the gym community. The second assumption is that when men do not have any information about a female boxer, they immediately revert to the default position of suspicion and skepticism. That is, men of the gym require that a woman prove herself to them. She must show that she is a diesel fighter and earn that label. In the absence of knowledge, men do not presuppose that a female athlete is committed because she has decided to become a member of the gym. In some cases, it can even come as a shock to men when women are skilled and hold their own in the ring. One afternoon, Matthew spars with a female fighter whom Ricardo trains. He hits her with strong punches, and she works hard on both defense and offense. In between rounds, Matthew turns to me and, leaning on the ropes, says with surprise, "She's good!" The astonishment with which he speaks belies the standard from which Matthew considers this female boxer to be a departure. Women, naturally, are not thought to be focused, skilled athletes. When they are, it is perceived as unusual.

The third assumption is that when male boxers work with female boxers, men see themselves as the actors in control. Men imagine they have the power to determine how hard a woman should be hit in a spar and how rigorously she should work. Matthew does several rounds with Ricardo's fighter and then leaves the ring. As he exits, I ask how he approaches spars with women. He says he does not mind sparring with women but he does not hit them with the same intensity as he would with a male fighter at his weight and level. He also does not go easy; his goal is to "keep them honest." That Matthew considers it his responsibility—and not the responsibility of the female boxer's trainer or the athlete herself—to keep a woman fighter "honest" assumes that he knows more than his sparring partner. The spar represents an imbalance of power—men determining the course of the spar—rather than the meeting of two equals. This locates authority with men and creates an asymmetrical relation of power between men and women in the gym and in the sport.

SUBCULTURES OF BELONGING: UNDERSTANDINGS OF AND RESPONSES TO SUPPLEMENTAL POSITIONING

Female boxers are aware of men's attitudes about their presence in the gym and their place in the sport. They understand the sexism at work and the patriarchal power behind men's views and actions. Language is cited as one locus of inequality. Female fighters comment on gendered language that challenges their participation in the sport. Danielle points out that "derogatory" phrases, such as "don't fight like a girl" and "women don't do this [particular fight techniques like throwing bodyshots]," are uttered often and undercut women's legitimacy. The male gaze is also understood as sexist. Being viewed as sexual objects rather than athletes and being hit on—demonstrating the double standard of simultaneously making sexual advances toward women and labeling them as "gym hos"—plague female fighters. This attention often is considered unwelcome. Danielle tells me, "As a woman just dealing with being hit on and stuff—it's like 'Ugh, for Christ's sake. Just right now, just hold off. Just stop.' And I feel that way with the men at the gym. It's kind of like people are watching in a sexual way. And that I don't like." After Leah was hit on in another gym, she joined Gleason's hoping that its reputation for having a vibrant women's community would protect her from unwanted advances. She reportedly told the Gleason's worker who answered her phone call that "I need a trainer who is not going to try to fuck me." Though Gleason's has a less intense atmosphere than her first gym, she still thinks it is sexualized and "very testosterone-pumped." She concedes, "I'm used to it [the sexualized environment] now, but for a time it was overwhelming. The energy is like 'ugh.' Sometimes it's just like 'Fuck. I can't deal with this anymore. All these sweaty men.' "

Maya attributes the attention she receives to men's inherent desire to flirt. She doesn't solicit interest but also doesn't find it surprising when she receives it. She thinks:

> Personally I get a lot of attention at the gym. I don't do it willingly. It's not nothing that I say, "Yeah, I'm a come to the gym and I want everybody to look at me." It's not that. I come to the gym and everyone is so nice and everybody want to know who you are. And being a female . . . you know? And I think I'm

cute, so being a female . . . guys, they notice you. And they tell you things like, "Oh, you look nice today." Just being nice, and I think that's all right. They may try to flirt with you and chat but that's guys.

To Maya, innocent flirtation between men and women is the natural byproduct of heterosexual coexistence and hence part of gym life. Maya's comment also suggests the ambivalence women have about transgressing gender norms. And the experiences of Danielle and Leah reveal a struggle between a sexual id and an aggressive fighting one; women are not allowed to have both.

Women fighters note that they are considered less important to trainers than male boxers and that they receive less attention in training, in competition, and in other arenas of the sport. They also believe they are coached differently than men. Jennifer noticed that her workouts were less rigorous than those of her male teammates and that her trainer focused more on them than on her. When it came time to spar and to prepare mentally for a difficult fight, her trainer pressured her less in the ring than she thought her male counterparts were pushed, which she found immensely frustrating. When trained, female fighters note being unnecessarily coddled, and when they try to engage in a discussion about pugilistic exercises, the discourse becomes gendered. In particular, what is perceived as excuse giving is coded by trainers as feminine and accepted from women. In chapter 3, I showed how excuse giving is not accepted by trainers from their male fighters and, accordingly, shut down quickly. The following dialogue is an example of how excuse giving is expected from female boxers and how discussions of training are invested discursively with gender. By the end of the discussion, Ricardo has reiterated the basic paradigmatic dynamic between trainers and fighters: that trainers have the interpretive power and fighters do not. But it takes much longer to assert this dynamic than with male boxers. Notice also Ricardo's gendered attitude towards Leah, another female fighter, who has hurt herself when hitting the heavy bag.

Ricardo begins a discussion with me about Lily's spar.

RICARDO: She [Lily] should have done better.
LUCIA: Really? She's tired. She can't help that. She said she's tired.

Ricardo mocks me with the voice of a little girl.

RICARDO: "She said she's tired."
LUCIA: She said she was tired in there, Ricardo.

RICARDO: Why would you believe her? Maybe she *felt* tired, but she's been rested. Don't let her give you a sad story like she's been on the treadmill all weekend. Or fucking working out all weekend.

LUCIA: You don't think she can feel tired?

RICARDO: I don't know. I'm saying you shouldn't, but you don't give me no excuses. You get in the ring.

LEAH: I think I hurt my elbow.

Ricardo mocks Leah with the threat of intimacy.

RICARDO: What, so you've come for medical attention? Oooooh, you OK, Leah? You all right? Do you want me to kiss your little elbow?

LEAH: It's not the first time I've done this. I keep doing it.

RICARDO: You've got to figure out why.

Always with advice to give, Harry enters the fray, without looking up from the book that he's reading.

HARRY: You need to know why.

Lily returns from several rounds of intense physical activity on the heavy bag, exhausted and out of breath. Ricardo raises the mistakes of her spar.

RICARDO: OK, so what did you do wrong then?

LILY: What?

RICARDO: What did you do wrong? What do you need to correct? What do you need to do more of? Right next time? You don't know?

LILY: I've got to run.

RICARDO: What do you mean you've "got to run?" You're putting her down for running? That you didn't throw your jabs? That you didn't step forward?

LILY: I was tired. My fucking legs felt like lead weights. When I got in there, I didn't get hit as much this time.

RICARDO: I thought you did.

LILY: What?

RICARDO: I thought you did. I thought you got hit *more* this time. Or you might have gotten hit cleaner this time. So you just got to capitalize on what when you bang her?

LILY: What?

RICARDO: She can't take your punch better than you take hers. You just got to believe in your ships and move forward. Stop letting her off the hook, man.

LILY: I wasn't letting her off the hook. I just told you my fucking *legs* were fucking *tired*.

RICARDO: That's letting her off the hook.

LILY: No it's not. It's *me*. It's *my* fault. It's nothing to do with her.

RICARDO: Well letting her off the hook is your fault. If you bang her twice and move back, that's letting her off the hook. If you bang her three times and don't move forward, that's letting her off the hook. If you don't jab first, you can't mow her down. That's you let her off the hook. Yeah? You've just got to fucking be on her constantly. Constantly. Until she's like, "Get off, back off! Back up. Give me some room to breathe." Don't let her get off the hook. Don't give her room to breathe. If she starts running around the ring, cut her off. Bam. You did it in the first round. She tried to go this way, and she tried to go that way, and *boom*, she ran right into your left hook. But you got to get on her more. Like a rash. Smart rash. Not just follow her and let her tee off on until she gives the other way. Told you, just like Winky [Winky Wright]. That's what he did. Close up. Boom, boom, boom, boom. Pop pop. Close up.

Lily gets angry and is exasperated.

LILY: I know, babe. I know what I was *supposed* to do.

RICARDO: That's fine.

LILY: I just didn't do it because I didn't have any fucking legs, *OK*?

RICARDO: It's OK.

LILY: You keep telling me what I needed to do. I *know* what I needed to do.

RICARDO: But you *do* need me telling you what you needed to do.

LILY: No I don't.

RICARDO: You *always* need telling what you needed to do.

LILY: I don't need telling what I needed to do.

RICARDO: Hey, listen. Do you think that Sugar Shane Mosely didn't need telling what to do? Everybody needs telling what to do and when to do it.

LILY: I don't need you telling me what to do. I already know what I did wrong, but I have no fucking legs when I got in there.

RICARDO: Do it right. That's all. It's not a dig at you. You cut her off and backed her up. You just needed to do it more. That's all. You had some good moments. You need a whole—how many rounds did you do?

LILY: Three.

RICARDO: You'll wake up by the middle of the wake.

Lily stops and thinks for a second. She changes her line of reasoning.

LILY: Did I look bad?

RICARDO: *Now* you want me to criticize you?

LILY: I'm just asking. I don't need the—

RICARDO: You didn't look bad. You just didn't look as good as you could have, should have, can do. You didn't come out busted up, which is good.

LILY: I didn't. I came up less busted than last time.

RICARDO: The day wasn't that bad then.

LILY: She said I nearly stopped her with a body shot.

RICARDO: What kind? You don't even know, do you?

LILY: Straight left.

RICARDO: What did I tell you? Get low. When she's doing all this prancing around, go right there. Shoot right there. I don't want to be negative, but don't fucking reach down to punch her in the belly. There's nothing in it. Just jab upstairs and throw the left downstairs. OK? Then you back her up, and then you hit on the sides, OK? Don't reach when there's nothing there. That's what you did. That's my biggest criticism, because when you're down there and there's nothing [in] that punch that will hurt her. And when you're down, she punches you. And it looks bad. Jab to the face and then throw the hand to the body. Pause. Nice guns.

LILY: My shoulders hurt like shit.

Ricardo laughs.

RICARDO: Mine, too.

LILY: I want to be good, Ricardo!

RICARDO: You are good. You just have to get—

LILY: I want to go in there and make somebody cry.

RICARDO: You will. All you need to do is keep going forward. All right? There's no room for backing up. And God help you if you back up when Fiona comes out there. There is no need to back up when she's coming up. You don't need to be standing and looking at these people, weighing that much. Good.

What is noteworthy about this interaction is that Lily herself picks up some of the gendered language, ultimately exclaiming that she wants to make someone "cry."

Finally, some women perceive that they are their trainers' last priority and that they are neglected because they are not interesting athletes with which to work. Women are typically the last gym members to be given important exercises, such as sparring, and training them is at the end of their trainers' lists of things to do. That is, trainers will work with female athletes only when their work with male athletes has been completed. When I ask Joanne why this is, she answers, "Why? 'Cause we weren't taken seriously. [Men say,] 'She's not a fighter. She's not a fighter.' The same line you get." After taking a gender and sport class in college, Joanne noticed the disadvantages and discrimination women in sport face. Though she is quick to point out that she doesn't want to complain, she expresses annoyance that women in the gym do not get enough attention for the hard work they put in.

Sexism pervades competition sites. At the *New York Daily News* Golden Gloves, women recount overhearing degrading comments by event organizers. Such sentiments usually focus on how much officials oppose women boxing. Caitlin recounts, "Tom heard it—I didn't hear it—but my boyfriend Tom heard the main organizer guy [say,] 'This [women's boxing] is the worst thing that ever happened to boxing.' " When Lily is asked if she is too old to compete by a *Daily News* administrator who knows her age, she understands the quip as sexist. Chloe, who worked for the Golden Gloves, said that the men who worked at the event "got lit" at dinner right before the fights and, without inhibition, would express their hatred of women's boxing. In the position of witnessing both male and female bouts, Chloe saw differential treatment. Women fighters were treated terribly by event officials. For example, when one female boxer was looking for her coach, a high-ranking official asked her, "What, do you need him to put on your makeup for you?" In contrast, officials treat male fighters with respect and are lenient with them and their trainers, bending rules and letting regulations slide. Officials would allow the scales for weigh-ins to stay open for hours after they were supposed to close at men's bouts but not at women's. According to Chloe, female boxers and their trainers were given a hard time at every turn.

Discrimination against female boxers can manifest in subtle but significant ways. When a casting crew comes to Gleason's Gym to recruit boxers for Oscar De La Hoya's reality show, they only audition men. Joanne is furious that women are not included and thinks that a reality show on women's boxing would help promote the sport and draw attention to the work of female athletes. To Joanne, a lot of men were not taking the process seriously, while there were "scores of female boxers" who trained rigorously every day. After hearing one man say that he hadn't "worked out in forever" but "is just doing this [auditioning]" while she and other female fighters sacrifice to train and fight, Joanne is outraged. She experiences this man's flippant treatment of the auditions as personally insulting. She tells me, "I really and truly am bothered by this." The continued practice of employing round-card girls at events also troubles female boxers, especially when women have to fight in those same events. Joanne says:

> First of all, let's just say, "round-card girls." Hello? I have to fight, and there's going to be a half-naked girl between rounds showing a card? So you have the audience saying, "OK, I have to look at that [round-card girl] and compare it to that [female athlete]," 'cause automatically they're going to 'cause I'm still a girl. And they're still looking at my legs. Amateurs don't have round-card girls, but I've actually fought in an amateur bout that had round-card girls, and it bothered the hell out of me, especially in an amateur bout! As a female, it's tough.

In response, women have created a space in Gleason's Gym and a place in the sport. They have formed interclass and interracial subcultures of belonging and have developed strategies for supporting each other as well as soliciting the support of their male teammates. Within the gym, they have created a network of solidarity that fosters an ethic of care. They work collaboratively—even if they are on different teams, which is uncommon for male fighters—during spars and encourage each other as they make their way through the various components of a pugilistic workout: running on the treadmill, shadowboxing in front of the gym's large mirrors, working the gym's various bags. They compliment each other on skillful moves and remark on progress made. If a boxer is having a difficult day, they give pep talks. These practices create a space where women feel supported and nurtured. Joanne remarks:

> This [the gym] is where I feel—like when I say "home," this is home, too. I feel it. And it's just incredible because, it's like where I've been and other places. It was like everybody had the missing link but now it's all together now. It feels like finally—emotional, physical, mental—everything just kind of came together, and I feel safe. Like really humbly safe in my own life.

Though significant encouragement takes place on the gym "floor," even more care is provided in the women's locker room. Here, beyond the earshot of men, women can let down their guard and be more vulnerable. In the locker room, they are more likely to cry and express anxiety about competition, frustration with trainers and male teammates, and feelings of failure. It is not uncommon to walk into the locker room and see a female fighter in tears being comforted by an army of women. Several days before the Golden Gloves begins, Jennifer bends under the pressure and starts to cry. Four women surround her and talk with her about why she is scared and why she should feel prepared, given the training she has put in. These women's comments soothe Jennifer.

It is also not uncommon to see women socializing and celebrating together in the locker room. Layla reflects:

> The women's locker room is another kind of gym. Maybe if two people just took a class together, they'll be discussing the class. Sometimes that will branch out into a little bit of socializing. But just the atmosphere, particularly among the women, is just incredibly supportive and much more—there seems to be a general spirit of everyone rooting for each other whether it's in your work or your life that, you know, "Oh, Layla, I saw you on TV." It's very—it's just very positive. There's a general spirit of community that you, you know, you feel. People greet you.

Women also work to earn respect from their teams, which are composed of male boxers and trainers as well as other women. In this case, there is cross-gender support. Many women think of their teams as extensions of their families, spending time with them on weekends and celebrating holidays together. Joanne says:

> Christmas, Christmas Eve, my birthday, and New Year's Eve, I was with him [her trainer] and his family. They embraced me. Not that—I mean my family—it's, you know, I got issues, you know what I mean? But his family embraced me. And that birthday that I had with no alcohol was the best birthday ever. I mean, I just sat and looked at the table, and Roberto [male boxer on her team] was there, and Roberto was looking at me like, "Are you all right?" And I wanted to cry. And if you ever saw *Antwone Fisher*, when he walks into the room and everybody's there, the family? That's how I felt. I was like, "So this is what it is. Not to have your father drinking or somebody putting you down or negativity." It was all positivity. Everybody was happy and genuine. I was happy.

Jennifer explains:

> It's cool. I love hanging out with Jack, and now that I'm into this, now I watch boxing. Every time there's a big fight—like, I didn't get to go this Saturday because it was my grandmother's eightieth birthday—but whenever there's

> a good, big fight on TV, we'll go to Jack's house: Mila, Bob, myself. Eva and Myriam are always invited. Whoever wants to come, and we'll get together on Friday nights at Jack's house because he has DirecTV or whatever. And it's fun.

As women move on from the gym and pursue other aspects of their lives, they continue to follow and support each other by going to fights and cheering. They also provide encouragement on social networking sites. This cadre of female fighters uses Facebook to monitor each other's progress and to congratulate each other on victories.

GENDER AND THE GYM

Women's integration into the gym challenges men and women's assumptions about gender and forces both to confront the codes and norms of femininity and sexuality. Heteronormative suppositions about gender confront women in the gym at every turn. They are excluded de facto from the community and from the sport and have to fight for inclusion. This inclusion is set on narrow terms: they must act "like men" by becoming diesel fighters or they must seek legitimacy under the banner of family by joining one of Gleason's many teams. To develop into a diesel fighter, a woman must degender and desexualize herself. She must overcome fear of aggression, pay close attention to choice of clothing, patterns of sociality, and decisions about cross-gender relations. Gym hos, in apposition, are dismissed because they do not degender or desexualize themselves. They are condemned because of their tight clothing and social personalities. They are then highly sexualized by the men of the gym.

These classifications illuminate the power of gendered assumptions, especially in relation to sexuality and femininity. The gym's hierarchies demonstrate that women's bodies cannot be both sexual and powerful. Female fighters must demonstrate lack of sexuality in order to belong and in order to escape objectification. They also must be forceful, which violates another norm of femininity and which they must work hard to develop. For woman boxers, it is impossible to have a fighting body and a sexual body. As I will discuss in chapter 6, whereas proximity to masculinity is an asset in identity formation for white-collar male clients, it is an obstacle for women. The only route to belonging in Gleason's Gym for women is to enact a gender-suppressed performance.

The gender-suppressed performance required of women and the ambivalence of men to women further reveal the ways the pressures of postindustrialism in New York City, where gender relations are rapidly changing, are filtered into the gym. Bruce Silverglade needed female members to keep the gym afloat. At the same time, postindustrial structural circumstances gave women access to new social possibilities and relations of power. With the proliferation of urban fitness and advertisers' direct marketing to women, sport became ever more attractive to female participants. New forms of family—whether because women forfeit marriage, because they desire alternative familial configurations, because of male incarceration, or because of men's abandonment—placed women as primary earners and heads of household. The feminization of white-collar jobs and the increase in "pink-collar" positions gave women more spending power just as men's employment declined. These transformations are reflected in Gleason's: women entered spaces, such as the urban gym, and assumed roles, such as boxers, long considered masculine. As much as women *fear* aggression, one could also interpret a *wish* for aggression in their decision to join the sport. This desire and accompanying integration has unleashed complicated and contradictory dynamics in the gym, which are played out through pugilistic practices. The transformation of gender relations, then, has been met with unease from the gym's men, and their responses are sometimes admirable, often not.

Chapter Six

BUYING AND SELLING BLACKNESS: WHITE-COLLAR BOXING AND THE CULTURAL CAPITAL OF RACIAL DIFFERENCE

"The science of Boxing is now become so fashionable, that some of the first personages in the kingdom are known to patronize it."

—AMATEUR OF EMINENCE, 1788

ON A WEDNESDAY EVENING, GLEASON'S GYM CLOSES FOUR hours early in preparation for a special event. Scott Stedman and Jeff Koyen, the editors of *L Magazine* and the *New York Press*, respectively, two small "alternative magazines," are taking a feud between their publications from the page to the ring. For the past four months, Koyen has attacked *L Magazine*, insulting everything from the fashion choices of the editorial staff to the supposed sexual activities of the editor's mother. To defend magazine and mom, Stedman will settle the score in a pugilistic encounter at Gleason's Gym.

Tonight is fight night.

A handful of boxing trainers remain past 6:00 p.m. to help run the event. As three hundred young, white professionals exceptionally dedicated to the latest style trends descend on the gym, it is unclear which group of people is more surprised by the other. Self-professed hipsters train at Gleason's Gym, and trainers and competitive fighters alike coexist with a variety of gym users. But this mass of fashionable twentysomethings gives even the most unflappable gym trainer pause. I watch with Mike, Harry, and Ricardo as an army of women clad in slip-like dresses, heavy woolen tights, metallic sandals, and crocheted hats and men wearing guayabera shirts and fedoras march into the gym. With eyes on the audience and arms crossed across his chest, Ricardo leans to me and whispers, "Where do you even get this stuff?" I shake my head. We decide this clothing must come from deep in the recesses of Williamsburg.

During the fight, female spectators sit dour-faced, arms folded, their crossed legs wagging in affectation and detachment. Behind me, one of them needs a restroom and mutters to her friend, "Do they even *have* bathrooms in places like this?" Overexcited men scream profanities and air-punch combinations during the rounds. At the seconds-out, one of the audience's loudest asks me earnestly, "How is he doing?" with little understanding of his friend's performance in the ring. The gym's owner announces each bout and takes his opportunity with the microphone to promote the gym. Half of the membership, he says, is made up of "people like you" who "live, work, and play in DUMBO."[1] He plugs the excitement of never knowing who may be training in the gym on any particular day: Hollywood actresses, championship fighters, businessmen, and television network executives.

Making boxing gyms ("places like this") available for corporate showdowns and attractive to young, white, and wealthy people ("people like you") is part of a trend in the sport of boxing called "white-collar boxing."[2] This phenomenon, which may be one of the few sports named for the professional status of its participants outside the sport itself, began in the mid-1980s in New York City when a number of white male businessmen, lawyers, and doctors expressed eagerness to pay substantial sums of money to be trained in the city's most famous gyms. Trainers and fighters, most of whom were men of color, stepped up to act as instructors, and created for themselves jobs in a restrictive postindustrial labor market. Gyms quickly instituted white-collar classes, programs, and leagues, and, at a time when the number of amateur and professional boxers in New York City dwindled, the number of white-collar clients expanded dramatically, keeping urban gyms afloat with their dependable membership dues.

This chapter examines the social practices, social relations, and implications of white-collar boxing. It considers its history, the economic possibilities that it offers, and the ways trainers and their clients understand and operate within this new pugilistic industry. I argue that a specific racial and gender identity is actively constructed through the commercial exchange of the training session. Blackness is a site of cultural capital that is valued and exchanged and, simultaneously, engenders new forms of anti-black racism.[3] When upper-middle-class and upper-class white professionals pay for the expertise of "authentic" black trainers, they are imagining and consuming a notion of blackness defined by the body, narratives of suffering, histories of criminality, and experiences of racial inequality. Clients presume an authentic black identity, and, in turn, produce a form of black masculinity. This construction of black masculinity is predicated on the very sufferings of racial segregation and class exclusion that prevent men of color from generating an income by other means in the first place.

FROM GENTLEMAN BOXER TO WHITE-COLLAR CLIENT

Journalistic accounts of white-collar boxing give the impression that recreational boxers—those who do not compete as amateurs or professionals—only recently began to take up the sport.[4] In fact, recreational boxing has a long history. While interest in pugilism has waxed and waned across the centuries, almost from the inception of the modern form—which is commonly dated to 1719, when James Figg won the first championship bout in Britain—recreational athletes learned to fight. In the eighteenth and nineteenth centuries, as competitive boxing became more disciplined and the rules of the sport increasingly rationalized, recreational pugilists taught themselves the sport's techniques from training manuals in the privacy of their own homes. A number of texts from the 1700s and 1800s suggest that middle- and upper-class English and American men studied the sport to protect themselves from physical assault.[5] In 1784, the author of *The Art of Manual Defence, or System of Boxing: Perspicuously Explained in a Series of Lessons, and Illustrated by Plates* complained of the "licentiousness," "rudeness," and "scurrility" of "the lower order of society" and their penchant for confronting upper-class men strolling the streets of London.[6] Acknowledging the physical disadvantage of upper-class men against their working- and lower-class attackers, who, it was believed, had mastered the sport, the manual's author suggested the former learn its methods:

> It is therefore an object of some utility and importance of a man to acquire a dexterity in Boxing in order to defend himself against such rudeness, and to protect those whose weakness, age, or sex renders them liable to the insults of the rabble, and deprives them of all power and effectual resistance.[7]

The ability to defend oneself became a way to negotiate class conflict and uphold a genteel masculinity through force by protecting one's body and the bodies of the weak and dependent.

Based upon the rhetorical features and cost of these manuals, it is fairly certain that the readership was upper-middle- and upper-class men and not competitive fighters, who were overwhelmingly from an emerging working-class and lumpenproletariat and therefore could not afford the publications' costs. Given the texts' proliferation in multiple editions and printings, it also can be assumed that there was at least moderate demand. But by the late nineteenth and early twentieth centuries—with the formation and popularization of proper boxing gyms, elite athletic clubs, and all-purpose gymnasiums as well as the incorporation of public education programs in various social institutions—men interested in training to box studied pugilism in formal settings. Men of schools such as Yale and Harvard boxed at university while the exclusive New York Athletic Club hired famous prizefighters to instruct wealthy gentlemen in sparring.[8] Historian Gail Bederman writes that by the 1880s, recreational boxing was considered "respectable enough" to be offered in Young Men's Christian Association (YMCA) branches.[9]

Like their manual-reading counterparts of the eighteenth and nineteenth centuries, recreational boxers in the twentieth century expressed an interest in the sport's techniques. Men categorized as neither amateur nor professional, and often with little interest in competition, such as Ernest Hemingway and Miles Davis, toiled on their own and with trainers in the gyms of New York, Chicago, and San Francisco.[10] According to accounts of "old-school" trainers at Gleason's Gym, in the early to mid-1900s, recreational athletes constituted a relatively small proportion of gym memberships. However, by the end of the century, interest in the sport among recreational boxers exploded. With the eruption of the urban fitness industry, legions of business executives, lawyers, and doctors expanded their workout routines and joined urban boxing gyms to work with trainers and competitive fighters.[11]

Bruce Silverglade, the current owner of Gleason's Gym, and the gym itself are generally credited as originator and site of the white-collar craze that began in the 1980s.[12] The *Houston Chronicle* declares that "the official origins of white-collar boxing date to the late 1980s at Gleason's

---

Opposite: Title page from a boxing training manual circa 1880, Ann Street, New York City. In Owen Swift, *Boxing without a Master; or, Scientific Art and Practice of Attack and Self-Defence: Explained in So Easy a Manner that Any Person May Comprehend This Useful Art and Containing Descriptions of Correct Pugilistic Attitudes, as Practiced by the Most Celebrated Boxers of the Present Day* (New York: Frederic A. Brady, c. 1880). Courtesy of Beinecke Rare Book and Manuscript Library, Yale University.

12 1-2

BOXING

WITHOUT A MASTER;

OR, SCIENTIFIC ART AND PRACTICE OF

ATTACK AND SELF-DEFENCE.

EXPLAINED IN SO EASY A MANNER THAT ANY PERSON MAY COMPREHEND THIS USEFUL ART CONTAINING DESCRIPTIONS OF

CORRECT PUGILISTIC ATTITUDES,

AS PRACTICED BY THE MOST CELEBRATED BOXERS OF THE PRESENT DAY.

BY OWEN SWIFT,
PROFESSOR OF THE ART.

New-York:
FREDERIC A. BRADY, PUBLISHER,
24 ANN STREET.

Copies sent by Mail on receipt of price

WAITES' SCHOOL OF ARMS,

19, BREWER STREET,

PICCADILLY CIRCUS, W.

JEM MACE, JUNR.,

SON OF JEM MACE

(the retired Champion of the world)

and author of this book, gives lessons in

BOXING,

under the method herein explained,

AT THE ABOVE SCHOOL,

where he may be seen any day after 10 a.m.

TERMS UPON APPLICATION.

Mace's Professional Boxing Gloves, Dumb-bells, Punching-Balls, Etc., sent to any part on receipt of Remittance.

Advertisement for boxing lessons in London, England, 1880. In Jem Mace, Jr., *Boxing* (London: Phelp Bros., 1880). Courtesy of Beinecke Rare Book and Manuscript Library, Yale University.

Gym in Manhattan, where owner Bruce Silverglade openly encouraged doctors, lawyers and investment bankers to climb into the ring against their peers." *USA Today* pronounces that white-collar boxing "was born" at Gleason's Gym, and even the gym's official website asserts that it "created the concept of white collar boxing."[13] However, the legendary trainer Bob Jackson, who worked with Cus D'Amato at Gramercy Gym on Fourteenth Street in Manhattan for decades, taking over when D'Amato passed away, believes that he coined the term "white-collar boxer" before Silverglade used it. He remembers:

> White collar would have started in Fourteenth Street ten years before I moved here [Gleason's Gym]. What it was was there was no white collar. You were either an amateur or a pro. Very few people would come up, but once in a while someone could come up. And we'd say, "Come on!?" but "OK, it costs seven dollars a month. You want to exercise, go ahead." "But I want you to train me." Ugh. And then it began to be that so many people came up asking to be trained that I thought "Hmmm."

Jackson polled his members to assess the level of interest in boxing among recreational athletes and, after an overwhelming response, asked his amateur and professional fighters to teach group lessons. The term "white-collar" was coined when Jackson began advertising. When asked by *The Learning Annex* what to call the gym's classes, Jackson decided to define the participants by what traditional gym enthusiasts were not.[14] He thought, "Well most of the people aren't blue collar, they're white collar. And there you are! White-collar boxing!"

Jackson's primary interest was not financial gain but rather quieting the noisy demands of white upper-middle- and upper-class men. To him, these recreational athletes were more of an annoyance than economic opportunity. He recollects, "[B]elieve me when I tell you I didn't want to make money. And I didn't want to train all those people. So I hired all the fighters and used them as trainers. With all the money that came in, I paid the fighters." The development of white-collar boxing was an efficient solution to his logistical aggravation: it satisfied both the recreational boxer, who could be trained by those with expertise, and the struggling fighter, who was compensated for his time.

Whether it was Jackson or Silverglade who christened "white-collar boxing," the former gives credit to the latter for the establishment of a white-collar boxing league. The competitive series was the outgrowth of a bout of trash talking between two men who trained at Gleason's Gym in 1988. At that time, Aaron was a banker and Doc an attorney and veterinarian. Aaron explains:

> This guy Doc, who had three pro fights, wanted to fight me for $500. So I said, "OK, I'll fight him for $500." Then we said—of course this wasn't an amateur and it wasn't a professional 'cause we're not sanctioned—so this will be the first white-collar fight. He was a veterinarian and lawyer, and I was a Wall Street banker. So we were both from the kind of business—or the professional world.

Aaron advertised the show, and it was a great success. Because his age prevented him from competing as amateur or professional and he wanted to fight, he suggested that Gleason's institute a white-collar series, which he promoted and financed for a time. The league was instantly popular, and Silverglade has run shows ever since. He holds monthly cards, keeps an active mailing list of participants who come from around the country, and recruits partners from around the world.

The first white-collar show consisted of five rounds of three minutes, which is the typical format for a professional fight or an open amateur bout.[15] Today white-collar boxers fight three two-minute rounds. They sport sixteen-ounce gloves, wear headgears, and occasionally don special head equipment outfitted with a nose bar so they will not break their noses. As they hop from foot to foot in their corners, Bruce Silverglade announces them by name and occupation: "And in the blue corner—John Doe—a neurologist from Boston. . . ." At the end of the fight, both participants receive a trophy and have their hands lifted by the referee, as there are no winners or losers declared. These special shows boast ten to fifteen matches and draw crowds of between seventy-five and one hundred people, largely comprising friends, family, and other white-collar athletes. Silverglade believes they represent an important "next step" for exercise addicts who want to do more than just train.

What started as a bet in 1988 swiftly became a lucrative local phenomenon, and boxing programs and classes materialized in fitness clubs throughout New York City. Silverglade recalls, "Then there was a lot of publicity on my white-collar shows and on white-collar boxing, businesspeople training at Gleason's. And it became very popular, so Equinox and all these clubs started boxing programs." Silverglade did not consider this development to be harmful to his business or even competition because of the inevitable pull to his gym. An athlete would try a boxing class in a health club and enjoy it. After taking classes—and possibly paying for a private lesson with a fitness trainer—the hobbyist would be hooked and want a more rigorous experience. Eventually he or she would seek out Gleason's Gym because of its reputation as the oldest operational boxing gym in the country and a rigorous fighting institution. Silverglade recollects, "And I didn't mind at all. I was very happy for it because what happened—those gyms became the minor leagues of Gleason's Gym."

While boxing programs popped up in New York City health clubs, white-collar gyms and leagues surfaced around the country and then around the world. In Barcelona, Dubai, Hong Kong, Dublin, Liverpool, London, and Winnipeg, gyms cultivated white-collar clients. The United Kingdom's first white-collar show took place in the summer of 2000 and was billed "Capital Punishment."[16] Today "The Real Fight Club," the United Kingdom's white-collar league, has 500 members in London and 4,000 members in the United Kingdom.[17] In southern England alone, white-collar shows attract as many as 2,000 people. Adrian King, an organizer of bouts, keeps a database of 3,800 people in the region, 600 of whom are active members.[18] The first white-collar card in Winnipeg, Canada, located in the Exchange District, quickly sold out its 250 tickets.[19]

Some gyms hold white-collar "fantasy boxing camps" where participants reenact carefully chosen aspects of classic professional training regimens in pristine mountain getaways. In Dublin, former Olympian and professional Cathal O'Grady organized an intense eight-week program in which Irish businessmen "lived" the sport. After six weeks of training in a Dublin gym, attendees relocated to Kutsher's Golf and Country Club in the Catskills, where, in a different era, famous heavyweights prepared for championship bouts. Participants were trained by Olympic trainers, consulted sports psychologists, met with nutritionists, and paid 10,000 euros for their adventure.[20]

Gleason's Gym has a similar camp. Each fall, Silverglade takes a group of white-collar boxers to retreats in the Catskills or the Poconos to learn the sweet science from ex–world champions, such as Mark Breland, and famous trainers, such as Hector Roca. Participants endure a rigorous training schedule and intense indoctrination into the sport. Gleason's website promises that the experience "will include intensive boxing discussions, coaching sessions, ring craft, sparring and training drills" and that "[a]t the end of the camp you will have the chance to showcase your new-found skills in our White Collar Boxing Show." But lest the fantasy boxing camp simulate too many features of traditional training, many austere and stoical aspects are scrapped, and participants are assured a certain level of comfort. Far from Brad Pitt and Edward Norton's dilapidated tenement colony or the damp and dreary restaurant basements where bouts of *Fight Club* were slugged out, Gleason's fantasy camp promises an inventory of luxurious amenities and nonboxing entertainments. The website offers a multitude of enticements:

> Kutsher's provides an environment that offers the finest in dining, entertaining, sports and recreation. Attendees of the Fantasy Camp will have full access to all the facilities that Kutsher's offers, including Bicycles, Canoes, Exercise Room, Fishing, Miniature Golf, Indoor and Outdoor pools, health club and saunas at no extra cost. Kutsher's Resort also has a PGA Standard Championship golf course available at an additional charge to guests. Horseback riding, mountain biking, tennis and water-skiing are also available to guests at a nominal charge. Guest services including baby sitters, a nursery, day camp, children's pool, pre-teen program and game room are available to those who wish to bring their family.

The cost for the three-day excursion is $1,850 for participants willing to share a double room, $2,550 for participants who bring one guest, and $3,150 for participants who bring two guests.[21]

White-collar memberships have become important to the survival of urban boxing gyms. The sport has declined in recent years, which has meant fewer gym memberships and less money to pay overhead. Bruce Silverglade estimates that between 2003 and 2004, there were roughly 400 registered amateurs in the Greater New York area; when he was president of the Metropolitan Amateur Boxing Federation in the early 1980s, there were 2,000. He blames skyrocketing rent prices and insurance premiums,[22] the consolidation of power of major promoters such as Don King and Bob Arum, and the alphabet belts[23] created by TV networks for the lack of investment in grassroots boxing. Gym owners desperately needed a new source of income, and white-collar clients provide the necessary revenue. At Gleason's, white-collar fighters constitute 65 percent of the 1,000-person membership, which continues to grow. According to an article on the gym in the *New York Post* in October 2005, "Enrollment in the white-collar boxing program grows each year and last year registered a rock solid 10 percent increase over the prior year."[24] This is true for gyms in other cities as well. *USA Today*'s Chuck Johnson writes that white-collar memberships "are the main source of revenue of many boxing gyms in large urban areas, from New York to Detroit to Los Angeles."[25]

TRAINERS AS ENTREPRENEURS: MARKETING AND SUBJECTIVITY

If Bruce Silverglade and Bob Jackson are responsible for the inauguration of white-collar boxing, Gleason's trainers are the workers responsible for sustaining this pugilistic industry. Silverglade estimates that roughly eighty trainers work at Gleason's Gym at different points in time, and, of these, forty make their livings entirely from income earned at the gym. During my fieldwork, there were roughly eighteen trainers who worked in the gym on a consistent, full-time basis. Most trainers are men of color, though this involves a number of racial and ethnic self-identifications such as Hispanic, Latino, black British, African Caribbean, and African American. There are trainers who have emigrated from Guyana, Britain, Panama, Guatemala, Nicaragua, Puerto Rico, Russia, and Palestine, but the majority of the gym's trainers grew up in Brooklyn, the Bronx, and Queens.

Most trainers did not aspire to work in the gym full-time but rather created their positions when a combination of talent, experience, opportunity, and chance intertwined. As white-collar boxing became popular, trainers realized that if they coached these new members in large enough numbers, they could support themselves entirely from income earned in the gym. They first worked outside jobs and as trainers in their spare time, and then quit their full-time jobs and became full-time workers in the gym as soon as they could. Karl worked in construction, Harry in food service, Ed in school safety, Jeremy in security, and Mike in a number of low-wage jobs—all while frequenting the gym during their free time. When they acquired enough white-collar clients, they became full-time trainers. Other trainers went full-time after they retired from outside occupations. Joseph worked for Verizon for almost twenty-five years and took an early retirement. Bob was a corrections officer and worked as a trainer part-time at Gramercy Gym for more than three decades. Once he retired, he settled into full-time training, first at Gramercy and then at Gleason's. Legend surrounding a well-known trainer at Gleason's is that a friend who was a boxing trainer pulled him out of an unemployment line. After years of being an assistant second, he is now one of the gym's most famous trainers.[26]

A contingent within the group of full-time trainers worked out of the Bed-Stuy Boxing Center before coming to Gleason's around 2000. Because Bed-Stuy did not have white-collar clients, its trainers worked part-time. In 1998, Harry had a fight with the gym's management and was kicked out. He relocated to Gleason's Gym, where he promptly apprehended the income potential from the upper-middle and upper-class clientele. Over the next several years, he recruited roughly a dozen trainers from Bed-Stuy, who were eager to generate an income using their training talents. For reasons discussed later in this chapter, the relationship of these trainers to the near-mythic status of Bedford-Stuyvesant is significant. But suffice it to say that this wave of trainers notices immense differences between Bed-Stuy and their new base of operation. Karl explains:

> It's different because you get paid. You're not just working for the glory of it. Just for the—to get somebody a pair of gloves or to get your name out there. You get paid for it. I work with lawyers and doctors, and it's been successful for me, really. I got some good fighters. I'm making money right now. I'm good.

While these trainers have fond—even nostalgic—feelings for the gym in Bedford-Stuyvesant, making an income is a decisive factor for moving to Gleason's. Trainers also work with other professionals at Gleason's, which, as referenced in Karl's quote, many trainers appreciate. When asked whether he prefers what he and others describe as the "family atmosphere" of Bed-Stuy or the bottom-line business of Gleason's Gym, Karl responds:

> Well, I love Bed-Stuy. Bed-Stuy will always be my home, with George Washington.[27] I love him, and that will always be my home. But I like this—this common sense. The bills gotta get paid, and I can't pay the bills on love and life. You know what I mean? I do what I want to do, and I get the same attention, I just get paid for it.

Trainers charge clients between $20 and $75 per hour or per session.[28] Harry bills $30 per hour, while Jeremy asks for $40 per session. Trainers, however, are likely to offer good deals for longer-term contracts, giving big discounts for paying monthly rather than by the day. Karl explains:

> It depend on who you are and what part of the game you into and what you looking to—who you want to fight or if you are a white-collar fighter and you just want to sweat or if you want to learn the technique. It depend on what you want out of boxing. That's how I work with you, and I give you a price. It could be anywhere from $25 a day to $50 a day. A week it could be anywhere from $300 a week to $200 a week.

Mike charges a flat rate of $60 per week or $200 per month depending on how much a client would advance up front. Some trainers will agree to "doubling up"—training two clients at once—at a considerable reduction for each party. If someone is perceived to have a lot of money, he or she might be charged more. Harry was paid over $1,000 per month to train a *Comedy Central* comedian, though this required him to leave the gym each day to train his client in Manhattan. Whatever the price a trainer quotes, in practice it is rare for a trainer to reject a bid from a client. Most trainers need an income so desperately and consider their financial predicaments so sensitive to weekly and monthly fluctuations that they will settle for what a client proposes if it promises regularity.

White-collar clients are a crucial source of income for trainers because of the uneven compensation from competitive fighters. Professionals give their trainers a percentage of their earnings from fight nights, but these earnings are unpredictable. They offer the possibility of a decent or even generous paycheck at some point, but usually they do not provide the bulk of a trainer's earnings. Male amateurs are even more precarious with their payments. These fighters tend to pay when they can and if they can, which amounts to very little for a trainer. They are likely to pay in-kind in a symbolic gesture, with a soda, CD, DVD, or magazine. More often than not, they cost their trainers money. Many trainers pay the gym dues of their struggling amateur fighters on a regular basis as well as cover tournament registration fees, traveling expenses, and even the cost of equipment. Women pay like male clients.

When trainers discuss their relationships with clients they situate their work in a political economy where they possess expertise and status. Some trainers see clients as dilettantes and patronize them rather than take white-collar boxing training seriously. They devise subtle ways to humiliate clients, which are both punitive and appealing marketing tools. These trainers humor their clients in training sessions and even try to get over on them. Trainers know that the practices that boxing clients perform are different than those of competitive fighters and, it is imputed, not as legitimate. Ed sees clients as people who "just" work out. He tells me, "Clients basically want a nice workout. We're just training to keep in shape. I'm not even gonna ask you to box." Ed's comment belittles the "nice" white-collar training regimens and patronizes the clients by not "even" asking that they box.

Karl takes Ed's hints to their logical conclusion, "With the white collars, I just give them pads and make them sweat. All they really want to do is sweat and have a good workout. Hit the bag, and make them feel like they're really doing something." Karl makes clients "feel" a certain way, which is different than giving them a training regimen that accomplishes "really doing something." He creates the illusion of a feat; that is, that white-collar clients have actually completed a rigorous workout when they have not. He dismisses clients' physical activities as watered-down versions of what real fighters are taught and practice.

Mike sends his male amateur pugilists into the ring to "play with" white-collar boxers. His words conjure the image of a cat batting at a mouse; for its own amusement, the cat allows the mouse to entertain the hope that it has a chance of escaping the encounter unscathed when, in reality, the outcome is set. Letting the white-collar boxer "win" the spar supposes that if the partner were allowed to really fight, the white-collar would not have a chance. For example, when a reality show comes to Gleason's Gym to film the fulfillment of a fantasy of a professional Scandinavian soccer player—to fight in Madison Square Garden—the production crew asks for a sparring partner. Anthony is recruited because he matches the contestant's height, could be trusted to be "gentle" and, no doubt, meets a stereotypical image of a black heavyweight. Anthony understands his role, and bids farewell to the regulars of Mike's corner with a big smile, informing us that he has "to go do some acting." There is humor in this knowledge. Just before Anthony goes off to do his "acting," Mike jokes that he should hit the contestant "just to see what he does." Without skipping a beat, Anthony deadpans that he suggest to the contestant, "Now, let's get serious," after two rounds of sparring (striking a serious facial expression, slapping his gloves together twice, and bouncing rapidly from foot to foot to demonstrate an increase in the spar's intensity). Or, Anthony thinks, he could feign anger should the contestant manage to land a punch, threatening, "Oh, you want to play like *that*?!" To keep clients happy and, by extension, to protect their income, trainers treat clients as if they are strong and powerful and the center of gym life. Patronizing white-collar clients and making them feel legitimate and in the loop is the gym's public secret.

Other trainers do not humiliate clients by mocking them but rather market their work as a fee for service between two equal parties. These trainers define their relationships to white-collar boxers in purely financial terms and seal their interactions in the economic bubble of the gym. To these trainers, working with clients is simply a way to make an income. Harry refuses to see the exchange as anything other than a professional arrangement, and in doing so, he negates the gym's social relations and relations of power. When I ask if he likes working with white-collar clients, he answers with an economic rationale: "That's how I pay my bills." The subtext of Harry's response is that training clients is not about likes or dislikes, personalities, or preferences. It is merely about income. It is only after he has first firmly located his clients in an economic sphere that he will answer the social component of my question: "Some of them I do, some of them I really don't care for." But Harry believes he approaches the "liked" and the "disliked" equally because it is an exchange and not a place for favorites. Harry's comments echo Mike's explanation of the gym's economy: "White collars pay the rent and trainers." These economic arguments make clear why trainers do not threaten white-collar clients with termination if they fail to execute an instruction as they do with amateurs and professionals: to do so would risk losing money. But trainers also have such little investment in their clients' physical prowess that ceding to their desires is simply part of the job.

Not all trainers relegate trainer-client relationships to either pure patronizing or only financial exchange. At the same time as Mike talks about his male amateur fighters' "playing with" white-collar boxers, he comments on race relations in the gym and appreciates the presence of clients in his community. White-collar boxing, he thinks, brings together people of different racial, class, and gender backgrounds who, in the world outside the gym, do not usually have occasion to meet. "Look at Sunshine [his nickname for a female boxer]," he explains. "Do you think Anthony and Sunshine would ever have been speaking? Leah [a female boxer] and Adrian? Or Omar joking with Leah? Or even you and Karl? You get access [to people] you wouldn't have met."

The subject position of the person gaining "access" is apt to change. In the preceding paragraph, it is white women who get access to black men. Mike thinks it is good for female boxers to interact with those of other racial backgrounds. But Mike also sees his amateur fighters of color as gaining access:

> They [white-collar boxers] meet a lot of guys in the gym. I know a lot of guys I had been training over the years [amateurs], and they have a white-collar guy in the morning, and I say, "Adrian, go spar with this guy," and the guy likes Adrian, and he move around and play with him. This guy owns a fucking company. And I say [to the white-collar client], "Yo, can I get something for this guy because he looking for work?" and he say, "Yeah, OK, I can do something." A lot of guys get jobs like that. The union.

Not only can interactions between white white-collar men and amateur fighters of color lead to jobs, which are virtually nonexistent for black youth in postindustrial New York City, but they can also lead to union jobs—some of the most coveted positions because of their security and benefits. The advantages of "access," according to Mike, are a *mise en abyme* for the social and economic structure of the gym: clients get access to racial difference and amateur boxers and trainers get access to various possibilities and derivations of work.

THE SOCIAL PRACTICES AND RELATIONS OF WHITE-COLLAR BOXING

Gym trainers work with white-collar clients in a substantially different manner than with amateur and professional boxers. Because clients pay for their training sessions and believe they know enough to select the components of their workouts, they dictate the terms of their exercise. Jeremy puts it most aptly, "With a client, you really can't push 'em." Competitive fighters defer to their trainers. Clients, on the other hand, rarely defer to trainers, choosing instead to set the limits of their workouts: duration, components, pitch, and intensity. In practice, this means that white-collar workouts are easier and abbreviated versions of amateur and professional training sessions. When Harry trained the comedian, he drove to midtown Manhattan from Brooklyn in the middle of the day to work with his client for roughly twenty minutes. Upon arrival, he would be whisked into an office and would wait until the comedian was ready to see him. The client would tell Harry what his workout would be—usually preferring padwork—as well as the duration of each "round." These instructions were nonnegotiable: If Harry tried to extend the round, the comedian would protest, "That's enough" or "I can't do anymore." Training sessions were often more social than physical, and Harry and his client bantered more than they exercised, sharing stories of drug use and recovery, popular news events, and historic prizefighters.

Trainers tweak gym practices to support their clients' illusions of control. As stated earlier, in spars, trainers construct a scenario in which their clients can attack their opponents but cannot be hit back. Trainers ask their most experienced male amateur fighters to work with clients but not to touch them. Clients, then, can punch but cannot be punched back: amateurs feint and fake to give the impression that they are sparring but they never strike. This is a strange practice for a fighter. A spar traditionally consists of two people working offense and defense together. A spar in which one person can hit while the other can only duck and weave is a very different ring exercise. But it is one that both trainer and fighter take seriously. For example, for several rounds of Anthony's spar with the fragile Scandinavian soccer player, he was tender with his intimidated partner. But in a later round, Anthony accidently hit the contestant in the stomach, causing the contestant to crumble in pain to the canvas. For a moment everyone watched, frozen in shock, and then slowly expressed a range of emotions: the contestant looked up from the canvas at Anthony betrayed; Anthony glanced at the contestant apologetically and then at Mike shamefully; Max, Anthony's teammate, giggled hysterically—his hand covering his mouth trying to smother his laughter—and Mike quietly muttered "no" and shook his head in disgust. The reactions to this transgression are telling, and this exception proves the rule. The contestant felt deceived because the production staff had assured him that he would not be hurt by the heavyweight, who had been selected precisely because he looked like he *could* hurt him. Anthony felt bad because he knew he was not to wound the novice. (In his defense, he had faked the same punch only a moment before and the contestant had slipped it. Thinking the contestant understood the drill, he threw the same punch again.) Mike was angry because he had given strict instructions to Anthony ("lightly, Tony, I mean lightly") that were not followed. Perhaps unconsciously the violation frustrated Mike because his income is dependent on his fighters not injuring his clients. Max's laughter belies how nonsensical it is to suppose that a misunderstanding of this sort would not happen when someone with no boxing experience or knowledge of the semiotics of the ring would spar with a competitive athlete.

The control clients believe they possess is commonly uninformed, and white-collar boxing can be more brutal and bloody than amateur or professional fighting. Aaron remembers, "They're real fights, and we're trying to kill each other 'cause we don't want to lose." Shows at Gleason's Gym urge participants to ease up when mismatched, referees intervene to protect the less skilled, and trainers encourage the more experienced to work on defense. The tone of bouts is that of a hard spar rather than an aggressive attack, and the atmosphere feels safe. But at other gyms, white-collar fights can be gruesome. The participants of the Waterfront Boxing Gym (now Trinity Boxing Club), a glamorous institution with exposed brick walls, recessed lighting, hardwood floors, and cutting-edge exercise equipment designed specially for white-collar boxers, demonstrate little defense and significant offense. As in *Fight Club*, matches are hyper-masculine spectacles that deteriorate into slugging and bloody chaos. Instructed by cackling corner men to "never back down" rather than protect a chin, nose, and jaw or even throw in the towel, clients charge with aggression, adrenalin, and little skill. They often get hurt. The risk of bodily harm and minimal medical supervision in white-collar shows has prompted officials to question their safety, especially for men in their forties, fifties, and sixties.

White-collar boxers tend to pluck the more aggressive and enchanting practices of boxing, such as padwork and sparring, and jettison the boring components, such as shadowboxing, roadwork, or even developing defense. In doing so, they neglect the regimenting and disciplining aspect of pugilism that is not only central to traditional training but also meaningful to traditional boxers' senses of purpose. Trainers who inhibit their fighters' abilities to retaliate protect white-collar clients from the potential repercussions of their patchy training and reinforce the clients' pugilistic selections. Together these selections help white-collar boxers feel tough, aggressive, and powerful, even though this feeling is artificially constructed. A new form of boxing is produced. That a white collar is called a "client" and not a "boxer" or "athlete" signifies a new boxing ritual.

The practices of this new ritual shape the social relations between clients and trainers. As explicated in chapter 3, being a boxing trainer is about knowing, sometimes with uncanny ability, what trainees do not: when to push a fighter; what components to include in a workout; when to ease up. This expertise carries with it authority. Clients' control of the training session not only disregards trainers' skill but also ignores trainers' social status in the gym community. In addition to athletic knowledge, the position of a trainer is about life knowledge. As many trainers are from an older generation than their fighters, they have a perspective on life and advice to give, which they readily share with their fighters. This knowledge produces reverence and respect. Clients' rejection of the first form of trainer knowledge disregards the second form and, in doing so, does not recognize the trainers' social position. This misrecognition limits the types of communication, friendships, and intimacies possible and produces asymmetrical power relations based on financial incentives. Instead of the relationship being formed through the trainers' expertise, the relationship is founded on the consumption of a service and the expectation of being served. David Grazian writes of a similar phenomenon in blues nightclubs:

> These clubs attracted predominately white patrons who valued the experience of "slumming" in a seemingly exotic and sexualized world represented by the era's dominant stereotypes of black men and women. For this reason, the kinds of social encounters in which whites engaged with blacks tended to be highly patronizing and offensive, and were often rooted in the misperception that black entertainers (and, to a certain extent, black customers) naturally enjoyed dancing and smiling for paying consumers as a means of sharing their god-given birthright of hot sensuality and cool soul in exchange for their humanity.[29]

RACIAL FANTASIES AND MASCULINE MOTIVATIONS

White-collar clients span a number of generations: they range from their twenties to their seventies. They are often exercise addicts who seek thrills and want to push boundaries. Many have played college sports and after graduation plow through a series of high-risk sports and intense physical exercises before trying pugilism. William, for example, prefers boxing to other sports because he wants not only to work out but also to develop and perfect a skill. Aaron was a tournament tennis player and a ranked skier, who raced dirt motorcycles at his vacation home in the West Hamptons. When the chauffer of his Rolls-Royce was killed in a motorcycle accident, Aaron's wife forbade him to race. Aaron suggested boxing—another violent sport—as a substitute to rib his wife: "I say, 'OK, I'm giving away the motorcycles and taking up boxing.' I swear it was just a joke. She said, 'Fine, take up boxing.' I said, 'I think I will.' "

Clients articulate gendered and racialized themes when talking about their interest in boxing and gyms. Before William, an extremely successful business executive, stepped into Gleason's Gym, he possessed an "attraction" to boxing gyms. He was drawn to the sport because of its "soul." He stresses this when I ask about what he hoped to gain from training to fight: "There was an attraction in it. There was something—there's something a bit soulful in boxing and in boxing gyms and working out that I was attracted to." Part of the clients' attraction is a gendered investment in self-defense and anxiety about their manliness. Like their manual-reading counterparts of the eighteenth and nineteenth centuries, training gives clients the skills to inflict violence, which many believe are necessary to be a man. William asserts, "It's a very basic skill. A fighting skill. You know, as a guy, I really should know how to throw a really hard punch if I need to." Part of William's concern, which he argues is innate to men, is his own fear of violent confrontation. He continues, "I think somewhere inside every man, and maybe every woman, there's a fear of physical confrontation that sort of lives inside you and how you would react when that would happen."

Clients seek not only the skills of self-defense to respond to violent confrontation but also the simulation and rehearsal of such violent encounters. The experience of pain is central to their investments in pugilism and its institutions. William craves the release that absorbing blows precipitates:

> It's really hard. You put yourself into it—and I think I push myself fairly hard—and, you know, it's a bit painful. I know I'm going past what most people would push their body to in a workout, and there's something sort of purifying about that. I think there's things in boxing—people enjoy the pain. They have to enjoy the pain, or they wouldn't be here. There's something—I don't know—to religious people it's like those people who slap themselves on the back. There's something about causing themselves pain that's supposed to purify their souls. It's really fucking jarring when someone punches you in the face. You endure it, and when you're done, you think, "I feel substantially better about myself."

To William, inflicting and receiving violence becomes purifying:

> Uh, I probably have a hard time articulating why, but I like the vibe of the—the sort of vibe of the place. You know, it's funny: it's a very pure place. And you wouldn't look at it from the walls and the floors and the bloody canvases and the buckets full of spit as pure, but sort of, the intent there is pure. And I think there's a thing, like, when I worked out that I feel sort of purified when I'm done. Both from a physical standpoint—from the amount that I actually sweat, to, um, an emotional standpoint from feeling purified that there's probably more of a release in punching someone or something than there is in lifting a weight or a sort of amount of time on a treadmill. And there's a sort of simplicity of the pursuit.

William finds explaining why he feels good when he hits or has been hit difficult, and to aid his explanation, he calls on certain visual signifiers in the gym: spit, sweat, blood. His inability to fully explain the centrality of embodied experiences, such as pain, suggests something larger about his investments in the gym, beyond the fact that violence and pain are things that he is looking for because, as a man, he should know how to fight. William could have gone to any health club in New York City to learn how to respond to physical confrontation. Why did he choose Gleason's?

William's explanation mobilizes terms, such as "soulful" and "pure," and visual markers that are familiar tropes in primitivism.[30] The bloody canvas and spit buckets, for example, are representative of primitive purity. William qualifies these representations by saying, "you wouldn't call it pure," but he is, in a sense, doing just that—invoking the body's spilt fluids, substances, and secretions as cues to the purifying work that goes on at the gym. In describing the blood-and-spit aesthetic of the gym, it is as if his investment in the physical, embodied violence of the gym transmogrifies into a metaphysical, even moral, ideal.

Clients do not always explicitly link aesthetic investments in the gym with race in the same way that they are connected to gender, but race is a subtext.[31] Some clients are more explicit. In an article in the *Washington Post*, Aaron characterizes boxing as "primitive—it's tribal."[32] When I ask him about his first time at Gleason's Gym, he immediately relates what one might call his own aesthetics and metaphysics of the gym to race. In telling me how he began boxing, he remembers, "I go to Gleason's Gym, which is next to Madison Square Garden and take some lessons. Everyone in there is black, Puerto Rican, killer looking." Before interacting with anyone from the gym, Aaron has an idea of what racial difference means. It is equated with violence and deviance. It is then connected with, among other things, inherent toughness and masculinity:

> It's strange. It's not that the tough fighters have changed, it's that all of the white-collar guys are proud to be members of their low-class club. We want to be low class. We want to be in a shitty gym. We don't want to be at Equinox and Reebok with all the pretty people.

Aaron sets up a binary: whiteness is equated with beauty, wealth, and—it is imputed—weakness, and is set against blackness, which is equated with toughness, violence, and poverty. People like Aaron do not go to boxing gyms, they go to health clubs, and for this reason, the gym is attractive, a challenge. It is exotic, unlike anything to which the clients are accustomed.

Clients can be obsessed with the perception that their wealth has made them weak. Aaron is convinced that his class position of multimillionaire emasculates him. He worries, "[I]t's like everybody expects the little prissy—I should play polo because boxing is dangerous—and I don't want to go that route. I want to go somewhere that's tougher and more direct. . . . I could make $4 billion, but that still doesn't make me tough." Compounding his anxiety and self-image of masculine weakness is a philosophy of human nature that rewards domination. In explaining his philosophy, he joins William and other clients in using a gendered and racialized discourse of primitivism. He philosophizes:

> Well, in the male psyche there's a desire to be an animal and tough, which you see in the history of wars and killings and all that goes on. I mean, that's inbred in all of us, and even if we pretend it's not or we manage to get some Buddhistic facade, there's still some potential under there to kill. And to hurt. And I think that it comes out clearly. A lot of guys are afraid to accept that in their own lives, so they don't come here. But I think to cure yourself of that, you should come here. You know? And to somehow rise above it rather than to read Buddhist and cover up your yearning to kill and hurt with some philosophical oatmeal.

With Hobbesian reasoning, Aaron makes the gym a place to return to primitivity, or an animal state of nature. His antidote to the natural propensity for violence is not learning the skills of self-defense or experiencing pain for purification, as William relates. It is dominating and enacting violence towards the men of color with whom he has already equated toughness and violent intention. Aaron not only wants to frequent this "shitty" gym with killer-looking black and Latino men, but he seeks to subjugate them as well:

> It doesn't matter if you're poor, rich, or whatever. That's why it was a real thrill when I was beating up amateurs from Bed-Stuy. I'm scared, at that time. I was scared to walk in Bed-Stuy. I wouldn't go in Bed-Stuy. I'd never been in a subway in those days. I know nothing about this world, and I'm beating these guys up.

Because Aaron invests racialized men who are from dangerous sections of Brooklyn (as decoded in his representation of Bedford-Stuyvesant) with hypermasculinity, he can use them to assert his manliness. Defeating the representatives of an admired, marginalized form of masculinity is the vehicle by which Aaron can develop his own masculinity. Aaron believes, "This is pure male domination."[33]

The assumption of white-collar boxing is that proximity to the masculinity of the racial Other can help clients construct an identity. Clients narrate their motivations for boxing in a number of different registers, which can be more or less obviously racialized. For William, boxing is about purity; for Aaron, it is about male domination. Other clients, especially those who feel constrained by political correctness, seek out boxing for its "multiculture" or its promises for "primal return." However, boxing is racialized and gendered for most male white-collar clients, and though there is a spectrum along which they fall, when they explicate their interests in the sport, that spectrum is centered on a notion of black masculinity.[34] Whether white-collar men join the gym to be "one of the guys" or to dominate those same guys, there is an image of "the guys" that animates their decisions. Clients try to establish their own sense of manliness through a relationship to some idea of racialized masculinity. As Hazel Carby argues, abstract constructions of black masculinity are the vehicles for white men's personal growth and self-exploration.[35]

White-collar clients make Gleason's trainers and boxers of color the arbiters of the purity and primitivity that they seek from boxing. In attributing other abstract notions such as masculine aggression and toughness to these men, the clients presume an authentic black identity, and, in turn, construct a form of black masculinity. This masculinity is an embodied state of violence ("killer looking") and marginalization (again, as represented in the perceived social and economic circumstances of neighborhoods such as Bedford-Stuyvesant). It is conquerable with money and a little training and, thus, is for sale. Rather than drawing on the expertise of their trainers, clients produce and then consume an abstract notion of black masculinity in an attempt to know themselves better, specifically to prove their own manliness. Yet in looking for an authentic version of black masculinity, a fairly inauthentic representation of the sport is simulated.[36] As the fantasy camps, abbreviated training sessions, and no-hit rules of sparring show, the practices of boxing that clients use to construct and consume this form of black masculinity are not those of amateur or professional pugilists.

BUYING BLACKNESS AND RACIALIZED CONSUMERISM

The social philosopher Andre Gorz argues that a lack of work, coupled with an unequal distribution of free time, has created conditions in which the wealthy are able to buy time from the poor.[37] He suggests, "For a section at least of those who provide personal services, this type of social stratification amounts to subordination to and personal dependence upon the people they serve. A 'servile' class, which had been abolished by the industrialization of the post-war period, is again emerging."[38] The work of this emergent class, made up of housecleaners, waitresses, cooks, deliverymen, and personal shoppers, creates time for the economic elite, which they use for cultivation of self, consumption, and their own pleasure. Because the economic elite can generate in salary considerably more than they pay for domestic tasks, they purchase leisure time, which pushes those who have been marginalized and distanced from formal labor into a servile position. Gorz calls this process the South Africanization of society or "the realization of the colonial model within the metropolitan heartland."[39]

Trainers' work with white-collar clients is part of this sector of personal services.[40] At the most basic level, trainers provide for the white-collar clients' pleasure, and the white-collar clients' pleasure gives trainers work. There is little sovereignty in the trainer's role as they do not control the regimens of their clients. One could argue that money alone shapes the relationships between trainers and clients, but professional boxers also pay their trainers. So what is different in the case of the white-collar pugilist? Whereas the professional seeks the expertise of the trainer, expertise is secondary for the white-collar client. Consumption is primary.[41]

If boxing is a service industry, this is a racialized form of consumerism. White-collar clients' pleasure is structured through preconceptions. Ideas about masculinity, Bedford-Stuyvesant, criminality, violence, and boxing inform their quest for embodied purity and primitivity. These ideas enable the commodification of black masculinity and some notion of authentic racial identities. Here commodification is not just about labor power. Trainers' labor is commodified, to be sure, but their ontological being is also fetishized into a commodity. Clients buy the cachet of men who they believe fit the form of an authentic black masculinity. The trainer's expertise *is* important to this cachet, but it is a preconditional attribute rather than one that is utilized in the exchange with the white-collar client. Training amateurs and professionals merely qualifies trainers, a credential that constructs them, curiously, as both possessors of technical expertise and conduits to base and brute physicality.

Commodification produces further marginalization because there is no upward mobility for the servant class. Its members do not jump up to join the economic elite; these jobs hold people. All of the worst stereotypes animating white-collar boxing are predicated on positions of exclusion. Clients are drawn to a perceived peripheral relationship of men of color to the social or economic mainstream, or by the thrill of being in proximity to the dangerous, the wild, and the most clichéd tropes of primitivism. White-collar boxing is enabled by social and economic forms of racism and creates and then coexists with an ontogenetically grounded form. Blackness is valued and exchanged, and, in turn, generates new types of anti-black racism.

EPILOGUE

> "Human beings are driven not only to struggle to survive by making and remaking their material conditions of existence, but also to survive by making sense of the world and their place in it."
>
> —PAUL WILLIS, 2000

"WHEN THE BELL RINGS, COME OUT SWINGING." I LISTEN to the last line of Harry's voicemail greeting and bite my lip as I wait for the beep. I leave my message in a sputtering, nonsensical monologue. I am wiggling out of a scheduled workout, something that I have been doing for years. Sometimes I have a "headache"; other times I am sick to my stomach. On occasion, I am too tired or I need to "focus on my research." In my more dramatic moments, I have just recovered from a bloody nose and I am concerned that it could start bleeding again if I am punched. My cancellation doesn't bother Harry. He has long given up on me as a boxer and I pay him my training fees upfront at the beginning of the month in a lump sum. By the time I reach the gym to start my participation observation research, he will have forgotten that we had agreed on a training session earlier in the morning.

Harry also will not care about my cancellation because it happens to him all the time. Scores of boxing enthusiasts join Gleason's Gym eager to master the noble art. They find a trainer with whom to work, buy all the gear, and bound into the gym ready for action. Many think that taking up the sport will be easy, but it takes only a training session or two to disabuse them of this notion. Boxing is an extremely frustrating sport to learn. It requires the rare ability—at once intellectual and physical—to instantaneously translate heard information into bodily movement. It requires developing strategy on a moment's notice, thinking several steps ahead, and executing these moves while adapting to an opponent's decisions. Corporeally, boxing requires sophisticated and manifold technical skills, swift reflexes, great strength, and nymphlike agility. Psychologically, it requires near fearlessness and the capability to remain calm in situations in which most reasonable people would rightly panic. These requirements are met only by undertaking some of the most rigorous training of any sport and repeating the regimen over and over again until you are dripping with blood and sweat and dizzy with exhaustion. Not surprisingly, boxing trainers expect a fair amount of attrition.

The people I have written about in this book are different. They return to the gym time and time again when other people quit. They work to realize their goals and remain undeterred, if not unnerved, when they hit obstacles. They are exceptional; in the parlance of social science research, they are self-selecting. The qualities they possess enable them not only to become great athletes but also, I have tried to show, to create a range of social and economic possibilities in the gym to buffer the vicissitudes of postindustrial New York. The outcomes among gym participants are mixed, of course—the result of their material conditions and the life circumstances, aspirations, and desires that brought them to join Gleason's in the first place.

For many amateur boxers—poor men of color who have been all but shut out of a restrictive labor market—the gym offers a place to improvise work that provides opportunities for building individual and collective forms of identity and for forming intimate social relations with other men.[1] This work departs from conventional social scientific understandings of the concept; in many sociological schemas, the social and psychological features of work and the economic sustenance it provides are co-constituting.[2] While some of these social and psychological effects and benefits may accrue along with material recompense in some forms of labor, the connection does not hold in the context of Gleason's Gym. As shown, the sort of work that pays the bills, when available, rarely delivers the potential for the recognition, status, dignity, and sociality that amateurs cherish and seek in the urban gym; whatever social and cultural capital or moral and emotional fulfillment participants achieve from training their bodies is not a product of any sort of economic gain.

For the trainers of Gleason's Gym, even the work relationships that most closely adhere to a traditional economic transaction, namely those between trainers and white-collar clients, where there are overt monetary exchanges, are made possible by the other nontraditional work relationships. The phenomenon of white-collar boxing at Gleason's is driven by the cultural cachet—attended by no small amount of racial stereotyping—of training in proximity to amateurs working without wages and in a gym with a revered and hard-core boxing reputation, a reputation bolstered by the presence of those so committed to the sport that they work at it full-time without getting paid.[3]

The women who join and commit to the gym are as serious and self-selecting as their male counterparts. Over the past thirty years, they have marched into urban gyms, such as Gleason's, which historically banned them, to claim their right to engage in pugilistic exercises and develop the attendant identities and social relations. Often met with sexism, sexual advances, indifference, and ridicule, they generate their own possibilities from the sport. Through their training, they find out who they are, learn how to defend themselves, and discover how to trust themselves. As discussed in chapter 5, the selves they craft are strong, certain, and rooted in an intimate knowledge of their bodies and minds. For these women, rehearsing and enduring violent encounters in the safe and controlled space of the gym helps them understand violence and prepare for its arbitrary unleashing. Though profoundly ambivalent about brutality, female fighters style a number of tactics and strategies for resolving their uncertainty and developing into highly successful fighters. They also carve out a protected space for themselves in the urban gym, creating camaraderie, support, and community in the process.

White-collar clients, or *nouveau clientele*, do not always engage the same pugilistic rituals as competitive boxers, but they, too, create their own social possibilities in Gleason's Gym. With anxiety about their masculinities and substantial amounts of money, they fuel the political economy of white-collar boxing. While this economic arrangement reveals the entrepreneurialism of trainers, who are men of color with limited job prospects, it also illuminates some of the ways wealthy white men see low-income black men. With a multiplicity of new meanings of blackness circulating in the postindustrial economy, white-collar clients have novel resources in which to actively construct a specific racial and gender identity in their workouts with gym trainers. Paul Gilroy suggests that blackness, once a sign of inferiority and worthlessness, has gained cultural capital in an increasingly global political economy. He observes that "racial differences not only became integral to the process of selling and advertising things, they helped to name and fix various products in an elaborate system of racial symbols."[4] In addition to reifying "race," commercial uses of racial difference also produce new forms of racism. As argued earlier, when clients employ "authentic" black trainers, they fashion and commodify a concept of blackness that is primarily corporeal, defined by narratives of racial subjugation and criminal pasts. In white-collar boxing, blackness as a form of cultural capital is valued and bought. These particular pugilistic practitioners, then, generate instances of misrecognition and preclude opportunities for conviviality.

These differences in the ways people use the gym are evident in their outcomes. As with every relationship, boxers and trainers change, as do their investments in pugilism and the meanings of the urban gym. For example, after a period of depression, which he attributes to spending too much time in the gym, Mike tried to limit his hours at Gleason's and to cultivate outside, nonboxing relationships. He labored "only" from 6:00 a.m. to noon and from 3:00 p.m. to 8:00 p.m. and, for a short while, trained people at Mendez Boxing Gym instead of Gleason's. He continued to coach Max, who successfully turned professional, until Max was reincarcerated for a gun possession. He also trained Michael and Lily, both Golden Glove champions, and several other talented male and female amateurs. Eventually he left the New York City fight scene for Las Vegas, which offered a more vibrant sporting milieu. His transition went well. He currently runs a booming mixed-martial arts (MMA) program and is looking to buy his own gym.

Harry continues to work as a trainer but has taken up different work patterns. He served for years as head trainer to John Duddy, a now-retired middleweight from Northern Ireland with an excellent knockout record who drew huge crowds and who had the potential to offer Harry a handsome salary. But just as Duddy became famous, Harry was relieved of his responsibilities by Duddy's management, who wanted a big-name trainer and hired Don Turner, best known for training Evander Holyfield, and then Pat Burns. This decision took a huge emotional toll on Harry. He now takes on fewer amateur and white-collar boxers but remains devoted to Omar, Wells, Leon, and Lawrence, who do not compete but dabble in gym life now and again. Harry focuses primarily on professional fighters, albeit with less investment, and on a happy note, he was married several years ago.

The boxer-trainer relationships have changed as well, and almost all the remaining fighters either work with different trainers or have left the gym altogether. Scott, whom Mike trained for years, switched to working with Harry and then stopped boxing altogether. He got married, obtained work papers, and had a baby. His job and family responsibilities keep him from training. He follows the sport closely and frequently has people over for big fights. He has not lost his passion: The last time I went to his house to watch a fight on television, he paced around his living room when a Mexican fighter competed, covering his eyes and muttering "I am so nervous, I can't think." Anthony also stopped working with Mike. First, he worked with another of Gleason's trainers, and then he left the gym entirely in favor of another coach. He, too, has a family and works long hours, which affect his ability to train. Kenny stopped training after a falling out with Harry; their relationship was irreparable. Cedric lost interest in boxing, which left Harry worried about Cedric's future and disappointed about not being able to shape it.

Adrian cannot box anymore because he has bleeding on the brain. He was hit on the head with a lead pipe in a street altercation, and the several-years-old injury was discovered in a pre-fight examination just as he was turning pro. For years, he continued to visit the gym two days a week, though he had difficulty going to Mike and Harry's corner, where his former team members continued to train. He spent some time homeless, sleeping on trains when possible, and eventually was sentenced to months on Rikers Island. He would call me from jail and speak of deep depression but vowed never to be forcibly confined again. Eventually he found stable accommodation through a nonprofit organization that also treated an undiagnosed mental illness. Several months ago, he emailed me to say he was traveling the country. Diego moved to Florida with aspirations to go to college, but the last Mike heard, he had been back living New York and was re-incarcerated on Rikers Island on a parole violation. Diego's story is painfully common; many boxers experience unwanted and unwarranted stints in city jails and upstate prisons.

Among the women I knew, Maya and Joanne continue to compete and have successful professional careers. Lily won the Golden Gloves under Mike's direction and retired, though she will compete occasionally for charity. Danielle also retired after another Golden Gloves championship and is pursuing a graduate degree while starting a family.

DUMBO, the neighborhood Gleason's calls home, continues to gentrify. Now dubbed "Silicon Beach" by David Wallentas's Two Trees Management because of the density of technology firms—sixty-five companies in a five-block radius—the affluent area is growing, even boasting job vacancies in a post-2008 economy. While New York City's official unemployment rate stands around 9 percent, according to the DUMBO Business Improvement District, seventeen technology companies are desperate to fill 329 jobs.[5] As DUMBO has gentrified, so too has Gleason's Gym. White-collar boxing is thriving, and the proportion of clients in the total membership is steadily increasing—between 60 and 70 percent at any particular moment—changing the gym's tenor. Gleason's still offers fantasy camps and monthly competitions. In April 2012, Gleason's participated in "The Battle of the Barristers," a fundraiser for the Wounded Warrior Project and Gleason's Give a Kid a Dream program.[6] Twenty staff members from the Manhattan District Attorney's office fought, and according to the *Wall Street Journal Online*, "The event featured a regulation-sized boxing ring in the middle of the Broad Street Ballroom, a venue adorned with marble mosaic columns and a fresco-style mural that normally hosts galas and corporate functions. Professional lighting shone down on the fighters, and seats installed around the ring gave it a Las Vegas feel."[7] Gleason's also remains a popular destination for the culture industry; within the past several months, the popular TV show *White Collar* filmed at the gym, and it was the setting for photo shoots for Victoria's Secret, Sugar Ray Leonard, and Hugh Jackman.

The social context, meanings, and possibilities of Gleason's Gym—along with my analyses of them—are as historically contingent and defined by social and personal circumstance as are the lives of the gym members with whom I collaborated. The relationships and practices developed at Gleason's are so intense that they are often unsustainable in the long-term, born of great need and, in most cases, more need than they can satisfy to remain tenable. Though the gym offers many possibilities that are deeply meaningful for a time, these possibilities wither and wane as people move through life stages. The meaning making at Gleason's Gym helps people mediate the injuries of racial, class, and gender hierarchies, but it doesn't change those hierarchies. Instead, it operates within them. This is the landscape of postindustrial New York City, offering poor men of color, women, and white-collar men the ephemeral possibilities of new identities at the same time it packages and commodifies their lived experience.

Methodological Appendix: Ethnographic Research in the Urban Gym

I began conducting ethnographic research at Gleason's Gym in January of 2001. Initially I was interested in women's integration into the historically masculine space of the urban boxing gym and their participation in the sport. Gleason's Gym was a logical site of research because it was one of the first New York City gyms to offer women membership and because a high proportion of female fighters trained there. In addition, from my contact at *Ring Magazine*, Eric Raskin, I knew that the gym's owner, Bruce Silverglade, strongly supported women's boxing. Silverglade also had recently given a talk at Oxford University, and I hoped this would make him amenable to my ethnographic project.

Just one visit to Gleason's Gym made my research plan expand dramatically in scope. It took me only hours to realize that this community was adjusting to far more than female participation and that many important social phenomena related to class stratification, gender subordination, and racism were being expressed in and out of the gym's four rings. For the first six months of my research, I visited the gym once a week for a five-hour period. I became increasingly interested in the political economy of the gym as I noticed that some trainers were able to eke out an income from training sessions with white-collar clients. I began to study the economic and cultural components of this work, examining how the trainers understood their labor as well as how they, as "no-collar" workers, might be vulnerable to the whims of upper-middle- and upper-class fitness trends.[1] I also became interested in how laboring in the gym for so many hours a day allowed the trainers to develop deep bonds with amateur athletes. It seemed to me that the permanence and stability of trainers' workdays allowed them to undertake an informal social work with the boxers who sought their guidance. As several trainers told me, if they had been forced to work outside the gym, they would not have had the time for and access to so many amateur fighters. I wanted to know more about the social relations of the gym, especially between trainers and amateurs, many of whom used boxing and the urban gym to recover from criminal pasts and to avoid criminal futures.

After I had visited the gym several times, both the trainers and the fighters pressured me to try the sport myself so that I might understand boxing from a different perspective. For the next two years, I continued to frequent the gym once a week for roughly five hours per visit, but I broadened my participation in the gym by training to box. Gym regulars persuaded me that to comprehend, even cursorily, the bodily dimensions of pugilism—especially as they relate to discipline, pain, and dependence on a trainer—I would have to possess at least a preliminary understanding of pugilistic practices. I worked with Harry, a trainer whom I met on my first day of research. Harry taught me the basics of the sport, and my typical workout included running and climbing the StairMaster, shadowboxing, hitting the heavy bag, doing padwork,[2] undertaking stomach and strength exercises, and occasionally sparring with one of the male amateur or professional fighters on Harry's team, On the Ropes.[3]

In my fourth year of research, I immersed myself in the gym community completely and conducted ethnographic fieldwork full-time. From September 2003 to September 2004, I spent between six and fourteen hours in the gym five to six days a week, observing participants, interviewing people, and working with fighters, trainers, and clients. I developed close relationships with two trainers—Harry and Mike—and with the fighters of their teams, On the Ropes and Team One Boxing, respectively. I established a good rapport with other trainers in the gym and interacted with them on a regular basis. However, the sensitive nature of my interests, the intensity of boxing training, and the spacious layout of the gym, which prevented me from observing all social and athletic happenings at once, necessitated that I attach myself to one or two trainers and establish in-depth and consistent contact with them and with their fighters. Harry and Mike are both exceptional teachers and interlocutors, and they allowed me to append myself to their teams. Each day they would explain their goals, their methodologies, their concerns, and their successes, briefing me on their lives and the lives of their fighters. They answered my many insistent and ignorant questions about the logic and logistics of their work and, during the amateur fight season, took me to fights with their teams.

On a typical day, I would arrive at Gleason's Gym mid-morning and settle into Harry and Mike's part of the gym, where groups of amateurs, women, and professionals prepared to box. Such preparation can take ten minutes to two hours, depending on the degree of a fighter's sociability and the trainer's schedule. I would observe and participate in this sociality and then follow the boxers and their coaches to the various sites of their workouts: the heavy bag, the speed bag, the mirrors for shadowboxing, the floor for padwork, the ring for sparring, and the weights area. On Tuesdays, Thursdays, and Saturdays—common days for sparring—I would watch and sometimes record the spars. As I became more integrated into the community, I was recruited by trainers and fighters to help in training sessions by videotaping spars, lacing up and taping gloves, applying grease, tying shoes, and cleaning mouth gears. On rare occasions, I was placed in charge of a spar, working either with one fighter or with both sparring partners.

During the height of the amateur fight season, which stretched between January and April, I accompanied Harry and Mike to Golden Glove bouts in New York City and the Greater New York area. I rode with these trainers and their athletes in their cars, on the subway, and on trains, observing their interactions prior to fights. Where possible, I went into locker rooms to witness pre-fight preparation. I observed fighters and trainers during the fight and traveled back from the bouts with them to see how they coped with loss or celebrated victory. I also had the opportunity to attend several "smokers"—unsanctioned, illegal bouts—and apprenticed as an assistant second.[4] My job at the smokers was to pull the stool through the ropes before the head trainer stepped into the ring and to have the spit bucket and water bottles ready for the fighter. When the seconds-out bell rang, I removed the bucket, water, and stool before the round began.[5] On occasion I was allowed to work as an amateur cutman, applying grease to a fighter's face in between rounds—a tricky task designed to prevent cuts and excessive bleeding. I found both roles extremely stressful.

As I slowly became a gym regular, I was given a number of other tasks around the gym. I was recruited by Bruce Silverglade's assistant to work at monthly white-collar club and amateur shows, and my responsibilities included registering fighters for the shows and tournaments, ensuring that each fighter was armed with and returned the proper ounce gloves for their weight division, and selling tickets at the door. I sometimes helped with tasks associated with the everyday running of the gym, such as creating and updating an amateur's USA Boxing fight book, helping with mailings, and checking in members at the door. Occasionally I was asked to help fighters and trainers with tasks associated with the completion of paperwork—obtaining passports, filling out job applications, registering for tournaments, and acquiring driving directions to fights. I did some GED tutoring and a lot of babysitting. In the beginning of my time at the gym, people would request that I watch their children as they trained, but by the end of my tenure, several fighters would simply deposit their toddlers into my arms or leave their children in my "corner" of the gym.

Throughout my time at Gleason's Gym, I continued to train to box with Harry and occasionally with Mike. My progress was unimpressive, I hated the workouts, and I was a source of great frustration for my trainers. But I did learn a lot about the bodily dimensions of the sport, especially about the anxiety of hitting another human, the shock of and anger at being punched, the exhaustion of a round, and the complete reliance on a trainer for instruction, encouragement, and guidance. I developed a deep appreciation for the skill and commitment necessary to be a successful boxer and the frustrating process that sharpening one's technique can entail.

Though training was a component of my research, it was not my primary focus or the primary means by which I collected data. I did not train intensely, and I never intended to compete. I found that on the days I devoted time to training, my regimen precluded recording and understanding any gym phenomena except my own personal fitness, fatigue, and failure. I realized that one of the dangers of focusing too heavily on one's personal relationship to boxing is the tendency to universalize experience and understand an individual relationship to training as that of all boxers. The introduction of women and white-collar clients to Gleason's has produced a new political economy of boxing and a new form of pugilism in general, which generated different data.

I am frequently asked what it was like to be a white middle-class woman conducting research in a gym frequented by men of color. This question always baffles me because I believe people develop solidarity in a number of ways. People develop communities, friendships, and loyalties on the basis of many experiences, histories, and backgrounds. Though in the United States, we are socialized to understand solidarity as emerging from identity—race, class, gender, sexuality, and (dis)ability—at Gleason's Gym there were, and continue to be, several bases for my relationships. For some boxers, especially female fighters, my experiences as a competitive Division I athlete made me an empathetic discussant about competition anxiety. Though track and field is a very different sport than boxing, apprehension about competition in both produces uncomfortable emotions, which can be mitigated by discussing their aspects. For other boxers, it was being able to pass long periods of time talking about anything from Jennifer Lopez's romantic relationships, Ronald Reagan's funeral, exotic New York City pets, and recent fights to outrageous rent prices, the difficulties of locating dignified employment, the racism of the United States' criminal justice system, and the imperialism of the US invasion of Iraq. As a nontraining member of the gym and thus a free pair of arms, and as a woman, I was someone with whom some male boxers could trust their babies and children. Asking about and being updated frequently on a child's growth and development produced strong friendships. But probably the most important way that I developed bonds with most fighters and trainers was, very simply, to listen to them and to be interested in their struggles and their dignity. I found that people responded positively to a respect for and support of their aspirations as they attempted to create purposeful work and identities for themselves in the gym.

It is important to note that how I became accepted by this community is less about me and more about the community itself. At Gleason's Gym, one usually is accepted if one cares about people, treats others with respect, is willing to pass time, joke, and deliberate, and is committed to the sport of boxing. Though it may seem overly idealizing to say so, this community functions despite differences in class, race, ethnicity, gender, and sexuality. And yet the development of my access to and friendships at Gleason's Gym did shape the type of data I collected. I do not believe that there is one objective truth about the boxing gym but rather that there are multiple truths at any field site. These truths are shaped by the researcher's activities and understanding of the social world as well as by a complicated and near inexplicable coagulation of researcher and participant personalities, politics, and worldviews. To be sure, I do not think that all narratives of social life at Gleason's Gym would be equally plausible or that all accounts of training ought to be categorized as *fictocriticism*.[6] Rather, I believe that there are dominant readings of the urban gym that depend on where and how one conducts research. Gleason's Gym can be understood in a particular way because of the situated knowledges my participants possessed *in* Harry and Mike's corner of the gym and that I developed conducting research *from* Harry and Mike's corner.[7]

Come Out Swinging is derived from the situated knowledges of Harry and Mike's corner—a small plastic table with a bunch of plastic chairs scattered in front of rows of lockers, tucked in the back of Gleason's Gym. Methodologically, it emerges from four years of participant observation research and over one thousand pages of coded field notes, fifty open-ended and semistructured interviews with fighters, trainers, clients, and other gym regulars that ranged from one and a half to three hours in length, and several episodes of video solicitation. It also is derived from five months of archival research on boxing training manuals from the eighteenth, nineteenth, and twentieth centuries in the Beinecke Rare Book and Manuscript Library at Yale University.

Notes

PREFACE

1. I use the term "of color" not to suggest fixed or stable racial and ethnic categories but rather to mark processes of racialization as well as opportunities for racist thought, discourses, and practices to shape the lived experience of people in the gym. I use the terms "black" and "Latino" when study participants identify or self-identify as such or when the literature specifies. My participants overwhelmingly self-identify as black.
2. Delaney 1999.
3. Gleason's Gym 2010a (accessed Aug. 20, 2012).
4. See, e.g., Wacquant 2009; Pager 2007; Western 2006; Mincey 2006; Orfield 2004; Wacquant, Loic 2004; Wacquant 2001; Wilson 1996, 1987.
5. Dworkin and Wachs 2009.
6. Gilroy 2010.
7. Title IX mandated equal funding for girls and boys in educational programming and in activities receiving federal money, such as sports. For more on the history and significance of Title IX, see Title IX Info 2012 (accessed July 15, 2012).
8. My ethnography differs from Loic Wacquant's ethnography, *Body and Soul: Notebooks of An Apprentice Boxer* in several ways. First, the relationships between Gleason's Gym and postindustrial Brooklyn differ from the relationships between the Woodlawn Boys Club and Chicago's Southside. According to Wacquant, the Woodlawn Boys Club "offers a relatively self-enclosed site for a protected sociability where one can find a respite from the pressures of the street and the ghetto, a world into which external events rarely penetrate and onto which they have little impact" (p. 26). Gleason's Gym is not a self-enclosed space and cannot "protect one from the street" or function as

"a buffer against the insecurity of the neighborhood and the pressures of everyday life" (p. 14). Rather my Brooklyn gym is open to the complexities, troubles, and challenges of "the streets." The problems of the outside world intrude, and, as I will show, boxers and trainers spend significant time in the gym negotiating the vicissitudes of life outside the gym (for more on this point see Hoffman and Fine 2005). Second, the demographics of Gleason's Gym vary greatly from the gym where Wacquant conducted fieldwork. At Gleason's, there are women and white-collar clients, two groups that do not appear at the Woodlawn Boys Club. The presence of these two groups has changed the political economy, social relations, and relations of power within the urban gym. Hence the lived experience of gym culture is different in Gleason's than in Woodlawn. Third, Wacquant's participants and their outcomes postprison diverge from many of my participants and their outcomes. Wacquant's comrades hail largely from Chicago's working class and appear to experience a unidirectional movement from criminality to desistance once they become members of the gym's "island of stability and order" (Wacquant 2004:26). Many of my participants are not working class but are characterized more as subproletariat or even lumpenproletariat. They did not enjoy the "stable families that cultivate a set of working-class habits and virtues" (Geurts 2005:145). My participants also experience quite different outcomes when they reenter society from jail or prison, largely returning to criminal labor despite significant and full participation in gym routines, regimens, and culture. And except for the interruption of forced confinement (or because of it?), a member of the subproletariat can maintain "a sense of discipline, a physical and mental asceticism" (Wacquant 2004:44); one can be a drug salesmen and an accomplished Golden Glove champion. Finally, the data I collected as a female ethnographer who did not engage in rigorous boxing training are different than the data Wacquant collected and shape my perspective as well as the analyses and interpretations that I make.

9. These collections of principles, practices, and relations constitute what E. P. Thompson calls a "moral economy." In his work on the eighteenth-century bread riots, Thompson analyzes the "*mentalité*" that led to mass action and argues that in this *mentalité* was an underlying notion of rights (Thompson 1993:260). In *The Making of the English Working Class*, he writes: "In 18th-century Britain riotous actions assumed two different forms: that of more or less spontaneous popular direct action; and that of the deliberate use of the crowd as an instrument of pressure, by persons 'above' or apart from the crowd. The first form has not received the attention, which it merits. It rested upon more articulate popular sanctions and was validated by more

sophisticated traditions than the word 'riot' suggests. The most common example is the bread or food riot, repeated cases of which can be found in almost every town and county until the 1840s. This was rarely a mere uproar, which culminated in the breaking open of barns or the looting of shops. It was legitimised by the assumptions of an older moral economy, which taught the immorality of any unfair method of forcing up the price of provisions by profiteering upon the necessities of the people" (Thompson 1966:62–63). Thompson draws a distinction between political economy, or the development of the free market, and the existence of an older paternalistic order and argues, "Actions on such a scale . . . indicate an extraordinarily deep-rooted pattern of behaviour and belief . . . these popular actions were legitimised by the old paternalist moral economy" (p. 66). He continues, "In considering only this one form of 'mob' action we have come upon unsuspected complexities, for behind every such form of popular direct action some legitimising notion of right is to be found" (p. 68). In *Customs in Common*, Thompson contends: "It is possible to detect in almost every eighteenth-century crowd action some legitimising notion. By the notion of legitimation I mean that the men and women in the crowd were informed by the belief that they were defending traditional rights or customs; and, in general, that they were supported by the wider consensus of the community. On occasion this popular consensus was endorsed by some measure of licence afforded by the authorities. More commonly, the consensus was so strong that it overrode motives of fear or deference" (Thompson 1993:188). What is meant by a moral economy of the gym is a collective, though not always uncontested, sense of what the community considers fair and just. It claims and actualizes a set of rights unavailable outside of the gym and sets and enforces social norms, obligations, and behavior. Like the participants in E. P. Thompson's eighteenth-century bread crowd, men and women of the gym assert and defend certain customs. The gym's moral economy is both an answer to postindustrial capitalism and unique in its own right: an anticapitalist indictment and a system of morality. As Paul Gilroy suggests, a moral economy need not deny political economic conditions—indeed, such conditions are responsible for the groupings of people in the gym. Gilroy argues moral economy does not "downplay the fundamental significance or scope of political economy but [contests] the limited place provided in that paradigm for questions of morality and political culture. Those components of social and economic interaction lie at the heart of the critique of consumer capitalism and its freedoms" (Gilroy 2010:7).

10. Willis 2000; Dworkin and Wachs 2009.

CHAPTER ONE. SURVIVAL IN A CITY TRANSFORMED: THE URBAN BOXING GYM IN POSTINDUSTRIAL NEW YORK

1. Because the term *postindustrial* is used in contradictory ways, some scholars argue the term amounts, essentially, to empty rhetoric (Wilensky 2003). Other scholars warn that the term is not a neutral description but rather "a cultural artifact, a discursive practice serving attempts to make sense of the political, economic, social, and cultural changes of the contemporary period. . . . [I]t serves certain interests while offering an interpretation of the world, and so its meaning should be, and is, contested" (Neisser and Schram 1994:44). Some caution the "post" inaccurately suggests the complete obliteration of industrial production (Wilensky 2003; Kester 1993:76; Mollenkopf and Castells 1991:6), while others lament that the term is ahistorical. Richard Gillam writes, "For to speak of a postindustrial society, in which everything is new, unprecedented, is also to imply that only the present (and the future) have to count. The study of the past thereby loses credibility; those who feel dislocated—'unstuck in time'—can take refuge in largely ahistorical analysis" (Gillam 1982:78). Finally, some suggest that discussions about the postindustrial manifest teleological assumptions of technological inevitability. Grant Kester writes, "Underlying many of these celebrations, critiques, analyses, and descriptions [of postindustrialism] is a common set of assumptions about technological innovation and material progress" (Kester 1993:76). Kester worries that the vanishing use of class suggests that the social consequences of capitalism are resolved, rather than displaced to the periphery: "One of the most significant results has been the gradual erosion of class as an analytic category in postindustrial culture, and a corresponding confidence in the triumph of technology and rational planning over the 'crisis' tendencies of the capitalist economy" (Kester 1993:75–76).
2. Vitale 2008:95; Venkatesh 1994:160.
3. Saskia Sassen suggests, "US direct foreign investment in off-shore manufacturing facilities grew immensely over the decade of the 1970s[,] indicating that an increasing number of US manufacturing jobs are now abroad" (Sassen 1990:469).
4. Bailey and Waldinger 1991:43; Mollenkopf and Castells 1991:30.
5. Mollenkopf and Castells 1991:7.
6. Bailey and Waldinger 1991:46.
7. Sassen 2001:79.
8. Lloyd 2010: 41; Mollenkopf and Castells 1991:6.
9. Sassen 2001; Lazzarato 1996.
10. Sassen 2001:xx.

11. Persuad and Lusane 2000:26.
12. Ibid., 23.
13. Persuad and Lusane 2000:22; Neisser and Schram 1994:43; Venkatesh 1994:176.
14. Wilensky 2003:5. Randolph B. Persuad and Clarence Lusane assert, "Involuntary contingent workers in particular, such as security guards, sales clerks and office cleaners, who now number tens of millions, are the most vulnerable of all workers, at the beck and call of capital, and considered disposable labour" (Persuad and Lusane 2000:23).
15. Persuad and Lusane 2000:22; Neisser and Schram 1994:43.
16. Persuad and Lusane 2000:27.
17. Sassen 2001:85.
18. Ibid. 82; Sassen 1990:467.
19. Rose 1994:27; Bailey and Waldinger 1991:46.
20. Wacquant 2009:57; Neisser and Schram 1994:43.
21. Wacquant 2009: 56. Persuad and Lusane argue that historically, manufacturing—especially in automotive and steel—provided workers who had little educational training with jobs that paid a living wage. This benefited black families who, because of racist laws and practices, had not had the same educational opportunities as whites. As a result, between the 1930s and 1970s, black workers relied heavily on manufacturing jobs for social and economic advancement (Persuad and Lusane 2000:23). This may be a slightly optimistic view of the economic circumstances of blacks in these four decades. However, the point that paths to social and economic advancement were blocked with the advent of postindustrialism is an important one.
22. Krough 1991 cited in Venkatesh 1994:160; Pager 2007; Pager and Quillian 2005; Venkatesh 1994:160; Mollenkopf and Castells 1991:8.
23. Eckholm 2006.
24. Mollenkopf and Castells 1991:8.
25. Richard Lloyd writes, "Already by 1980, new patterns of development in older industrial spaces of the industrial past reimagined around the residential and consumption requirements of a new class of urban residents, white-collar (or 'no-collar') workers in the growth sector of the postindustrial city" (Lloyd 2010:29).
26. Mollenkopf and Castells 1991:8.
27. Vitale 2008:63-64.
28. Rose 1994:27.
29. Tricia Rose argues that as many US cities reorganized economically, they simultaneously lost massive amounts of federal funding for social-welfare programs and social services and faced fiscal crises. She explains New York

City's crisis: "As John Mollenkopf notes, 'during the 1970s, the US system of cities crossed a watershed. New York led the other old, industrial metropolitan areas into population and employment decline.' The federal funds that might have offset this process had been diminishing throughout the 1970s. In 1975 President Ford's unequivocal veto to requests for a federal bail out to prevent New York from filing for bankruptcy made New York a national symbol for the fate of older cities under his administration. Virtually bankrupt and in a critical state of disrepair, New York City and New York State administrators finally negotiated a federal loan, albeit one accompanied by an elaborate package of service cuts and that carried harsh repayment terms. 'Before the crisis ended,' David Walkowitz notes, '60,000 city employees went off the payroll, and social and public services suffered drastic cuts. The city had avoided default only after the teachers' union allowed its pension fund to become collateral for city loans' " (Rose 1994:28).

30. Persuad and Lusane 2000:22. They continue: "The 'economy is great' discourse also masks and justifies the retreat by the state from responsibility for the elimination of poverty, marginalization and immiseration. However, the new ideology of 'personal responsibility,' which increasingly dominates the popular media and discourse within the public sphere, generates a cultural response that wins many to the belief that state responsibility towards the poor and subaltern should be eliminated. A 'winner-takes-all' mentality grows with media-driven beliefs that the market is the only source of capable of addressing human social needs" (Persuad and Lusane 2000:24). For another detailed account of the implications of personal responsibility discourses and ideologies, see Wacquant 2009.

31. Wacquant 2009:93. Persuad and Lusane write, "Welfare reform was consistent with the new imperatives of capital which was increasingly ridding itself of nation-state boundaries and, more critically, of regulation. In addition, privatisation became the solution to the nation's social problems. And along with privatisation came racialisation" (Persuad and Lusane 2000: 31).

32. Of the connection between welfare retrenchment and the explosion of crime control, Loic Wacquant argues, "the downsizing of the social-welfare sector of the state and the concurrent upsizing of its penal arm are functionally linked, forming, as it were, the two sides of the same coin of state restructuring in the nether regions of social and urban space in the age of ascending neoliberalism" (Wacquant 2009:43). For a smart account of the emergence of New York's "quality of life" campaign and focus on crime and social control through personal responsibility narratives, see Alex Vitale's *City of Disorder: How the Quality of Life Campaign Transformed New York Politics.* Vitale defines quality-of-life policy makers as having policies that "were to reject the

central role of the state as a force for both social reform and planning and the culture of tolerance. Instead, they relied on market principles through the privatization of public spaces and services and an overall shrinkage of government. In addition to privatization, they supported, at least rhetorically, greater community and business control of the delivery of government services and of planning at the expense of expert planners" (Vitale 2008:30).

33. In some states, as in California, one of the so-called strikes could be from prior decades. In others, the three strikes can take place in a single event. Michelle Alexander writes, "First and second strikes are counted by individual charges, rather than individual cases, so a single case can result in first, second, and even third strikes" (Alexander 2012:91).

34. Truth-in-sentencing laws mandate that offenders serve the majority—usually 85%—of their prison sentences. In some states, such as Wisconsin, truth-in-sentencing laws replaced parole. In many states, "good time" has been eliminated and "bad time" added onto sentences.

35. Alexander 2012:93; Petersilia 2003:22.

36. Western 2006; Western et al. 2002:165. David Garland demonstrates how the free market and the emergence and popular support of conservative politics beginning in the 1980s shaped the crime industry rather than an objective incidence or prevalence of crime. He contends, "The private actors of civil society developed their own adaptations to the new pervasiveness of crime, their own routine precautions and social controls, and it is these adaptations (rather than the crime rates themselves) that account for the political and cultural salience that crime has taken in recent years" (Garland 2001:x–xi).

37. Parenti 1999:213.

38. Wacquant 2009:16, 37.

39. Alexander 2012:7; Pager 2007; Western 2006; Mauer and Chesney-Lind 2002; Davis 2000; James 2000; Mauer 1999b.

40. Lloyd 2010:15. For a brilliant ethnographic account of how artists marshaled postindustrial resources to transform the Chicago neighborhood of Wicker Park, see Richard Lloyd's *Neo-Bohemia: Art and Commerce in the Postindustrial City*.

41. Grazian 2003:2.

42. Ibid., 115.

43. Currid 2007:3; Garland 2001:77–82.

44. Currid 2007:10.

45. Lloyd 2010:90.

46. Ibid., 34. Currid suggests, "Cultural producers understood—and quickly—the links between their symbolic capital and economic gains, which is how rapper Diddy and Jennifer Lopez managed to create clothing empires,

Stephen Sprouse painted graffiti-covered bags for Louis Vuitton, and artists like Futura and Lee Quinones designed sneakers for Nike and Adidas respectively" (Currid 2007:40).

47. Willis 2000. Dworkin and Wachs write, "Scholars argue that 'male body panic,' or male preoccupation with appearance, has become more prevalent with the advent of consumer culture in the postindustrial era" (2009:66).
48. Dworkin and Wachs 2009:2.
49. Ibid., 70, 38.
50. Ibid., 38–39.
51. Ibid., 63.
52. Ibid., 11. It is also noteworthy that these politically charged narratives were increasingly fostered by popular culture and Hollywood. See Jeffords 1993 and Dyer 1997.
53. Farrell 1996.
54. Ackman 2002.
55. Included in the category of "serious boxing gym" are the Times Square Gym and Kingsway Boxing and Fitness in Manhattan and Gleason's Gym in Brooklyn (Delany 1999:xi; Hamill 1996).
56. Ackman 2002.
57. Amateur boxing is also referred to as Olympic boxing.
58. Though the number of gyms registered in both years is the same, the actual gyms registered are different. In 2004, there were six gyms registered in Brooklyn, five in the Bronx, seven in Queens, and ten in Manhattan. In 2005, there were six in Brooklyn (and even these six were different than the year before), six in the Bronx, nine in Queens, and seven in Manhattan.
59. The Golden Gloves tournament was by founded in 1923 by the *Chicago Tribune* sports editor Arch Ward as a citywide amateur competition. The event took place in the Chicago Stadium and was sponsored by the *Tribune*. Because boxing was ruled illegal in Illinois in 1924, the second tournament did not run again until 1928, when boxing once again was legal (primarily so Chicago could host the September 1927 Dempsey-Tunney fight), and it has run annually ever since. In 1927, the *New York Daily News* started its own tournament in New York City, and the winners of the Chicago and New York tournaments competed for a national Golden Gloves title. Other newspapers in regions all over country began their own tournaments in the 1930s (Hickok Sports 2006; Seconds Out 2004; both accessed July 22, 2011).
60. Again, the gyms and programs in this category are usually devoted to white-collar boxers, but sporadically a professional fighter will spend time at a fitness club like Crunch in order to escape the pressures of competitive gyms and to take advantage of the quiet and resources. For example, junior

welterweight Sechew Powell trains out of Gleason's with coach Angel Rivera, but because Rivera is also a trainer at Crunch Gym in Manhattan, Powell will often use Crunch as his base.

61. Trinity Boxing Gym rate schedule, http://trinityboxing.com/ny-ratesschedule (accessed August 8, 2011).

62. For example, limited space means that the gym can fit only one or two rings. This, in turn, means that fighters often have long wait-times to get into the ring to shadowbox or spar. Long wait-times discourage fighters from working out at the gym and maintaining their commitment to that particular gym. Over time, this limits membership and the gym's financial resources.

63. Gleason's Gym 2010a (accessed July 22, 2011).

64. Mee 2004.

65. The Swank case is a good example of how much publicity can be generated from a celebrity simply saying she trained at Gleason's Gym. Bruce Silverglade reports a dramatic increase in gym memberships among white-collar boxers and competitive women at Gleason's Gym since *Million Dollar Baby* was released. This has enormous financial repercussions for the gym, which supports itself through membership dues and depends on word-of-mouth publicity. This also has important implications for the gym's trainers, who will earn between $20 and $75 per session working with new gym clients. Other gyms around the country have experienced a similar surge in interest among female boxers. In an April 2005 article, "'Million Dollar Baby' Gives More Women Fighting Spirit," the *Chicago Tribune* reported a tripling in female registrations for the 2005 Chicago Golden Gloves Tournament, as well as an increase in inquiries at Chicago gyms such as JABB Boxing Center (Hirsley 2005).

66. Rhoden 1991.

67. Hindo and Cohn 2004.

CHAPTER TWO. WORK WITHOUT WAGES

1. During the 2003–2004 academic year, Gleason's membership dues were $55 per month for amateur boxers and $70 per month for professional fighters and white-collar clients. Because this fee is cost-prohibitive for many amateurs, their trainers often pay their dues.

2. This chapter focuses on amateur men and not amateur women. Because amateur women do not have the same social circumstances as amateur men, they do not have the same relationships to prison, education systems, social welfare, and social housing. This chapter examines how amateur men use the gym to respond to those social circumstances.

3. I use Richard Sennett's characterizations of dignity, status, and prestige. Sennett argues that status, prestige, recognition, honor, and dignity are aspects of respect. Status refers to one's place in a social hierarchy. Status dictates whose needs are legible and who is recognized. Prestige "refers to the emotions which status arouses in others." Recognition is a complicated term often used in legal discourse but expanded upon by scholars such as Rousseau to encompass "mutual acknowledgment . . . of social behavior as much as of legal right." Sennett suggests that recognition is not sufficient for understanding mutual need. He uses Bourdieu to define honor, which "supposes 'an individual who sees himself always through the eyes of others, who has need of others for his existence, because the image he has of himself is indistinguishable from that presented to him by other people.' " Dignity is linked with labor. Sennett writes that the dignity of work has "become a universal value," explaining, "The historians Linda Gordon and Nancy Fraser phrase that value as follows: 'The worker tends to become the universal social subject: everyone is expected to "work" and to be "self-supporting." ' Any adult not perceived as a worker shoulders a heavier burden of self-justification" (Sennett 2003: 53–58).
4. For this line of argument, see Willis 2000, Wilson 1996.
5. The Crime Bill of 1994, or Public Law No. 103-322, was designed to "increase police presence, to expand and improve cooperative efforts between law enforcement agencies and members of the community to address crime and disorder problems, and otherwise to enhance public safety" (Library of Congress 2012). "Tough on crime" practices abolished rehabilitation, for the most part, and fixated instead on an array of new penalties and policies, such as three-strike rules, truth-in-sentencing laws, victim impact statements, sentencing guidelines, and "zero tolerance." Longer sentences than ever before were imposed, and the number of nonviolent acts considered criminal expanded, which increased the prison population, even as crime rates dropped (Petersilia 2003). A provision in the Violent Crime Control and Law Enforcement Act of 1994 allowed states to evaluate the "adult nature of the crime" and bypass juvenile court, sentencing sixteen- and seventeen-year-olds to years in maximum security prisons in New York State (Library of Congress 2012).
6. Horton 1972:24.
7. Wynn 2002.
8. Parenti 1999. In 1982, 350 college programs operated in US prisons; by 2006, eight remained (Fine et al. 2001 [accessed July 15, 2012]).
9. Parenti 1999:43.
10. Pager 2007.

11. According to my participants, finding and keeping work remains one of the most stressful aspects of postprison supervision. Michelle Alexander finds similar stressors: "In fact, a study by the Vera Institute found that during the first month after release from prison, people consistently were more preoccupied with finding work than anything else. Some of the pressure to find work comes directly from the criminal justice system. According to one survey of state parole agencies, forty of the fifty-one jurisdictions surveyed (the fifty states and the District of Columbia) required parolees to 'maintain gainful employment.' Failure to do so could mean more prison time" (Alexander 2012:148.) For some of the most comprehensive review—qualitative, legal, and historical—and analysis of postindustrial parole, see Scott-Hayward 2011. Fall. For a historical overview of how the initial mission of parole supervision—the encouragement of disciplined workers—has transmogrified in a postindustrial labor market with high levels of joblessness, see Simon 1993.
12. Katherine Newman argues that workers of color are more likely to be fired in recessions than white workers.
13. I focus on some of the individual repercussions of forced confinement, such as the material conditions and identities of fighters, rather than the social or political repercussions, which Patricia Allard rightly calls "post-conviction penalties." For a thoughtful discussion of postconviction penalties or collateral consequences, see Mauer and Chesney-Lind 2002; and Travis 2000.
14. Willis 2000:86.
15. Ibid., 87–88.
16. Ibid., 92.
17. Dworkin and Wachs 2009; Willis 2000:95.
18. According to Georg Bauer, boxing athlete and scholar, "In some countries, the techniques are also different in amateur boxing. A cross, for instance, is rarely taught in Austrian Olympic boxing gyms but is part of the regular inventory in professional boxing gyms. Professional fighters' trainers have told me to keep both heels on the ground and twist my hip with every punch in an almost comically exaggerated fashion" (written personal communication, July 29, 2012).
19. Booth 2000.
20. Ibid., 11.
21. Ibid., 8.
22. Arinde 2004.
23. The amateur men I discuss in this chapter explicitly refer to themselves as boxers by profession. Not all amateur men in Gleason's Gym talk about boxing as their job. Firefighters and police officers, for example, who constitute

a relatively small percentage of amateur fighters, consider boxing a leisure pursuit and explicitly referred to it as a pastime.

24. Hamill 1996.
25. Sherman 2005.
26. See Wacquant 2004.
27. For a detailed description and incisive analysis of the many ways low-income men and women generate income and make ends meet outside of the formal economy, see Venkatesh 2006.
28. According to Joan Petersilia, meeting the terms of parole can be so challenging and the penalties of their violation so harsh that some prisoners in Massachusetts are choosing to forfeit the possibility of parole and instead choosing to serve out their entire sentences (Petersilia 2003). Some standard conditions of release for US Code offenders are: reporting to the district specified on the certificate of release and to the assigned probation officer within three days; obtaining written permission from the probation office in order to leave the district; notifying the probation officer within two days of changing residences; submitting "complete and truthful" written reports to the probation officer at the beginning of each month; refraining from violating any law or associating with those participating in criminal activity; if arrested, reporting to the probation officer within two days; working regularly unless excused by the probation officer and supporting dependents; reporting within two days with any changes to employment; avoiding possessing or purchasing illegal substances; avoiding visiting "places where such drugs are illegally sold, dispensed, used or given away"; avoiding socializing with others with criminal records unless given permission by the probation officer; avoiding possession of firearms; permitting searches and confiscation by the probation officer at his or her discretion; making "a diligent effort to satisfy any fine, restitution order, court costs or assessment, and/or court ordered child support or alimony payment that has been, or may be, imposed" by the probation officer; submitting to drug tests (United States Parole Commission 2004) (accessed 2004.)
29. Stephen "Donny" Donaldson argues that men of small build are preyed upon in prison (Donaldson 2001).
30. Though many amateur fighters can provide complex critiques of society, their analyses are not accompanied by arguments for social justice, liberation, or other forms of freedom. They place few demands on an outside world that has foreclosed access to a decent wage. The re-creation work in the gym naturalizes the world as is. When discussing unemployment, incarceration, and failed educational systems, amateur boxers acknowledge racial inequality but also accept this expression of social and economic injury as

an inevitable feature of modern life. Racial segregation and urban marginality are conceptualized as damaging yet natural by-products of power. Mike argues that "if it were the other way around, we [racialized people] would be complaining about the white people livin' in Bed-Stuy." Anthony philosophizes that history is both "cyclical" and "inevitable," and this fact eclipses any sort of intervention into history's legacy of racial and class oppression.

CHAPTER THREE. TOUGH LOVE AND INTIMACY IN A COMMUNITY OF MEN

1. Unlike professional boxers or white-collar clients, most male amateur fighters do not pay for their boxing instruction and overwhelmingly are a financial liability for their trainers. At best, amateurs cost their trainers money in time—when trainers could be working with clients or even up-and-coming professionals—and at worst, amateurs cost their trainers money for boxing-related expenses, such as gym memberships and tournament fees, and for non-boxing-related expenses, such as MetroCards, meals, utilities, and even tuition for college.

Not all trainers will work with amateurs because of the emotional and financial involvement. Jeremy does not like training amateurs because he considers them "hard-headed" and "stubborn." Aaron sees boxing as a business and will only coach people who can pay: "I'm not looking to do any freebies. I'm not naive enough to think that some fucking kid is going to stay with me five years later as I train him for free. And I'm not so fucking succubus that I want to suck off someone else's skill. I fought myself. That's it. I don't need some fucking kid to win something for me. . . . I love the work I do. I do it because I love it. I would almost do it for free but I won't because, as you know, I won't do anything for free because it's just inherently wrong."

Other trainers take on a few amateurs but remain wary of devoting their entire practice to "charity cases," Ricardo's characterization of amateur fighters. Ricardo is a former European Boxing Champion who trains primarily white-collar clients, occasionally taking on the highly talented amateur but with reservations. Karl acknowledges that training amateurs puts a trainer in the position of being "a psychologist, a father, a business manager," but he tries to avoid being a mentor: "I try to avoid that role. I really do because it's a business. Even though we can talk, and we can do this and that, it's still a business. I gotta go home, and I gotta pay my rent, and you gotta do what you gotta do. I still gotta pay my bills. But if I can see I can help you, and you trying, and you really worth it, and we're committed, I'll help you out every now and then. But don't make a habit of it. I will give money out—if you need help I will help you. But not chronically. Don't make a habit of it."

2. In this chapter, I use the masculine pronoun to refer to amateur boxers because the chapter focuses on the distinctly homosocial relationships that develop between male trainers and fighters. My analysis of mentoring and mediation does not apply to women or white-collar boxers because they are not in the same social-structural positions as the gym's male amateur fighters.
3. I use the term "kinship" rather than the more common term "fictive kinship" because all forms of kinship are fictive in a sense. And to call kinship that is not constructed on the basis of bloodline "fictive" is to normalize a concept that centers on traditional understandings of the family—in this case, the nuclear family. My use of "kinship" insists that the relationships forged in the gym are not simply compensation for a lack and that the intimacies are qualitatively different than mere coping mechanisms or substitutions for family positions. In *All Our Kin*, Carol Stack explores the domestic cooperation and exchange of goods and services between black kin in "The Flats." Though problematic in a few ways, among them that kinship is framed as a coping mechanism and thus is set against the normalcy of the nuclear family (which simultaneously disregards that every familial arrangement is a coping mechanism of sorts), Stack shows that the inventiveness and creativity of kin relatedness in the midst of urban struggle have existed for generations (Stack 1974). As Judith Butler writes, "The struggle to legitimate African-American kinship dates back to slavery, of course" (Butler 2000:73).
4. Having worked so closely with two trainers—Mike and Harry—I draw heavily on their experiences. But based on comparison with the broader body of my research, their understandings are not uncommon but rather generalizable to roughly twenty-five of the gym's eighty trainers.
5. Trainers believe that Mondays are bad days for sparring because fighters—both male and female—are likely to have partied or had sex during the weekend, tiring themselves out. Exhausted athletes will not be as alert in the ring so it is considered dangerous to have them spar. The prohibition against sex and drinking is historical; it appears as early as the late eighteenth century in boxing training manuals. Regarding competition preparation, a pupil of Humphreys and Mendoza writes of "taking constant care to avoid any thing like excess in either food, wine, woman, or even exercise" (A Pupil Both of Humphreys and Mendoza 1784).
6. Oates 1994:15.
7. It is interesting to note that sociologist Alex Vitale likens Mayor Rudolph Giuliani's decision to move away from urban liberalism (e.g., therapy, rehabilitation) to policing as "tough love." He writes, "When Giuliani took office

in 1994, he turned Dinkins's policing experiments into major citywide operations. He evicted dozens of homeless encampments, displaced squeegee men, and ordered the police to harass homeless people through the zero-tolerance enforcement of minor infractions. In the shelter system he attempted to transform the rules of accountability for homeless people by charging them for staying in shelters and threatening them with eviction from the shelter system, loss of benefits, and even separation from their families for failing to abide by work requirements calling for people to work twenty hours a week. 'Tough love' replaced housing and services as a new strategy for addressing homelessness and restoring order" (Vitale 2008:13).

8. Joyce Carol Oates writes, "A boxing trainer's most difficult task is said to be to persuade a young boxer to get up and continue fighting after he has been knocked down" (Oates 1994:13).
9. Though physically and psychologically demanding, these sparring scenarios are not reckless but exist within the clearly demarcated and designed limits the trainer carefully constructs. There are some injuries that trainers will not ask their fighters to battle through. Harry explains, "Certain situations, I pull them out. If you got a headache, you not boxing." Trainers also know when a fighter is really hurt and when he is exaggerating in order to be pulled out of the ring. This is when a trainer's skill as well as intimate understanding of his fighter comes into play. Harry tells me, "It's all about your reaction. I know how to read their pain. I know how to read *through* their pain."
10. For an insightful discussion on professional boxers' understandings of their social mobility as well as the relations of power imbrued in the labor of professional boxing, see Wacquant 1998.
11. Pager 2007.
12. Sandlin 2004.
13. George Washington is an important figure for many trainers at Gleason's Gym, especially Harry, Mike, and Karl. Washington established the club almost thirty years ago and is credited with building one of the most successful and nationally recognized teams of fighters in the 1980s. Several of Washington's protégés, such as Mark Breland, participated in the Olympics and won world championships. More important than Washington's record of athletic success are the relationships he developed with his amateur fighters. Washington is described as offering unconditional love to his boxers and supporting them through difficult times. He is considered—by both those he has trained and those he has not—as the epitome of the ideal trainer. Sadly, Washington passed away on June 16, 2006.
14. Other trainers have fond memories of care from coaches and older and more established fighters, which shape the relationships they forge with amateur

boxers. These trainers talk explicitly about the priceless attention and love their trainers gave them and explain why giving similar forms of attention to their fighters is important. Ed worked with "Trickman" Norris, first at the Times Square Gym and then at the Bed-Stuy Boxing Center. When Joseph trained at Gleason's Gym in the Bronx as a thirteen-year-old, a professional from his neighborhood in Corona, Queens, took him under his wing: "Lenny was a professional fighter who had—he lived out in my neighborhood, and he used to come up to the gym around 2 o'clock in the afternoon. So I would go up there—I would be up there around 11 or 12, and I would just stay there, banging the bag, punching out the bag—doing things on my own until Lenny got there and trained. Then he would bring me back everyday. I never forgot that."

Karl remembers how Willie Dockery made a significant impact on his sense of confidence: "I knew I could fight. But I didn't know how *good* I could fight. So I met this guy by the name of Willie Dockery, and he took me to camp. He took me to camp with [Leon] Spinks. . . . But when he first told me he was gonna take me to camp, I was like, 'This guy is not going to take me to camp. Are you crazy? I can't go up and work with them guys at their pace!' You know? The next morning, he was in front of my door blowing his horn talking about 'Come on, we going to camp.' So I said, 'If he believe it, I'm gonna try.' So I went to camp, and he used to talk to me every night 'cause me and him had the same room. And he used to talk to me about believing in me and knowing that there isn't anyone better than me. And I really picked up on some of the things he did and the way he made me feel. If someone don't make you feel like you're wanted or needed then you'll be like, 'This guy don't care if I box or not.' If he didn't care, he acted like he cared. 'Yo Karl, you the best, man. There is nobody better than you. You had a bad day today but tomorrow watch.' And he did it, and I believed in it. I believed in everything he said. If he had said, 'Jump off the roof, you won't get hurt, you'll just hurt your ankle,' I'd probably have believed it. You laughing, but I'm dead serious. I had that much trust in him. He helped me a lot in life."

15. I use the term "kinship" because amateur men and trainers use the discourse of kinship to talk about each other.
16. Butler 2000:72.
17. Kinship theory and studies is a large field. For the purposes of this book, I draw upon the writings of scholars who have challenged the taken-for-granted bases of traditional understandings of kinship (or kinship as "natural fact"). Marilyn Strathern writes, "The anthropological study of kinship since mid-Victorian and Edwardian times, as well as the (indigenous) models held

by others of the social class from which by and large the authors of such studies came, has drawn heavily on the idea that kinship systems are also after the facts, and specifically after certain well-known facts of nature" (Strathern 1992a:3). Using critical interventions such as feminist anthropology, post-structuralism, and postmodernism, some scholars have reconstructed kinship studies on the assumption that "[l]ike all epistemic devices, kinship helps to constitute what it describes so that even imagining its purchase on sets of phenomena, whether in Western societies or elsewhere, may be seen as ideological or circular, and thus complicit with an unreconstructed version of the anthropological project" (Franklin and McKinnon 2001b:1). Though David Schneider's *Critique of the Study of Kinship* (1984) is often considered one of the first critical examinations of kinship, Sarah Franklin and Susan McKinnon persuasively argue that the so-called death of kinship extends as far back as the 1950s and came from a number of areas, among them feminist studies of gender and kinship (see Collier and Yanagisako 1987; MacCormack and Strathern 1980; Rubin 1975), the rejection of structural-functionalism, and the reflexive turn in anthropology as a discipline (see Clifford 1988; Clifford and Marcus 1986; Marcus and Fisher 1986) (Franklin and McKinnon 2001b:3–5; Franklin 1998:102). Today, kinship study has been reimagined and re-theorized, and "new" kinship studies encompass more notions of kin relatedness, especially in contexts of reproduction, global capitalism, genetic technologies, and cyberspace.

18. Elijah Anderson argues that inner-city areas no longer boast "old heads" who mentor, socialize, and discipline young black men (Anderson 1999). Though I understand the interest in mentoring to be a symptom of a larger neoliberal agenda that prizes *teaching* people out of poverty instead of *providing* opportunities for social mobility, the kinship improvised in Gleason's Gym meets those needs. In a time when many decry the lack of mentoring, such kinship arrangements suggest that there are spaces where black men are able to express care for one another (Anderson 1999).

19. I borrow David Harvey's characterization of neoliberalism as "a theory of political economic practices that proposes that human well-being can best be advanced by liberating individual entrepreneurial freedoms and skills within an institutional framework characterized by strong private property rights, free markets, and free trade. The role of the state is to create and preserve an institutional framework appropriate to such practices. The state has to guarantee, for example, the integrity of money. It must also set up those military, defence, police, and legal structures and functions required to secure private property rights and to guarantee, by force if need be, the proper functioning of markets. Furthermore, if markets do not exist (in areas such

as land, water, education, health care, social security, or environmental pollution) then they must be created, by state action if necessary. But beyond these tasks, the state should not venture" (Harvey 2005:2). In particular, neoliberalism looks to the market to address structural inequalities, despite the fact that, as Harvey points out, "increasing social inequality [has] in fact been such a persistent feature of neoliberalization as to be regarded as structural to the whole project" (p. 16).

CHAPTER FOUR. PASSING TIME: THE EXPRESSIVE CULTURE OF EVERYDAY GYM LIFE

1. This time is overwhelmingly segregated by class. It is unusual for white-collar clients to pass time socializing in Mike and Harry's corner. While there is no formal prohibition against their participation, because these clients focus on themselves and their training rather than on talking with anyone other than their trainers, they do not linger before or after their workouts long enough to chat and develop friendships.
2. Lindquist 2002:3,124.
3. The folklorist Roger Abrahams profiles the "man-of-words" in his ethnographic work on verbal dexterity in the West Indies and suggests, "[T]he man-of-words not only provides the tone and subjects for traditional performances but also serves as the principal organizer of the activity" (Abrahams 1983:xvi).
4. See Chung 2003, Associated Press 2003, and CNN 2003 (all accessed July 22, 2011).
5. Abrahams notes, "Somehow creativity seem[s] less important than how a group managed to achieve meaning while celebrating community" (Abrahams 1983:xix).
6. Though dated, Annette Powell Williams's "Dynamics of a Black Audience" analyzes how conversational patterns can signify different meaning-making systems. On interruption, she writes, "This kind of activity constitutes inattention and disrespect to the white speaker, the worst thing that could happen. To a black speaker it means something else. It means that he is communicating with his audience and that they are communicating with him. He is stirring their emotions and they are reacting to what he has to say" (Williams 1972:102).
7. Lindquist 2002:126.
8. Roger Abrahams writes of a similar phenomenon in the West Indies. He contends, "This pattern of competitive interaction is observable in many other

traditional activities, such as the tea meetings previously described. More frequently held are riddling sessions (held at wakes or on moonlit nights), and *rhyming*, a trading of curses directed against the mother of another contestant, a practice commonly known as *playing the dozens* in the United States. These contests are so central to the sense of entertainment in the West Indies that they are observable whenever people congregate, whether for a special event or in the marketplace or rum shop. In all of these activities, little effort is made to declare a winner or a loser; it is the entertainment value of the battle that matters most" (Abrahams 1983:xvii).

9. Julie Lindquist writes, "The practice of argument not only allows one person to persuade others of the legitimacy of his or her claim to speak 'for' the group about something (and thereby to assure his or her own status) but also works to persuade participant-spectators that there is a common social investment, an assurance of collective identity" (Lindquist 2002:121).
10. Abrahams 1983:60.
11. Joking also is considered "nonsense behavior" (ibid., 1983:57).
12. Ibid., 60.
13. Ibid., 74.
14. Southpaw fighters are lefthanded. Southpaw is a fighting style in which the boxer jabs with his or her right hand instead of the orthodox style of jabbing with the left hand.
15. When writing about joking, Abrahams argues that "[t]here is no joking, then, unless there is an order that can be overturned or at least challenged by the establishment of new continuities and relationships." He continues, "But simply because a joke relies upon this previous social order indicates that it acts in response to certain pressures already existing within that order, tensions that are shared by the group who participates in the joking" (Abrahams 1983:74).
16. Abrahams suggests that "play is the activity by which one progressively learns how to cooperate with others" (Abrahams 1983:50–51).
17. Ibid., 73.
18. Ibid., 77.
19. Ibid., 58.
20. Expressive practice "provides an active way of guaranteeing a certain level of homogeneity of ideals and even of social practices" (Abrahams 1983:84).
21. I am grateful to Hilary Silver for pointing out the connection to Phil Brown's work. For more on legal consciousness, see Ewick and Silbey 1998. I am grateful to Michael Yarbrough for directing me to the connection to Patricia Ewick and Susan Silbey's work.

22. Lindquist writes, "That immediate, lived experience is valued . . . means that as a genre, narrative is authoritative. It enacts the common logic of productivity and immediacy and contains the densities and contradictions of moment-to-moment sociality. To tell stories in the contexts of arguments is to lay claim to an unchallengeable empirical reality, to appeal to the legitimacy of the link between life and story, world and word. When invoked as evidence in arguments, narratives affirm that participants exist on the same experiential plane (if not on the same philosophical one). In telling a story to 'prove' a point, an arguer makes an ethical appeal that says, in effect, Now here's my unmediated, not strategized point of view.' . . . Narrative serves to make sense of the world, in effect, to theorize without resorting to theory" (Lindquist 2002:157).
23. Ibid., 157.
24. Abrahams 1983:25.
25. Though there are gay and lesbian boxers, who open about their relationships, I was never privy to a discussion about problems with same-sex male partnerships. I was, however, privy to discussions about same-sex female partners.
26. bell hooks writes, "Conservatives and radicals alike seem to be better at talking about the plight of the black male than they are at naming strategies of resistance that would offer hope and meaningful alternatives" (hooks 2004:xv). She elaborates, "White-supremacist capitalist patriarchy's refusal to allow black males full access to employment while offering black females a place in the service economy created a context where black males and females could not conform to standard sexist roles in regard to work even if they wanted to" (p. 8).
27. Ibid., 27.
28. Ibid., xii.
29. Cited in ibid., 121–122.
30. Willis 2000.

CHAPTER FIVE. THE CHANGING POLITICS OF GENDER

1. The women of the gym cite annoyance at Christy Martin's lack of advocacy for the sport and argue that she cultivates an extreme form of femininity at the expense of support for boxing women. Danielle says, "Pisses me off. It's like, 'Come on. *Say* something.' "
2. I understand Jacques Derrida's concept of a supplement as a thing that exists to define the "natural" or "original" through addition, exclusion, or expul-

sion, thereby fortifying the natural's boundaries (i.e., that which the supplement is supplementary to). The supplement can also suggest a lack within the original or natural. Derrida describes "the two significations of supplementarity" as "substitution and accretion" (Derrida 1976:200).

3. "Woman boxer wins decision after eight-year legal battle," *USA Today*, April 22, 1992. Amateurs can compete until they turn thirty-five, at which point they become "master" boxers. See USA Boxing Metro 2011.
4. Fachet 1993.
5. Heiskanen 2012.
6. Women Boxing Archive Network 2011 (accessed July 22, 2011).
7. The *Daily News* understands the situation slightly differently. In an article written in 2011, they claim that Dee Hamaguichi missed the entry deadline (*New York Daily News* 2011) (accessed Aug. 17, 2012).
8. A walkover is a win awarded to a boxer when there are no other competitors.
9. Leidecker 2010.
10. USA Boxing 2011 (accessed July 22, 2011).
11. Gleason's Gym 2010a (accessed Aug. 20, 2012).

CHAPTER SIX. BUYING AND SELLING BLACKNESS: WHITE-COLLAR BOXING AND THE CULTURAL CAPITAL OF RACIAL DIFFERENCE

1. The phrase "Live, work, and play in DUMBO" is real-estate developer David Walentas' slogan for the district, and it appears on banners that hang from lampposts.
2. In this chapter, unless otherwise noted, when I discuss white-collar clients, I am referring to male clients. I focus on men for several reasons. First, when trainers talk about clients, they are referring to male clients; in gym discourse, "women" are considered their own category of gym user. Second, white-collar men—and not women—initiated the white-collar trend. In a sense, their participation paved the way for women to join the gym, in the sense that gym management and trainers imagined a new kind of "financial" member, a category that could be expanded to include women. But the originators of white-collar boxing were men. And third, white-collar men's reasons for boxing are quite different than their female counterparts. My goals in this chapter are to demonstrate how the service economy of boxing works and what is being bought in a training sessions. For white-collar men, their purchase not only of a training session but also of an abstract notion of black masculinity has to do with their own identities, specifically their own

sense of manliness. Women have very different interests in boxing and, obviously, do not have these same investments in acquiring masculine identities. For example, many women cite histories of personal trauma—rape, domestic violence, and food and body-image preoccupations—when they discuss their reasons for boxing. Boxing for these women is about reclaiming their bodies as a source of power and strength. They, in turn, practice boxing much more like amateur and professional boxers. Unlike male clients, female clients often do not attempt to control the terms of their training. And many young female clients go on to compete in the amateurs. Because they are buying expertise and not an abstract construction, female clients have different relationships with their trainers. Interestingly, many female amateurs, who began as clients, look down on white-collar boxing, seeing it as a "gimmick" and unserious, and argue that it actually delegitimizes women's boxing by association.

3. For an elegant discussion of the historical, political, and economic processes through which blackness became invested with cultural capital, see Gilroy 2010. Gilroy argues, "Blackness, which for so long had been entirely worthless, could be recognized as becoming endowed with symbolic value that nobody appears to have anticipated. Needless to say, new forms of racism emerged with these developments" (p. 9). Also see hooks 2004.
4. White-collar boxers quickly captured the attention of magazines and newspapers, and several alumni have written memoirs about their pugilistic journeys.
5. See, e.g., Parkyns 1713; Godfrey 1747; A Pupil Both of Humphreys and Mendoza 1784, 1788; Amateur of Eminence 1789; Fewtrell 1790.
6. A Pupil Both of Humphreys and Mendoza 1784.
7. Ibid.
8. Gorn 1986.
9. Bederman 1995.
10. Rhoden 2001.
11. Dworkin and Wachs 2009.
12. See, e.g., Johnson 2005 and Robertson 2005.
13. Robertson 2005; Johnson 2005.
14. The Learning Annex is a continuing education school in New York City, which runs a number of different types of classes for adult learners.
15. "Open" fighters are amateur boxers who have more than ten fights.
16. Steve Bunce points out that many of the participants of "Capital Punishment" earned salaries of millions of dollars. The same night of that show, a group of professionals participated in a show in York Hall. Most of those

boxers made less than 6,000 pounds. He writes, "Same sport, same city, but so different" (Bunce 2000).

17. Connellan 2005; Hari 2005.
18. Briggs and McIntosh 2005.
19. Martens 2005; *Province* (Vancouver) 2005.
20. Looney 2005.
21. Gleason's Gym 2010c (accessed Aug. 8, 2011).
22. Richard Wilner reports that Gleason's rent is $15,000 per month and insurance costs $12,000 per month (Wilner 2005).
23. Alphabet belts refer to the abbreviations of the numerous championship boxing belts awarded by a number of sanctioning bodies, such as IBA, IBO, NABA, NABC, NABF, WBF, and WBO. The alphabet sanctioning bodies emerged in the 1980s.
24. Wilner 2005.
25. Johnson 2005.
26. An assistant second is someone who helps the cornerman (or second), who assists the boxer in between rounds.
27. George Washington was the head trainer at the Bed-Stuy Boxing Center for decades. Deeply admired by his boxers, he is remembered as a role model. Many trainers say they became boxing coaches because of the time, energy, and care that George Washington gave to them.
28. These fees are in addition to membership dues.
29. Grazian 2003:29.
30. Primitivism has different meanings in different fields. I see primitivism as a modern and postmodern fascination with racial stereotypes considered, on the one hand, mystical, "wild, elemental," backward, and inferior and, on the other hand, a conduit to "liberation, and spontaneity, for a simultaneous recovery of ancient sources and an access to true modernity" (Clifford 1989:901). For a brilliant discussion of primitivism, especially of primitivism and the black body (including the black boxing body), see Clifford 1989. Also see Torgovnick 1990.
31. The connections among the primitive, race, and masculinity are explicated at length in Bederman 1995.
32. Wartofsky 2000.
33. Ibid.
34. Whatever plurality of racial identities trainers use to describe their loyalties and solidarities, they are conflated and then abstracted by clients into one category: black masculinity.
35. Hazel Carby makes this argument in *Race Men* (Carby 1998).

36. By “authentic” I mean a precise replication.
37. See Sherman 2007.
38. Gorz 1989.
39. Ibid.
40. Gorz suggests these personal services might become increasingly concentrated in hygiene and body care and in gyms and health and fitness establishments (ibid., 154).
41. In *Neo-Bohemia*, Richard Lloyd makes a similar point about waitresses who see themselves as co-equals with their clientele. He writes, “And yet, service workers at the North Side and other neighborhood bars are not co-equals with either Landise or the bar’s patrons—within the structure of the social situation, they remain subordinates, although the way that subordinate status plays out can be complicated” (Lloyd 2010:136).

EPILOGUE

1. I analyze work in Gleason’s Gym because it is the category and language through which these men understand and talk about their lives.
2. For instance, William Julius Wilson understands the social and psychological benefits of work—such as labor-force attachment, discipline, regularity, and perceptions of self-efficacy—to derive from the work that is the primary economic sustenance of the laborer, that is, the work that reproduces the material conditions of existence.
3. The unique forms of work fashioned in the gym suggest that a static class theory is insufficient for analyzing postindustrial labor. Amateur men and their trainers cannot be categorized into a fixed social structure, as they might be with such designations as “working class” or “lumpenproletariat,” and similarly the work they do cannot be neatly fit into a fixed work hierarchy. Sociological definitions of work, which often describe work through a series of binaries—service or manufacturing, informal or formal, legal or illegal, work or leisure—do not help us think about labor at Gleason’s Gym. This is not to say that these categories are not useful in other contexts but rather that gym work cannot be sufficiently understood by concepts and structures beholden to these binaries. For example, how might we talk about a worker who earns wages from a security job but considers himself, by profession, to be a boxer? Or a worker who considers his job to be boxing despite generating income from selling drugs, either chronically or episodically? Or a worker whose pugilistic labor is performed both in and out of prison? The

very multiplicity of work in Gleason's Gym demands new ways of conceptualizing postindustrial labor.

4. Gilroy 2010:8.
5. Calder 2012 (accessed Aug. 26, 2012).
6. The Wounded Warrior Project, http://www.woundedwarriorproject.org; Gleason's Gym 2010b.
7. Matthew Bogdanos, a Marine colonel, Bronze Star for bravery winner, and prosecutor, organized the event (*Wall Street Journal* 2012 [accessed Aug. 26, 2012]).

METHODOLOGICAL APPENDIX

1. Ross 2004.
2. Padwork consists of a trainer holding padded mitts, which the boxer hits.
3. Though boxers are considered members of Gleason's Gym, many trainers form individual teams to distinguish themselves from other trainers and boxers in the gym. Gleason's, then, is constituted by a series of small teams.
4. A second is a cornerman or cornerwoman.
5. The seconds-out bell indicates that there are ten seconds left in the one-minute rest period in between rounds.
6. Fictocriticism, which the anthropologist Michael Taussig has pioneered, can be defined as the amalgamation of fact, fiction, participant observation, archival history, memoir, and literary theory in a text (Eakin 2001).
7. Situated knowledge is the idea that knowledge that is learned, acquired, or produced in particular social circumstances for particular reasons. That is, the production of knowledge is a practice that depends not just on context but also on motivation and use by the knowledge maker. It recognizes that knowledge is partial and contingent on situation but asserts that women and minorities have a privileged view of the world by virtue of their marginal position. See Haraway 1988.

References

Abrahams, Roger (1983). *The Man-of-Words in the West Indies: Performance and the Emergence of Creole Culture*. Baltimore: Johns Hopkins University Press.

Ackman, Dan (2002). "And in This Corner, the Insurance Broker." *Wall Street Journal Abstracts*, August 21.

Alexander, Michelle (2012). *The New Jim Crow: Mass Incarceration in the Age of Colorblindness*. New York: New Press.

Amateur of Eminence (1788). *The Complete Art of Boxing according to the Modern Method: Wherein the Whole of That Manly Accomplishment Is Rendered So Easy and Intelligent, that Any Person May Be an Entire Master of the Science in a Few Days, without any Other Instruction than This Book, to Which Is Added, the General History of Boxing, Containing an Account of the Most Eminent Professors of That Noble Art, Who Have Flourished from Its Commencement to the Present Time*. London: Printed for M. Follingsby and M. Smith.

Amateur of Eminence (1789). *The Complete Art of Boxing &c. &c. to Which Is Now Added Capt. Godfrey's Treatise on the Same Subject*. London: Printed for M. Follingsby and M. Smith.

Anderson, Elijah (1999). *Code of the Street: Decency, Violence, and the Moral Life of the Inner City*. New York: W. W. Norton.

Arinde, Nayaba (2004). "Bedford-Stuyvesant Boxing Center Threatened." *Voices That Must Be Heard*, October 11.

Associated Press (2003). "Official: World's largest snake in Indonesia." CNN .com, December 29. http://www.stinkyjournalism.org/news/7-01-04/cnn_snake.htm.

Bailey, Thomas, and Roger Waldinger (1991). "The Changing Ethnic/Racial Division of Labor." In *Dual City: Restructuring New York*, edited by John H. Mollenkopf and Manuel Castells. New York: Russell Sage Foundation.

Bederman, Gail (1995). *Manliness and Civilization: A Cultural History of Gender and Race in the United States, 1880–1917*. Chicago: University of Chicago Press.

Booth, Wayne (2000). *For the Love of It: Amateuring and Its Rivals*. Chicago: University of Chicago Press.

Briggs, Billy, and Rosie McIntosh (2005). "Stressed Out at the Office? Take It Out on a Banker at the Fight Club; White-collar Boxing Bouts Seek Scottish Contenders." *Herald* (Glasgow), August 9.

Brown, Phil (1992). "Popular Epidemiology and Toxic Waste Contamination: Lay and Professional Ways of Knowing." *Journal of Health and Social Behavior* 33:269–271.

Bunce, Steve (2000). "I Wanna Be a Contender: White Collar Warriors Will Live Out Their Fantasies as Broadgate Prepares for 'Capital Punishment.' " *Guardian*, July 9.

Butler, Judith (2000). *Antigone's Claim: Kinship between Life and Death*. New York: Columbia University Press.

Calder, Rich (2012). "Tech Wreck: DUMBO Jobs Go Begging amid Biz Boom." *New York Post*, February 13. http://www.nypost.com/p/news/local/brooklyn/tech_wreck_O28uwbZUuJA7ruJqfMEsyI#ixzz24gOotBUS.

Carby, Hazel V. (1998). *Race Men*. Cambridge, MA: Harvard University Press.

Chung, Jen (2003). "Further Proof that Rat Dogs Are Ratty." *Gothamist*, August 6. http://gothamist.com/2003/08/06/further_proof_that_rat_dogs_are_ratty.php.

Clifford, James (1988). *The Predicament of Culture: Twentieth-Century Ethnography, Literature, and Art*. Cambridge, MA: Harvard University Press.

Clifford, James (1989). "Negrophilia." In *A New History of French Literature*, edited by Denis Hollier. Cambridge, MA: Harvard University Press.

Clifford, James, and George E. Marcus, eds. (1986). *Writing Culture: The Poetics and Politics of Ethnography*. Cambridge: Cambridge University Press.

CNN (2003). "Tiger, gator removed from Harlem apartment." October 6. http://www.cnn.com/2003/US/Northeast/10/04/nyc.tiger.

Collier, Jane F., and Sylvia Yanagisako, eds. (1987) *Gender and Kinship: Essays toward a Unified Analysis*. Palo Alto, CA: Stanford University Press.

Connellan, Michael (2005). "White-Collar Boxers 'Are Risking Injury or Death.' " *Independent* (London), August 1.

Currid, Elizabeth (2007). *The Warhol Economy: How Fashion, Art, and Music Drive New York City*. Princeton, NJ: Princeton University Press.

Davis, Angela Y. (2000). "From the Convict Lease System to the Super-Max Prison." In *States of Confinement: Policing, Detention and Prisons*, edited by Joy James. New York: St. Martin's Press.

Davis, Angela Y. (2003). *Are Prisons Obsolete?* New York: Seven Stories Press.

Delany, Samuel R. (1999). *Times Square Red, Times Square Blue*. New York: New York University Press.

Derrida, Jacques (1976). *Of Grammatology*. Baltimore: Johns Hopkins University Press.

Donaldson, Stephen "Donny" (2001). "A Million Jockers, Punks, and Queens." In *Prison Masculinities*, edited by Don Sabo, Terry A. Kupers, and Willie London. Philadelphia: Temple University Press.

Dworkin, Shari L., and Faye Linda Wachs (2009). *Body Panic: Gender, Health, and the Selling of Fitness*. New York: New York University Press.

Dyer, Richard (1997). "The White Man's Muscles." In *White: Essays on Race and Culture*. London: Routledge.

Eakin, Emily (2001). "Anthropology's Alternative Radical." *New York Times*, April 21.

Early, Gerald (1994). *The Culture of Bruising: Essays on Prizefighting, Literature, and Modern American Culture*. Hopewell, NJ: Ecco Press.

Eckholm, Erik (2006). "Plight Deepens for Black Men, Studies Warn." *New York Times*, March 20.

Ewick, Patricia, and Susan Silbey (1998). *The Common Place of Law: Stories from Everyday Life*. Chicago: University of Chicago Press.

Fachet, Robert (1993). "Women Fight Red Tape to Win Right to Box." *Washington Post*, October 14.

Farrell, Bill (1996). "Gleason's Nurses 'Sweet Science.'" *New York Daily News*, January 30.

Fewtrell, Thomas (1790). *Boxing Reviewed; or, The Science of Manual Defence, Displayed on Rational Principles: Comprehending a Complete Description of the Principal Pugilists, From the Earliest Period of Broughton's Time to the Present Day*. London: Printed for Scatcherd and Whitaker, Faulder, and Champante and Whitrow.

Fine, Michelle, Maria Elena Torre, Kathy Boudin, Iris Bowen, Judith Clark, Donna Hylton, Migdalia Martinez, "Missy," Rosemarie A. Roberts, Pamela Smart, and Debora Upegui, with a reincarceration analysis conducted by the New York State Department of Correctional Services (2001). "Changing Minds: The Impact of College in a Maximum Security Prison." Collaborative Research by the Graduate Center of the City University of New York and Women in Prison at the Bedford Hills Correctional Facility. March. http://web.gc.cuny.edu/che/changingminds.html.

Franklin, Sarah (1998). "Making Miracles: Scientific Progress and the Facts of Life." In *Reproducing Reproduction: Kinship, Power, and Technological Innovation*, edited by Sarah Franklin and Helena Ragone. Philadelphia: University of Pennsylvania Press.

Franklin, Sarah, and Susan McKinnon, eds. (2001a). *Relative Values: Reconfiguring Kinship Studies*. Durham, North Carolina: Duke University Press.

Franklin, Sarah, and Susan McKinnon (2001b). "Relative Values: Reconfiguring Kinship Studies." In *Relative Values: Reconfiguring Kinship Studies*, edited by Sarah Franklin and Susan McKinnon. Durham, North Carolina: Duke University Press.

Franklin, Sarah, and Helena Ragone, eds. (1998). *Reproducing Reproduction: Kinship, Power, and Technological Innovation*. Philadelphia: University of Pennsylvania Press.

Garland, David (2001). *The Culture of Control: Crime and Social Order in Contemporary Society.* Chicago: University of Chicago Press.

Geurts, Kathryn L. (2005). "Even Boxers Carry Mace: A Comment on Relationality in LoicWacquant's *Body and Soul*." *Qualitative Sociology* 28:143–149.

Gillam, Richard (1982). "The Perils of Postindustrialism." *American Quarterly* 35, no. 1 (Spring): 77–82.

Gilroy, Paul (2000). *Against Race: Imagining Political Culture beyond the Color Line*. Cambridge, MA: Harvard University Press.

Gilroy, Paul (2005). *Postcolonial Melancholia*. New York: Columbia University Press.

Gilroy, Paul (2010). *Darker than Blue: The Moral Economies of Black Atlantic Culture*. Cambridge, MA: Harvard University Press.

Gleason's Gym (2010a). "Gym History" tab. http://www.gleasonsgym.net/gleasonsgyminfo.html.

Gleason's Gym (2010b). "How We Give Kids Their Dreams." http://www.gleasonsgym.net/gleasonsgymdream.html.

Gleason's Gym (2010c). "Next Fantasy Camp." http://www.gleasonsgym.net/gleasonsgymfantasy.html.

Godfrey, Captain John (1747). *A Treatise upon the Useful Science of Defence: Connecting the Small and Back-Sword, and Shewing the Affinity between them: Likewise Endeavouring to Weed the Art of Those Superfluous, Unmeaning Practices which Over-run It, and Choke the True Principles, by Reducing It to a Narrow Compass, and Supporting It with Mathematical Proofs: Also an Examination into the Performances of the Most Noted Masters of the Back-Sword, Who Have Fought upon the Stage, Pointing Out Their Faults, and Allowing Their Abilities: With Some Observations upon Boxing, and the Characters of the Most Able Boxers within the Author's Time*. 2nd ed. London: Printed for T. Osborne.

Gorn, Elliot (1986). *The Manly Art: Bare-Knuckle Prize Fighting in America*. Ithaca, NY: Cornell University Press.

Gorz, Andre (1989). *Critique of Economic Reason*. New York: Verso.

Grazian, David. (2003). *Blue Chicago: The Search for Authenticity in Urban Blues Clubs*. Chicago: University of Chicago Press.

Hamill, Pete (1996). *The Times Square Gym*. New York: Evan Publishing.

Haraway, Donna (1988). "Situated Knowledges: The Science Question in Feminism and the Privilege of Partial Perspective." *Feminist Studies* 14 (3): 575–599.

Hari, Johann (2005). "A Hot-blooded Lord of the Ring." *Evening Standard*, September 30.

Harvey, David (2005). *A Brief History of Neoliberalism*. New York: Oxford University Press.

Heiskanen, Benita (2012). *The Urban Geography of Boxing: Race, Class, and Gender in the Ring*. New York: Routledge.

Hickok Sports (2006). "Golden Glove Championships." http://www.hickoksports.com/history/boxgoldgs.shtml.

Hindo, Brian, with Laura Cohn (2004). "Out of the Office, Into the Ring; White-Collar Boxing Is Exploding—And That's Good News for a Sport on the Ropes." *Business Week*, November 9.

Hirsley, Michael (2005). "'Million Dollar Baby' Gives More Women Fighting Spirit." *Chicago Tribune*, April 7.

Hoffman, Steven, and Gary Fine (2005). "The Scholar's Body: Mixing It Up with Loic Wacquant." *Qualitative Sociology* 28:151–157.

Hollier, Denis, ed. (1989). *A New History of French Literature*. Cambridge, MA: Harvard University Press.

Horton, John (1972). "Time and Cool People." In *Rappin' and Stylin' Out: Communication in Urban Black America*, edited by Thomas Kochman. Urbana: University of Illinois Press.

hooks, bell (2004). *We Real Cool: Black Men and Masculinity*. New York: Routledge.

Jackson, Jonathan, Jr. (1994). *Soledad Brother: The Prison Letters of George Jackson*. New York: Lawrence Hill Books.

James, Joy, ed. (2000). *States of Confinement: Policing, Detention and Prisons*. New York: St. Martin's Press.

James, Joy, ed. (2003). *Imprisoned Intellectuals: America's Political Prisoners Write on Life, Liberation, and Rebellion*. New York: Rowman and Littlefield.

Jeffords, Susan (1993). *Hard Bodies: Hollywood Masculinity in the Reagan Era*. New Brunswick, NJ: Rutgers University Press

Johnson, Chuck (2005). "Business with Punch." *USA Today*, November 10.

Kester, Grant (1993). "Out of Sight Is Out of Mind: The Imaginary Space of Postindustrial Culture." *Social Text* 35 (Summer): 72–92.

Kress, Gunther (1994). "Text and Grammar as Explanation." In *Text, Discourse, and Context: Representations of Poverty in Britain*, edited by Ulrike H. Meinhof and Kay Richardson. New York: Longman.

Lazzarato, Maurizio (1996). "Immaterial Labor." In *Radical Thought in Italy: A Potential Politics* (Theory Out of Bounds, vol. 7), edited by Paolo Virno and Michael Hardt. Minneapolis: University of Minnesota, Press.

Leidecker, Leyla (2010). "The Life of Million Dollar Babies." Pathfinder Entertainment.

Levine, Lawrence (1977). "The Hero vs. Society: John Henry to Joe Louis." In *Black Consciousness, Black Culture: Afro-American Folk Thought from Slavery to Freedom*. New York: Oxford University Press.

Levitan, Mark (2004). *A Crisis of Black Male Employment: Unemployment and Joblessness in New York City, 2003*. New York: Community Service Society.

Library of Congress (2012). "Bill Text 103rd Congress (1993–1994) H.R.3355. ENR." http://thomas.loc.gov/cgi-bin/query/z?c103:H.R.3355.ENR:.

Lindquist, Julie (2002). *A Place to Stand: Politics and Persuasion in a Working-Class Bar*. New York: Oxford University Press.

Lloyd, Richard (2010). *Neo-Bohemia: Art and Commerce in the Postindustrial City*. New York: Routledge.

Looney, Fiona (2005). "White Collar Fight Fans Take Rocky Road to New York in Boxing Dream; A Select Group of Irishmen Have Paid EUR 10,000 Apiece to Train to Take Each Other On in the Ring." *Sunday Tribune*, August 20.

MacCormack, Carol, and Marilyn Strathern, eds. (1980). *Nature, Culture, and Gender*. Cambridge: Cambridge University Press.

Mace, Jem, Jr. (1880). *Boxing*. London: Phelp Bros.

Marcus, George E., and Michael Fischer (1986). *Anthropology as Cultural Critique: An Experimental Moment in the Human Sciences*. Chicago: University of Chicago Press.

Martens, Kathleen (2005). "White-Collar Card 'Professionals' Ready to Box." *Winnipeg Sun*, November 8.

Mauer, Mark (1999a). "The Crisis of the Young African American Male and the Criminal Justice System." Paper prepared for the US Commission on Civil Rights, April 15–16, Washington, DC.

Mauer, Mark (1999b). *Race to Incarcerate*. New York: New Press.

Mauer, Marc, and Meda Chesney-Lind, eds. (2002). *Invisible Punishment: The Collateral Consequences of Mass Imprisonment*. New York: New Press.

Mee, Bob (2004). "Tyson Is Let Off Jail." *Daily Telegraph*, February 28.

Merriam-Webster's Dictionary, 10th ed. (1983) Springfield, MA: Merriam-Webster.

Mincey, Ronald B. (2006). *Black Males Left Behind.* Washington, DC: Urban Institute Press.

Mollenkopf, John H., and Manuel Castells, eds. (1991). *Dual City: Restructuring New York.* New York: Russell Sage Foundation.

Neisser, Philip T., and Sanford F. Schram (1994). "Redoubling Denial: Industrial Welfare Policy Meets Postindustrial Poverty." *Social Text* 41 (Winter): 41–60.

Newman, Katherine (1999). *No Shame in My Game: The Working Poor in the Inner City.* New York: Vintage.

New York Daily News (2011). "Women's Rights." November 15. http://www.nydailynews.com/sports/more-sports/golden-gloves/women-rights-article-1.977957.

Oates, Joyce Carol ([1987] 1994). *On Boxing.* Expanded ed. Garden City, NY: Dolphin/Doubleday Press.

Orfield, Gary (2004). *Dropouts in America: Confronting the Graduation Rate Crisis.* Cambridge, MA: Harvard Education Press.

Pager, Devah (2007). *Marked: Race, Crime, and Finding Work in an Era of Mass Incarceration.* Chicago: University of Chicago Press.

Pager, Devah, and Lincoln Quillian (2005). "What Employers Say versus What They Do." *American Sociological Review* 70, no. 3 (June): 355–380.

Parenti, Christian (1999). *Lockdown America: Police and Prisons in the Age of Crisis.* New York: Verso.

Parkyns, Sir Thomas (1713). *The Gymnastics of Inn-play, or Cornish-Hugg Wrestler: Digested in a Method Which Teacheth to Break All Holds, and Throw Most Falls Mathmatically: Easie to Be Understood by All Gentlemen, &c. and of Great Use to Such Who Understand the Small Sword in Fencing, and by All Tradesmen and Handicrafts, That Have Component Knowledge of the Use of the Stilliards, Barr, Crove-Iron or Lever, with Their Hypomochlions, Fulciments, or Baits.* Nottingham: William Ayscouh.

Persuad, Randolph B., and Clarence Lusane (2000). "The New Economy, Globalisation, and the Impact on African Americans." *Race and Class* 42, no. 1: 21–34.

Petersilia, Joan (2003). *When Prisoners Come Home: Parole and Prisoner Reentry.* New York: Oxford University Press.

Province (Vancouver) (2005). "White-Collar Boxing a Hit in Winnipeg: Lawyers, Stockbrokers, Executives Put Up Their Dukes in a Hot New Sport." November 9.

A Pupil Both of Humphreys and Mendoza (1784). *The Art of Manual Defence, or System of Boxing: Perspicuously Explained in a Series of Lessons, and Illustrated by Plates.* London: Printed for G. Kearsley; 2d ed. published 1788.

Rhoden, William C. (1991). "Miles Davis Provided Sweet Union of Sports and Music." *St. Louis Post-Dispatch*, October 27.

Robertson, Dale (2005). "In This Corner . . . ; Why Are Guys Like These Turning to White-Collar Boxing to Get into Shape? It Gives Them a Fighting Chance." *Houston Chronicle*, December 27.

Rose, Tricia (1994). *Black Noise: Rap Music and Black Culture in Contemporary America*. Middletown, CT: Wesleyan University Press.

Ross, Andrew (2004). *No-Collar: The Humane Workplace and Its Hidden Costs*. Philadelphia: Temple University Press.

Rubin, Gayle (1975). "The Traffic of Women: Notes on the 'Political Economy' of Sex." In *Toward an Anthropology of Women*, edited by Rayna R. Reiter. New York: Monthly Review Press.

Sandlin, Jennifer A. (2004). "'It's All Up to You': How Welfare-to-Work Educational Programs Construct Workforce Success." *Adult Education Quarterly* 54, no. 2: 89–104.

Sassen, Saskia (1990). "Economic Restructuring and the American City." *Annual Review of Sociology* 16: 465–490.

Sassen, Saskia (2001). *The Global City: New York, London, Tokyo*. Princeton, NJ: Princeton University Press.

Schneider, David (1984). *A Critique of the Study of Kinship*. Ann Arbor: University of Michigan Press.

Scott-Hayward, Christine S. (2011). "The Failure of Parole: Rethinking the Role of the State in Reentry." *New Mexico Law Review* 41 (Fall): 421–465.

Seconds Out (2004). "History of the Golden Gloves." http://www.secondsout.com.

Sennett, Richard (2003). *Respect: The Formation of Character in an Age of Inequality*. London: Penguin Books.

Sherman, Rachel (2005). "Producing the Superior Self: Strategic Comparison and Symbolic Boundaries among Luxury Hotel Workers." *Ethnography* 6, no. 2: 131–158.

Sherman, Rachel (2007). *Class Acts: Service and Inequality in Luxury Hotels*. Berkeley: University of California Press.

Simon, Jonathan (1993). *Poor Discipline: Parole and the Social Control of the Underclass*. Chicago: University of Chicago Press.

Stack, Carol (1974). *All Our Kin: Strategies for Survival in a Black Community*. New York: Harper Torchbooks.

Strathern, Marilyn (1992a). *After Nature: English Kinship in the Late Twentieth Century*. New York: Cambridge University Press.

Strathern, Marilyn (1992b). *Reproducing the Future: Essays on Anthropology, Kinship and the New Reproductive Technologies*. Manchester, UK: Manchester University Press.

Sum, Andrew, Ishwar Khatiwada, Frimpomaa Ampaw, Paulo Tobar, and Sheila Palma (2004). "Trends in Black Male Joblessness and Year-Round Idleness: An Employment Crisis Ignored." Report Prepared for Alternative Schools Network, Chicago.

Swift, Owen (c. 1880). Boxing without a Master; or, Scientific Art and Practice of Attack and Self-Defence: Explained in So Easy a Manner that Any Person May Comprehend This Useful Art and Containing Descriptions of Correct Pugilistic Attitudes, as Practiced by the Most Celebrated Boxers of the Present Day. New York: Frederic A. Brady.

Thompson, E. P. (1966). *The Making of the English Working Class*. New York: Vintage Books.

Thompson, E. P. (1993). *Customs in Common: Studies in Traditional Popular Culture*. New York: New Press.

Title IX Info (2012). "The Living Law." http://www.titleix.info/History/The-Living-Law.aspx.

Torgovnick, Mariana (1990). *Gone Primitive: Savage Intellects, Modern Lives*. Chicago: University of Chicago Press.

Travis, Jeremy (2000). *But They All Come Back: Facing the Challenges of Prisoner Reentry*. Washington, DC: Urban Institute Press.

United States Parole Commission (2004). "Standard Conditions of Release for U.S. Code Offenders." http://www.usdoj.gov/uspc/release.html. (Link now invalid; see United States Sentencing Commission 2010.)

United States Sentencing Commission (2010). "Federal Offenders Sentenced to Supervised Release." https://docs.google.com/viewer?a=v&q=cache:6cOSMO20slYJ:www.ussc.gov/Research/Research_Publications/Supervised_Release/20100722_Supervised_Release.pdf+&hl=en&pid=bl&srcid=ADGEESg3dKqQxLhIT6tJLOqk3NXc5Hn69rVQzmeY_T40OiV8xoyWmmYUR1FaRd7lCaxfyWG9WFKhecDAmUBysi5ljlnhqkThoQYbIMcOWZoRkH1imetTWJ2ALYhPSVn9U2Cw9UOU_G3w&sig=AHIEtbT8gCjHt7PbtRd0pyEcc5P_W4OS6w.

USA Boxing (2011). "The Evolution of Women's Boxing." http://www.usaboxing.org/about-us/the-evolution-of-women-s-boxing.

USA Boxing Metro (2011). "Masters Boxing." http://www.usaboxingmetro.com/masters.html.

Venkatesh, Sudhir Alladi (1994). "Getting Ahead: Social Mobility among the Urban Poor." *Sociology Perspectives* 37, no. 2 (Summer): 157–182.

Venkatesh, Sudhir Alladi (2006). *Off the Books: The Underground Economy of the Urban Poor.* Cambridge, MA: Harvard University Press.

Vitale, Alex (2008). *City of Disorder: How the Quality of Life Campaign Transformed New York Politics*. New York: New York University Press.

Virno, Paolo, and Michael Hardt, eds. (1996). *Radical Thought in Italy: A Potential Politics*. Minneapolis: University of Minnesota Press.

Wacquant, Loic (1995a). "The Pugilist Point of View: How Boxers Think and Feel about Their Trade." *Theory and Society* 24:489–535.

Wacquant, Loic (1995b). "Pugs at Work: Bodily Capital and Bodily Labour among Professional Boxers." *Body and Society* 1:63–93.

Wacquant, Loic (1998). "A Fleshpeddler at Work: Power, Pain, and Profit in the Prizefighting Economy." *Theory and Society* 27:1–42.

Wacquant, Loic (2001). "Deadly Symbiosis: When Ghetto and Prison Meet and Mesh." *Punishment and Society* 3, no. 10: 95–134.

Wacquant, Loic (2004). *Body and Soul: Notebooks of an Apprentice Boxer*. New York: Oxford University Press.

Wacquant, Loic (2009). *Punishing the Poor: The Neoliberal Government of Social Insecurity*. Durham, NC: Duke University Press.

Wall Street Journal (2012). "Fight Night Sends Manhattan's Prosecutors into the Ring." http://online.wsj.com/article/SB10001424052702303459004577360140692111270.html?mod=googlenews_wsj.

Wartofsky, Alona (2000). "Let's Do Lunch, and Three Rounds; Once a Month at Gleason's, No Professional Boxing but Plenty of Boxing Professionals." *Washington Post*, August 30.

Western, Bruce (2006). *Punishment and Inequality in America*. New York: Russell Sage Foundation.

Western, Bruce, Becky Pettit, and Josh Guetzkow (2002). "Black Economic Progress in the Era of Mass Imprisonment." In *Invisible Punishment: The Collateral Consequences of Mass Imprisonment*, edited by Marc Mauer and Meda Chesney-Lind. New York: New Press.

Vancouver Province (2005). "White-Collar Boxing a Hit in Winnipeg: Lawyers, Stockbrokers, Executives Put Up Their Dukes in a Hot New Sport." November 9.

Wilensky, Harold L. (2003). "Postindustrialism and Postmaterialism? A Critical View of the 'New Economy,' the 'Information Age,' the 'High Tech Society,' and All That." In *Rich Democracies: Political Economy, Public Policy, and Performance*. Berkeley: University of California Press.

Williams, Annette Powell (1972). "Dynamics of a Black Audience." In *Rappin' and Stylin' Out: Communication in Urban Black America*, edited by Thomas Kochman. Urbana: University of Illinois Press.

Willis, Paul (2000). *The Ethnographic Imagination*. Malden, MA: Blackwell.

Wilner, Richard (2005). "The Right Hook; Once-Novel White-Collar Boxing Turns Mainstay." *New York Post*, October 2.

Wilson, William Julius (1987). *The Truly Disadvantaged: The Inner City, the Underclass, and Public Policy*. Chicago: University of Chicago Press.

Wilson, William Julius (1996). *When Work Disappears: The World of the New Urban Poor*. New York: Vintage Books.

Women Boxing Archive Network (2011). "Chronological Events that Occurred in Women's Boxing." http://www.womenboxing.com/historic.htm.

Wynn, Jennifer (2002). *Inside Rikers: Stories from the World's Largest Penal Colony*. New York: St. Martin's Griffin.

Index